Changing Enemies

By the same author

ROXBURGH OF STOWE
LESLIE STEPHEN: THE GODLESS VICTORIAN
OUR AGE: PORTRAIT OF A GENERATION

Changing Enemies

The Defeat and Regeneration of Germany

NOEL ANNAN

HarperCollins*Publishers*

HarperCollins*Publishers*
77–85 Fulham Palace Road,
Hammersmith, London w6 8jb

Published by HarperCollins*Publishers* 1995
Copyright © Noel Annan 1995

The author asserts the moral right to be
identified as the author of this work

A catalogue record for this book
is available from the British Library

ISBN 0 00 255629 4

Set in Linotron Janson by
Rowland Phototypesetting Ltd,
Bury St Edmunds, Suffolk

Printed and bound in Great Britain by
HarperCollinsManufacturing Glasgow

For Georgia, Frederick,
Allegra and Felix

Will no one tell me what she sings? –
    Perhaps the plaintive numbers flow
For old, unhappy, far-off things,
    And battles long ago.

Contents

List of Illustrations

Acknowledgements

This book would not have been published but for the kindness of Professor Sheldon Rothblatt, a friend over many years, who invited me yet again to visit in 1994 the University of California at Berkeley. There I had nearly every day entirely to myself and I could work uninterrupted, the university library next door. Thanks to him I was able to convert a sketch of the first seven chapters into a working draft. So I owe him much.

I must thank the Trustees of the Liddell Hart Centre for Military Archives, King's College London, for permission to quote from the diaries of Field Marshal Lord Alanbrooke and from the papers of Major-General F.H.N. Davidson. I am especially grateful to Mrs Pam Wright who gave me permission to quote from the diary of Lieutenant-Colonel P.B. Earle. Sir Edgar Williams also generously put at my disposal a memorandum he wrote shortly after the war on intelligence in the field. Both the diary and the memorandum are held by the Imperial War Museum.

Anyone who writes about the work of military intelligence staffs is indebted to Sir Harry Hinsley and his co-authors for compiling the official history of British Intelligence in the Second World War. I am also grateful to Ralph Bennett who corresponded with me about his two authoritative books on military intelligence. Mr Martin Albu kindly let me see a chapter in an unpublished memoir written by his father, Austen Albu, about his days with the British Control Commission. I owe a particular debt to the German Historical Institute and to the work of Professor Adolf Birke and Eva A. Mayring who edited *Britische Besatzung in Deutschland* and asked me to contribute a chapter. The Institute of Germanic Studies kindly allowed me to reproduce material from the Bithell Lecture (1982) that I gave at their invitation. My thanks are also due to Frau Elke Husemann who read a chapter and corrected my memory of the dates of some events. Professor Sam Hynes and Mr Robert Baldock were good enough to read an earlier draft of the first seven chapters and gave me stimulating advice, even if it was contradictory. I must also thank those who have corresponded with me over the years and have given me useful material and advice: Lord Ashburton, Lady Berlin, Miss Marion Bieber, Mr George Brennan, Mr Trevor Davies, Mr Anthony Glees, Mr Stephen Graubard, Mrs Jean Howard, Professor Harold Hurwitz, Dr Barbara Marshall, Sir Iain Noble, Bt, Mr Matthew Pryor, Dr Rolf Steininger and Professor Ulrich Reusch.

I must thank Mr David Jones, the Librarian of the House of Lords and among his staff in particular Miss Parthenope Ward; and also the Librarian and staff of the London Library, who never failed to be resourceful and courteous. Yet again Douglas Matthews has been willing to compile an index for me. My publisher, Michael Fishwick, and Robert Lacey, a paragon among editors, have helped me and been a delight to work with. My literary agent, Gill Coleridge, has been invaluable. For the second time Harriet Croxton, wrestling with my handwritten manuscript, has typed many drafts and deserves a bar to the medal she won last time.

I am as ever grateful to my family. My daughter Juliet read the book in draft and I followed her professional advice. My wife watched over my syntax and over me.

NOEL ANNAN

Prologue

There is a marvellous scene in Shakespeare's *Troilus and Cressida* where Ulysses tries to persuade Achilles to stop sulking in his tent and join the Greeks on the field of battle. In silky tones Ulysses attempts to arouse Achilles' jealousy: he tells him that Ajax is now being hailed as the hero of the Greeks. Then he tries reason: fame is destroyed by time, 'For time is like a fashionable host, That slightly shakes his parting guest by the hand, And with his arms outstretched, as he would fly, Grasps in the comer.' But Achilles is not to be moved. He has private reasons, he says, for refusing to fight.

Quick as a flash Ulysses' tone of voice changes. The smooth cadences vanish, and we hear a note of menace: ''Tis known, Achilles, that you are in love with one of Priam's daughters.' 'Ha! Known?' 'Is that a wonder?' sneers Ulysses. 'There is a mystery,' he explains, 'in the soul of state . . .' That mystery is the intelligence services. The high command knows exactly what Achilles has been up to: 'All the commerce that you have had with Troy As perfectly is ours as yours, my lord . . .'

This book describes my involvement with the mystery in the soul of state. Every country has its intelligence service, that tries to penetrate the intentions of potential enemies at home and abroad. I was not part of what Ulysses calls 'the providence that's in a watchful state', i.e. counter-intelligence. Nor was I in the indeed mysterious business of running spies and spooks, still less at Bletchley Park where the age-old business of examining and breaking cyphers – well known to Walsingham, who ran Elizabeth I's secret services – reached a new peak of ingenuity. But I read much of what they produced, and tried to integrate it with the mass of information that poured in from different sources: from air reconnaissance and captured documents, from embassies and neutrals, from journalists and the reaction of the enemy to the operations of double agents and of deception plans. How much of this material is reliable, and how is one to interpret it? The interpretation of evidence became my job during the war; and after it for eighteen months or more in Germany I had to advise in the light of intelligence served up to me what was the best line to take in helping Germany to become a parliamentary democracy governed by the rule of law.

The second part of the book describes the beginning of the regeneration of Germany and the minor part I took in reviving German political parties. We had changed enemies. Soviet Russia was imposing communist regimes upon the Soviet Zone and in Eastern Europe. It was not in our interest to acquiesce in a central-ised Germany that would bring communism to the Rhine; nor in the interests of Germans to substitute for Nazism another one-party dictatorship. It was odious to find oneself in alliance with people who had been willing to go along with Hitler to keep communism at bay. But the best hope for the West was to encourage the Germans themselves to create a Western democratic state. It was also in Germany's interest.

All the Western Allies – America, France and Benelux – came to accept Germany's new status even when the two halves were united after the collapse of European communism. Except one. Britain was still doubtful. The British resented the economic miracle, they cherished nostalgia for the days of the war, they feared the state that between 1864 and 1939 had launched five wars. Yet anyone who has watched Germany since 1945 must see how genu-inely Germans have repudiated authoritarian government. I have never doubted that the character of Germany changed, and that what I saw there in 1945 was the death, resurrection and transfigur-ation of that country.

No one in operational intelligence should be complacent and congratulate himself. My memory of failures stifles any chortling over whatever success we had. Merit played no part in my being given this task. A chance meeting, a quirk of fate, altered the direc-tion of my life. Fortune plays a part in most lives; and it certainly did in mine. When I look back on those days I think of that sentence in Tyndall's translation of the Bible: 'The Lorde was with Joseph, and he was a luckie feloe.'

List of Abbreviations

CDU	Christian Democrat Union
CIGS	Chief of the Imperial General Staff
CSU	Christian Social Union (Bavarian party allied to CDU)
DMI	Director of Military Intelligence
DPs	Displaced persons
EAM/ELAS	Greek communist resistance forces
GRT	Gross registered tonnage
GRU	Soviet Military Intelligence
JIC	Joint Intelligence Committee
JIS	Joint Intelligence Staff
KPD	Communist Party of Germany
MEW	Ministry of Economic Warfare
OKH	German War Office
OKW	German High Command
OSS	Office of Strategic Services
SED	Socialist Unity Party
SHAEF	Supreme Headquarters of the Allied Expeditionary Force
SOE	Special Operations Executive
SPD	Social Democrat Party of Germany

CHAPTER ONE

❖

The Mystery in the Soul of State

They were playing cards or cleaning equipment in the hut that served as a barrack room when the sergeant came in and pinned a notice on the door. The officer cadets crowded round. But it was only a list of the names of those who had admitted they spoke foreign languages. They were ordered to report to the orderly room to show how well they knew them.

'What do they ask one?' I said to Peter Webber, who had been a contemporary of mine at King's, Cambridge and had studied modern languages.

'Oh, the same old phrases. In French "Tell him to wait until I come".'

'I see, the subjunctive.'

'This is the fourth time I've been tested since I joined the Field Security Police, and they never vary. In German you might get "I was at the meeting when the speaker was speaking", or possibly "I ought to have done it".'

Never was cynicism more accurate. At the interview next morning I was asked to translate every one of those phrases. 'But your German is much better than you said it was,' said my examiner.

Two months later at the end of the course in December 1940 the cadets again gathered round the door. Which regiment had they been posted to? I had hopes of being commissioned in the Rifle Brigade. To my dismay I found against my name something called the Intelligence Corps. Hardly anyone had heard of it – which was not strange, since it had been formed only that month.

'I'm told it has quite a nice cap badge,' said a school friend, John da Silva – who was in fact to spend his life in Intelligence. I thought that a frivolous observation.

It was now nearly Christmas, and the new officers were all sent on leave over the holiday before they joined their units. One day just before the New Year I was lunching with my father at our club where he introduced me to a member called Carl Sherrington. He was the son of a famous Cambridge physiologist who had won the Nobel Prize with E.D. Adrian, and made a living as a railway economist. He knew the capacity – that is to say how many trains a day could be run – of every railway line in Europe and America. Hearing that I was expecting to be posted to the depot of the Intelligence Corps, he said, 'But Kenneth Strong is itching to get his hands on people like you.'

Two days later I got a letter telling me to report to a Captain Sanderson at the War Office. He wore the ribbons of a veteran of the 1914–18 war and, characteristic of those days, had a moustache. He looked like a friendly, alert terrier. In a corner of the room sat a young officer peering into an epidiascope examining air photographs.

'I understand you know about railways,' said Sanderson, and looked somewhat disconcerted when I said I didn't. 'Well, then, your father does.' I recollected that at some time before 1914 my father had been associated with the Chesapeake and Ohio Railway. 'Ah, that must have been it,' said Sanderson, relieved that he now had a cast-iron case for getting me transferred to his department. 'Can you read German? Tell me what this means,' he said, thrusting into my hands a long report. At this point his phone rang, and while he answered it I was able to get the gist of the article.

'It's to do with transport in Europe,' I began.

'Excellent,' he said, without troubling me further. 'I am hoping you will hear from us soon.' Next week I found myself back in that room, having been ordered to fill a post in MI14. I was twenty-four years old.

The reason Captain Sanderson was so ready to recruit me was simple. MI14 was the German department in the Military Intelligence Division of the War Office. It was still a tiny unit, and even when I left two years later it numbered no more than twenty officers. The staff had hardly the time to wade through the torrent of paper that fell over their desks. For they were expected to advise the Chief of the Imperial General Staff (CIGS) what Hitler would do next. The Military Intelligence Directorate contained such well-known departments as MI5 (Security) and MI6 (the Secret Intelligence Service); and certain other sections specialised in obtaining information from a specific source – one, for example, interrogated prisoners of war and, having bugged their rooms, listened to their talk. But there was one department which nearly all the others served. That was MI3. It concerned itself with operational intelligence: it collected and interpreted all information from whatever source about the military forces and intentions of other countries – 3a dealt with Iraq, Iran and the Near East; 3b with Italy; 3c with the Soviet Union.

The German section had once been part of MI3, but it was now so important that it had broken away to become MI14. In MI14 one unit led by the second in command assessed German strategy and intentions. Another worked on what could be discovered about the operations of the German secret services, the Abwehr, Gestapo and Sicherheitsdienst. (Its head was a theatrical character, Brian Melland, and he was aided by Leo Long, an efficient young officer who was to be shamed years later when he was identified as one of the Cambridge spies. Long was a pupil of Anthony Blunt: self-confident, masterful and dismissive of fools.) Another section, vital for Bomber Command, identified the whereabouts and strength of the German anti-aircraft or Flak regiments. It was led by a former England cricket captain, G.O. 'Gubby' Allen. Crucial to the enterprise was the German Order of Battle section, which tried to estimate the number and character of the German divisions, and identify their commanders. Where were these divisions, and were they stationary or moving? The section I joined tried to answer the second of these questions.

After the spit and polish of my officer cadet training, the atmosphere of MI14 was anything but regimental. This was not surprising. It contained only three regular officers, and the only thing that was regimental about its chief, Lieutenant-Colonel Kenneth Strong, was his tartan trews. He looked like a beaver – an eager beaver bursting out of his uniform, with dark hair, a fine forehead, clever, shifty eyes and so chinless that he came to be known as the hangman's dilemma. Strong had been assistant military attaché in Berlin before the war, spoke German well and knew several of his contemporaries and elders on the German General Staff. His

3

reports from Berlin were so impressive that they were one of the factors, it was said, that persuaded Chamberlain to introduce conscription.[1] Strong won his reputation as an intelligence officer when he predicted the Germans would attack through the Ardennes in 1940. The French – our senior ally militarily and in intelligence work – scouted this bizarre idea.[2] Yet before the war, so Strong recalled, the senior officer present at the end of any lecture he gave would warn the audience against being over-influenced by his words on the strength of the German army; and he was forbidden at the Imperial Defence College to suggest that the German air force might give close support to their troops in the field.[3]

Strong's task was enormous. He had to build an organisation almost from scratch and shoulder a multitude of tasks, such as teaching the Military Operations departments what kind of army they were facing and how it would fight. He was tireless in explaining how the German General Staff was drilled in the tactic of the *Schwerpunkt*, or sudden concentration of armour and infantry to punch a hole in the enemy's line and exploit the breakthrough. He knew how efficient the German army was: 'You need three British battalions to equal one German. When will people learn this?' he used to say. But now his most pressing problem was to gauge how likely Hitler was to invade England. The unit in MI14 which I joined was there to put the evidence before him.

Captain Sanderson, the head of the unit, collated this evidence. But the crucial figure in the room was the man of my own age whom I had seen studying air photographs when I was first interviewed. This was Peter Earle, one of only three regular officers in the British Army who at the beginning of the war knew how to interpret air photographs; it was he who assessed the most crucial evidence by counting the fluctuating number of barges and other craft assembled in the Channel ports. If Strong made one think of a beaver, Earle had the air of a greyhound. He was lean and sensitive, with delicate hands and a quizzical expression. He was one of those Etonians who appear to be indolent but in fact develop curious talents and interests. Like Strong he was not a stereotyped regular officer. He disliked horses – 'nasty, unpredictable animals' – but knew a lot about fast cars. However squalid our conditions became (we were soon moved underground) his own corner of the

4

room somehow conveyed the calm of a country house. If some vulgarian patronised or oiled to him, his expression never changed; only his nostrils quivered. He was highly strung yet imperturbable – a quality much needed when later he became military assistant to the formidable and alarming Chief of the Imperial General Staff, Sir Alan Brooke. He was later to tell me that my predecessor was a devious, bone-idle and bad-tempered officer whom Strong had sacked by the well-used method of getting him appointed at a higher rank to a department in Military Operations, whence he departed by being again promoted to the rank of major in some other long-suffering organisation.

My prime task was to collate the evidence we got on the movement of German troops. What kind of evidence could we hope to get?

Military intelligence, so goes the well-worn joke, is a contradiction in terms. In fact it resembles a fountain, the jets of evidence spurting from different pipes. Air photographs; prisoner of war interrogations; captured documents; the reports of our own, and the gossip of foreign, diplomats; the observations of businessmen and industrialists travelling abroad, and the stories filed by foreign correspondents whose sources of information could be more reliable than those of our own diplomats. We studied newspapers, broadcasts and dozens of specialised periodicals that, unknown to their editors, rendered up secrets. Two organisations produced the most intriguing material. The first was MI6, whose spymasters recruited agents in Europe and elsewhere. The second was the by now famous, but then deadly secret, Government Code and Cypher School at Bletchley Park, where the radio messages sent between units of the German armed forces were decyphered.

Someone has to put all this information together and make sense of it if he can. It is not an academic exercise, although academic skills and techniques come in handy. The War Cabinet, the Chiefs of Staff and the Joint Planning Staff wanted quick answers to the questions they asked. What would be Hitler's next move? How strong would the German forces be were we to land in Sardinia –

and how quickly could they be reinforced? To answer such questions a staff had to be set up in each of the service ministries to estimate how many divisions, air squadrons, U-boats and capital ships the enemy possessed; where they were located and employed tactically; how many divisions were armoured, motorised or horse-drawn, and which squadrons were fighters, medium or heavy bombers. Almost anything that told us about the enemy's army was grist to the mill. And when – as was often the case – one source said one thing and another the opposite, we had to judge which was the more reliable.

Other ministries in Whitehall were expected to help the War Office, the Admiralty and the Air Ministry in their work: the Foreign Office injected political intelligence, the newly created Ministry of Economic Warfare (MEW) informed them about enemy production of weapons and identified bottlenecks or weaknesses in his economy. So a handful of officers and officials, each a spider, sat at the centre of their web and as each fly or item of intelligence got caught on a strand, they scuttled down to inspect and devour it, hoping that one day a fat bumblebee of information would land on the web and reveal what the other insects were about.

At the beginning of the war the British secret service stood higher in the imagination of foreigners than in Whitehall. The prestige of spies had waned. The masterful agent, who purloins the draft of a secret naval treaty from the private residence of a senior civil servant in the Admiralty, existed only in the imagination of the authors of thrillers. Foreigners took at face value the yarns of dozens of writers from Kipling and Buchan to Dornford Yates in which lean, bronzed British officers, often in disguise, outwitted the other side in the 'game': the Great Game. 'The only game in the world worth playing,' in Jim Maitland's words.[4] So much so that any event which thwarted their own plans was apt to be attributed to the British secret service. The reality was, alas, somewhat different. Sir Stewart Menzies, the legendary 'C', had no second-in-command to organise his office, with the result that he worked late hours and had had no leave for two years. The heads of the espionage and counter-espionage sections hated each other and were not on speaking terms. None of the staff of MI6 was a university graduate. Hugh

Trevor-Roper left a memorable account of the power struggles in MI6 during the war[5] and of the egregious characters who worked there; Graham Greene wrote of futile days in East Africa spent controlling agents whom he knew to be unreliable and corrupt and who provided worthless information. The tales of John le Carré told of a world of mirrors in which no one could be certain on which side agents were operating. These gifted writers turned MI6 into a black comedy. From the days when Sir Mansfield Cumming (the original 'C') set it up in 1909 its leaders rejoiced in sobriquets like Dummy Oliver, Blinker Hall, Biffy Dunderdale, Lousy Payne, Buster Milmo, Pay Sykes, Tar Robertson, Barmy Russel and Quex Sinclair (not to be confused with his successor but one, Sinbad Sinclair).*

Between the wars MI6's tiny staff was mainly engaged in identifying Soviet attempts to cause mutinies in the armed forces and to capture the leadership of the left and the trade unions. That famous clubland hero Bulldog Drummond was portrayed by Sapper as the leader of the Black Gang, a set of ex-army officers clandestinely kidnapping Soviet agents as they were infiltrated into Britain under the direction of the greatest of all villains, Carl Peterson. Intellectuals, horrified by Sapper's vision of life, denounced the gang as a bunch of fascists, but in fact they were pursuing a quarry that existed in real life. Christopher Andrew, the doyen of scholars of the intelligence community, concluded that the Zinoviev letter was not a forgery, even though the action of MI5 in briefing Admiral Blinker Hall to leak the letter to the *Daily Mail* was inexcusable.†[6]

The zeal of the intelligence services in such anti-Soviet activities was their undoing. Lloyd George sacked the head of Special Branch, Baldwin treated them with disdain (though his *éminence grise* J.C.C.

---

* In the period between Victorian times, when men called even their closest friends by their surnames, and the present day, when not to know someone's first name makes it almost impossible to address him without appearing supercilious or pompous, nicknames like Stubby, Toby and Tubby were used as a gesture towards informality, particularly in the Army and Navy.
† The letter, apparently signed by Soviet Politburo member Grigori Zinoviev, urged the British Communist Party to foment revolution. The publicity it attracted contributed to the defeat of Ramsay MacDonald's Labour government at the 1924 General Election.

Davidson employed retired MI5 officers to infiltrate Labour Party headquarters), and Chamberlain distrusted the former head of the Foreign Office, Sir Robert Vansittart's claims that an opposition existed in Germany waiting to overthrow Hitler on a sign from Britain. When members of this opposition came to London to meet Chamberlain, he said they reminded him of Jacobites in the reign of William III.

Intelligence is not the road to promotion in the armed services. Before 1914 only that outrageous Admiral Lord Charles Beresford understood its value to the navy, and got the Prime Minister, Lord Salisbury, to establish the Naval Intelligence Department in 1886. (In revenge the Admiralty cut the salaries of those who served in it.) As a result the Admiralty's record in the First World War was miserable, misreading intercepts and misleading Jellicoe and Beatty in action in the North Sea. The Commander in Chief of the army, Queen Victoria's cousin the Duke of Cambridge, Buller in the Boer War, and Haig and Henry Wilson in the First World War thought intelligence unnecessary. General French nearly lost the war in August 1914 by refusing to believe reports of the great enveloping movement by Kluck on the right wing of the German armies.

Nor was Whitehall much better prepared in 1939. The War Office and the Air Ministry had no technological sections. The War Office was informed that 1400 medium German tanks were in service: in fact only 300 existed. It was part of Hitler's propaganda to exaggerate the size of the German air force, and the Air Ministry fell for his boast that aircraft production would soar from 700 to 1500 a month: in fact in December 1940 only 780 aircraft were produced. This vast air force was intended, so it was put about, to flatten British cities as the Germans had destroyed Guernica, whereas in fact many of the aircraft were Stukas intended to give close air support to the army. Naval intelligence was much more accurate. Hitler began the war with fifty-seven U-boats, and the navy's estimate was only nine more.[7]

The estimates of Germany's economy were again wide of the mark. It was thought to be near collapse through overstrain. Goering's exhortation 'Guns before butter' was taken at face value, and the German people were pictured as having tightened their belts so far that they could hardly tighten them further in order to re-arm. Only a Hungarian refugee don at Balliol, Thomas Balogh, questioned these conclusions: in an article in the *Economic Journal* in September 1938 he argued that the sacrifice made by the German civilian population was much less than was imagined.[8]

The organisation of intelligence was not much better. Intelligence reports are misleading unless they are analysed and interpreted. Yet even when they have been analysed, intelligence is still a mine of controversy unless there is a single body to resolve the different interpretations which each ministry will put forward. In 1936 Sir Maurice Hankey set up the Joint Intelligence Committee (JIC) to give such a unified view, but the Planning Staff ignored it, and the Directors of Intelligence and the three armed services sent only their deputies to its meetings. Not until February 1940 were the Directors of Military, Naval and Air Intelligence all at the same meeting.[9] Each was briefed by his own staff, and each thought his own view of the situation was the most sagacious, so they did not bother to summon meetings of the JIC or ask it to provide an appreciation. The Foreign Office for long refused to share its political intelligence with the armed forces: indeed, it did not distinguish intelligence from the advice it gave to the Cabinet on foreign affairs. To diplomats intelligence and advice were a seamless garment.

The JIC was also burdened with too many responsibilities.[10] It dealt with plans to deceive the enemy, with internal security, with propaganda, with the treatment of prisoners of war, and with topographical intelligence. It jibbed only when it was proposed that it should mastermind the running of double agents. Too many summaries circulated, and a body on future operations duplicated its work. Much of its time was spent in struggling with the administration of intelligence, and it had no secretariat. Until the fall of France the JIC met the Chiefs of Staff only once, and it was never invited to join the Planning Staff in the War Cabinet Office.[11]

As war drew near, MI6's sources of information began to dry up. When Hitler marched into Austria and Czechoslovakia in 1938 the SIS network of agents in Vienna and Prague unravelled. Until 1937 our military attachés in Berlin had been able to glean considerable information about German military organisations and equipment: after that year their old haunts and contacts were sealed off.

9

The British network in Holland was penetrated by the Abwehr in 1935, and there was no advance warning of the Nazi–Soviet pact. There were indeed warnings from MI6 and the Foreign Office of the German invasion of Norway in April 1940, but earlier that month the War Office had brushed them aside. Paul Thummel, an old-guard member of the Nazi Party and a captain in the Abwehr, was MI6's most prized agent in the Czech network, but he could give no warning of the German attack through the Ardennes – though a woman in the Polish underground did. Whether it was this that alerted Strong I do not know, but it did not convince the French. By mid-1940 the military operations branch in the War Office did not believe what the intelligence sections told them, and hardly ever bothered to meet them.

Nevertheless, hope for the intelligence community was on the horizon. Even before war was declared some of the First World War veterans of Blinker Hall's Room 40 in the Admiralty began to recruit for the Government Code and Cypher School which had recently moved to Bletchley Park. Two classics dons were asked to select likely colleagues. Professor F.E. Adcock at Cambridge was diligent, Professor Last at Oxford was not, with the result that many of the earliest members came from Cambridge. Adcock was a fellow of King's, where I had been an undergraduate. He lured so many of the dons I knew best there – for instance the devotee of Horace, Patrick Wilkinson, and my own director of studies in history, Christopher Morris – that it did not require much imagination to guess what was going on. The staff was recruited by unabashed nepotism. Nigel de Grey and Dilly Knox of Room 40 days did not hesitate to recruit their sons; Evelyn Sinclair was the sister of 'Quex' Sinclair, a former chief of the Secret Intelligence Service. The dons were told to say that they were engaged on research into the civil air defence of London. It is certainly true that had security depended on the normal apparatus of passes and sentries, the secret would have not been kept long. One member of the staff who left his pass at home wrote on the temporary pass he was given the name 'Heinrich Himmler' and was admitted without demur.

Sir Stewart Menzies, the chief ('C') of MI6, under whom Bletchley nominally operated, once said that the best guarantee of security was to employ kinsmen of those known personally. Today such faith in the integrity of the old boy network may be met with sneers and the mention of Burgess and Blunt; indeed the 'fifth man', John Cairncross, did for a short time penetrate the organisation. Yet the secrecy of the work at Bletchley was preserved because the staff, realising how important it was not to gossip, were fanatically loyal to the institution. No one knew the whole story. Few knew, or had time to know, what the others were working on; and the various processes were so complicated that an individual had only 'tunnel vision' of the work on which he was personally engaged. At their peak the staff numbered 9000, but for thirty-five years none breathed a word to the media until F.W. Winterbotham wrote his book *The Ultra Secret* in 1974. Bletchley's success depended on one word: security. The work of the dazzling mathematicians and cryptographers would have gone for nothing had the Germans discovered that we had broken the secret of the Enigma machine.

The material which the cryptographers at Bletchley dissected was gathered by hundreds of men and women at listening posts scattered throughout the country. They worked in six-hour shifts listening to German radio operators sending messages by wireless telegraphy. It was slogging, unrewarding work to record a lot of unintelligible letters in morse. They came to recognise the individual operators by their quirks and idiosyncrasies in transmitting messages, by the frequencies they used and by their call signs. They could tell who sent an unsigned message from the style of the operators chatting to each other. Sometimes they could sense something fishy: in June 1941 the call signs of two construction companies, known to be in Holland, were transmitted from Poland, yet copious transmissions were still coming from Holland, and very few from Poland. The deduction was clear. The construction companies had moved to Poland and the transmissions from Holland were being faked.[12]

The unintelligible messages logged by our radio operators were sent to Bletchley where the cryptographers in Huts 6 and 8 got to work on them. The cryptographers had spotted the weaknesses in the Enigma machine, and the carelessness of those who operated it. They searched for cribs – some repetition, such as a weather report transmitted in much the same words at the same time of day week in, week out. With these and other devices they put together what they called a menu and fed this into the 'bombes' – electro-mechanical engines, the brain-child of a fellow of King's, Alan Turing. Turing and Gordon Welchman built on the work of the Poles and the French, and Turing was to invent the first automatic electronic digital computer that could store programmes.[13]

The bombes determined the wheel settings of the Enigma machines. When the German navy in February 1942 added a fourth wheel to the machines installed in U-boats, the bombes could not perform, and it was not until December 1942 that the cryptanalysts broke the new Enigma settings. Meanwhile the sinkings by U-boats of Allied convoys soared. This reverse in the Battle of the Atlantic was to have a profound effect on Allied strategy.

The bombes were dispersed over the countryside and serviced by a flotilla of 2000 Wrens. Year after year, with little chance of promotion, they worked, whey-faced, for four weeks of eight-hour shifts followed by four days' leave, getting electric shocks from the bombes and living in hideous conditions. Some collapsed, others had nightmares of breaking security, but they kept going by knowing that what they were doing was vital, in the way that most war work was not.

When the bombes had done their work and found the solution through permutation to the key on the Enigma machine which had been chosen for that day's transmission, what emerged were puzzling messages in German telegraphese. These were sent to Hut 3. If Bletchley had a centre it was there, where the second echelon of the staff got to work. Inevitably the books on Ultra concentrate on the triumphs of the cryptographers in Huts 6 and 8, but Ralph Bennett is right to point out that Hut 3 made the decrypts intelligible.[14] Linguists translated and emended the messages, and intelligence officers made sense of them. Some of the best linguists were schoolmasters accustomed to give top marks only to those boys who presented meticulously accurate translations. The intelligence officers were often dons who elucidated obscurities, abbreviations and map references. If a text was corrupt, they had to make sense of it. The duty officers in Hut 3, who worked an eight-hour shift, then had to paraphrase the Enigma translations into Ultra, so that if the Germans broke our own cypher they would not identify it as an Enigma message.[15] Only then did WAAFs teleprint the messages to the War Office, Admiralty and Air Ministry; and from 1941 to army group and army commanders in the field.

Among the first Enigma settings to be broken were those used by the German air force; and many of the messages that were decrypted came from 'Flivos', air force liaison officers attached to armoured divisions. What Flivos reported was of intense interest to MI14. In the first year of the war, however, the security surrounding Ultra sometimes defeated those whom it was meant to help. To explain how these German messages had been received, Bletchley invented a ubiquitous, highly-placed agent with the code name of 'Boniface', and displayed singular ingenuity in producing convincing situations in which this source might have got hold of the message that was passed to us in MI14: 'Source was able to look over the shoulder of GOC of X Fliegerkorps and read . . .' Once bad weather made an Enigma message almost unintelligible since several groups of numbers in the original signal had not been picked up, but the staff at Bletchley excelled themselves: 'Source was able to retrieve from a waste paper basket a badly charred document . . .' When such messages were first received the intelligence staffs gave no more credence to them than they would have to the utterances of a chuckle-headed spy. The navy, on the other hand, insisted on the original messages being sent to the Admiralty, but the intelligence staff there were as sceptical as the army about Ultra, and the muddles between the Home Fleet and the Admiralty remind one of the calamities of the Battle of Jutland, when the outnumbered German fleet inflicted heavy casualties on the Royal Navy. Struggles for turf were also inevitable. When Rommel landed in North Africa in February 1941, Bletchley Park (under the nominal supervision of Stewart Menzies) cut red tape, and Hut 3 communicated direct to Wavell's headquarters in Cairo. Sure enough in the winter of 1941–42 the War Office and Air Ministry tried to assert their control at a time when the battles between Eighth Army and the Afrika Korps were fierce and fluctuating. In the end MI6 won out, and the intellectuals were surprised to find a businessman, E.M. Jones, appointed as head of Hut 3, and even more surprised to find that his sagacity in reorganising duties relieved them of chores and gave them more time to do their own work.[16] Similarly, in Whitehall intelligence staffs became more professional and came to recognise how valuable Ultra could be as the numbers of messages they received multiplied. During 1943 the decrypts rose from 39,000 to 90,000, and in the last five months of the war over 45,000 went to the Western and Italian fronts. By that time 9000 people were employed at Bletchley Park. Long before then, 'Source Boniface' had faded away.*

Ultra was only one of the Bletchley products. Some staff worked on V cyphers, others extracted information about German troop movements from railway cyphers, which revealed consignment numbers – tedious hack-work, but ultimately rewarding. Dilly Knox broke hand cyphers, which the Abwehr used. These were invaluable to Melland and Long in MI14(d). Patrick Wilkinson worked on the book code of the Italian navy, an old-fashioned cypher that was far harder to break than machine cyphers. Late in the war Bletchley built the first true electronic computer, Colossus, that enabled the British at last to read messages sent by the German High Command, the OKW, to theatre commanders.

Bletchley was a community where age, sex, rank and appearance were irrelevant. The atmosphere was like a senior common room in one of the less stuffy Oxford or Cambridge colleges. Only those with sensitivity to the life of the intellect, like Hugh Alexander or Commander Travis, could succeed in the art of managing the menagerie of talent. There was only one criterion: could you do the job you were assigned? Women were treated as the equals of men – except, typical of Treasury rules, as regards pay: they were sometimes enrolled as linguists rather than cryptographers in order to get them equal pay. Many of them worked in dull routine jobs, like compiling the Index – a vast compendium of cross-references so that any message or unit or event could be traced in an instant. They could hold their own if challenged. Jean Howard, one of three women in the liaison section, was not to be cowed when a group of generals came to inspect the war map of the Russian border in early June 1941 and ridiculed the number of pins representing the

* It was part of intelligence jargon to refer to an agent as 'Source'. Colonel Strong's personal assistant, Lieutenant Cooley, who could be relied on to know what was cooking, was always referred to in MI14 as 'a well-placed Chinese source'.

massed German divisions: surely there were too many? They were taken aback when she replied that her training as an opera singer ill-equipped her to invent an order of battle.

The fact that so many at Bletchley knew each other had advantages. Patrick Wilkinson judged that the friendship between the two chess-players Hugh Alexander and Stuart Milner-Barry, or between Gordon Welchman and John Jeffries, prevented rivalry between sections that might have been at each other's throats because they were competitors. The young and obscure chalked up successes. Donald Michie, a classics specialist without mathematical training, straight from Rugby School, made a mark as an analyst and later became a professor of machine intelligence at Edinburgh. Mavis Batey decyphered the Italian Fleet signal that told Admiral Cunningham what he needed to know to win the Battle of Matapan. Peter Calvocoressi, whose sole virtue seemed to be that he could read upside down, and who was rated by the War Office as 'no good not even for intelligence',[17] was another success, along with his friend Jim Rose, the future literary editor of the *Observer* and chairman of Penguin Books. F.L. (Peter) Lucas, another King's don, wrote analyses of campaigns that were full of hints and hypotheses: they jogged the mind out of its rut.

Even more remarkable was Harry Hinsley, who had a sixth sense for deducing from the traffic and decrypts if something was up. In the spring of 1940 he tried to get the Admiralty to understand the significance of some decrypts that revealed that heavy ships were leaving the Baltic. He was ignored – until the aircraft carrier HMS *Glorious* was sunk off Narvik. From then on Hinsley, still an undergraduate, with an astonishing shock of hair and a cheeky grin, was *persona grata* at Scapa Flow and at the Admiralty.

Nearly everyone wore civilian clothes: some, Turing among them, were scruffy. The story circulated that when Churchill visited Bletchley in 1941 he met Turing and, turning to Alistair Denniston, said: 'I told you to leave no stone unturned in recruiting the best people, but I did not expect you to take me literally.'

One man transformed the standing of intelligence in Whitehall and throughout the armed services. That was Winston Churchill. From his experience at the Admiralty in the First World War Churchill was almost alone among politicians in understanding the value of intelligence. A cardinal rule of intelligence is never to allow officers, however exalted their rank, to see messages sent by top-grade sources before they have been interpreted by the intelligence staff. The CIGS never saw Ultra himself. Nor did Montgomery. Churchill, however, insisted that he be shown all Ultra messages of interest. Stewart Menzies, who had virtually nothing to do with the running of Bletchley, realised that his prestige and power as head of MI6 rested on serving up what the Prime Minister called the golden eggs, and he saw that he got them with his breakfast. As a result Churchill sometimes startled his Chiefs of Staff – not yet briefed by their Directors of Intelligence – by referring to some piece of news they had not heard.

Churchill paid several visits to Bletchley, one of which was to have a sequel. In November 1941, maddened by the inability of the administration at Bletchley to persuade Whitehall to exempt some young experts there from military service and to allow them to recruit twenty women clerks and some typists, Turing, Welchman, Alexander and Stuart Barry wrote a long personal letter to Churchill explaining their needs and why, for lack of them, the decrypting of Enigma, vital in the Battle of the Atlantic against the U-boats, was being delayed. Churchill immediately dictated a minute to General Ismay in the War Cabinet Offices: 'Make sure they have all they want on extreme priority and report to me that this has been done.'[18]

Churchill recognised that the problem was not so much the collection of information as the way to use it. Within a week of taking office as Prime Minister and Minister of Defence, he ordered the Chiefs of Staff to draw up a new directive for the JIC in which they were bidden to 'take the initiative in preparing at any hour of the day or night, as a matter of urgency papers on any particular development'.[19] The JIC soon found their conclusions subjected to scrutiny by Churchill's personal staff. On 5 July 1940 'The Prof' Lindemann, later Lord Cherwell, correctly challenged the Air Ministry estimate, endorsed by the JIC, that the German air force could deliver 4800 bombs a day. The tone of the Prime Minister's directive showed he wanted instant action. Like Ezekiel, Churchill breathed life into the dry bones of the JIC. Early in 1939 the War Office had proposed that the chairman of the JIC should be the

Foreign Office representative, the ostensible reason being that a neutral civilian would see fair play between the three armed services. The less charitable view of this decision was that the War Office was determined not to allow the Admiralty to take the chair. No wonder: Admiral Godfrey was the one Director full of ideas. His biographer, however, admits that he was not a man to conceal his contempt for less gifted colleagues, in particular the charming courtier and Guardsman, General Beaumont-Nesbit. But the War Office had not reckoned with the young man whom the Foreign Office appointed, William Cavendish-Bentinck. As the youngest of the JIC members, and a civilian, it took Cavendish-Bentinck time and patience to galvanise his colleagues, and only when Churchill spoke could he at last set up a secretariat under an elusive, secretive barrister, Denis Capel Dunn, and impose some sort of discipline upon them.

Such was the situation when I joined MI14. When I look back on those days and the years that followed, I see not only the remarkable stream of information that came from Ultra and many other sources. I also see the influences – some beneficent, some malign – that affected the interpretation of the evidence. I see the inevitable distortions and the immense efforts made by the operational intelligence staffs to produce a coherent explanation of the evidence that would convince army commanders, Supreme Headquarters, the Chiefs of Staff, the Prime Minister and the President of the United States. The Joint Intelligence Committee embodied an ideal: that each ministry would lay on the table its interpretation of the evidence, and after discussion a unanimous report would be signed which the Planners and the Chiefs of Staff could use. The ideal was frustrated. The War Office and the Air Ministry were both in the grip of what might be called an ideology – a theory of how the war could be won. The ideology was not constant: it fluctuated according to the fortunes of war. Indeed, within each ministry different interpretations were held, and the director of intelligence would be canvassed by one or other faction. Dejection in defeat affected the appreciation which Auchinleck and his staff made when the Eighth Army was driven back by Rommel to El Alamein. They looked over their shoulder and saw the German army advancing into the Caucasus, so they drew up plans to evacuate the Nile Delta and send troops a thousand miles to the north to protect the oil in Iraq and Iran. *Per contra*, the euphoria of victory in Normandy blinded Montgomery and his staff: they neglected the evidence from Ultra that the Germans were determined to hold on to the Scheldt estuary and stop Antwerp operating as a port.[20] I was to learn time and again that those of us who served in operational intelligence and tried to make sense of the information got it wrong. Had I been years older I might have felt as Shakespeare's Henry IV did:

> O God! that one might read the book of fate,
> And see the revolution of the times
> Make mountains level, and the continent –
> Weary of solid firmness – melt itself
> Into the sea ...
>   O! if this were seen,
> The happiest youth, viewing his progress through,
> What perils past, what crosses to ensue,
> Would shut the book, and sit him down and die.

But this happy youth had no intention of doing so. On that Christmas of 1940, like everyone else, I was full of boundless, unreasonable optimism.

CHAPTER TWO

MI14

The section in MI14 that I had joined had known what it was to work under pressure. After the fall of France in June 1940 the German army communicated by land lines and teleprinter, and the order of battle section could no longer get hard factual intelligence about the force that was being groomed for the invasion of Britain. MI6 was in difficulties. Many networks had disappeared or had been penetrated, and much of the information the intelligence department in Whitehall wanted was beyond the reach of agents. Paul Thummel in the Abwehr reported that the invasion of Britain was planned for 15 September 1940: gas would be used, and the disembarkation of shock troops would follow. On 12 August he informed us that the date of invasion had been postponed for a fortnight. It was again postponed, and then on 12 October it was scheduled for the spring of 1941.

But an Abwehr officer could hardly be expected to know the exact places on the English coast, from Norfolk to Devon, where the German army intended to land. MI14 was pressed to take every rumour, every theory into account. Carrier pigeons joined the Army, and Kenneth Strong found himself asked to evaluate the prognostications of an astrologer and a water diviner whom he nicknamed 'Smokey Joe'. (Smokey Joe did not last long, as the disposition of the German forces he provided was so ludicrous that he was paid off.*) The RAF declared that the Germans could not invade unless they had air superiority, and the Royal Navy was

---

* Smokey Joe operated from Yorkshire and claimed to be able by dowsing to determine the number of barges in Holland. Amazingly enough Peter Earle, *en route* in April 1945 to become one of Montgomery's Liaison Officers, found the sixty-two-year-old water diviner ensconced in the rear echelon of 21 Army Group. In what capacity he was then serving was obscure.[1]

confident that they could sink the German invasion fleet. The trouble was that the Navy's contribution was of the level that 'You can't sail a barge in a beam sea.' Almost the only factual evidence was provided by the young officer whom I had seen examining air photographs on the day of my interview. Captain Earle counted the barges and watched the remorseless build-up of their numbers in the French Channel ports and the emplacement for long-range artillery on Cap Gris Nez.

We now know that Hitler's thoughts had already turned to Russia even as the invasion of Britain was being planned. To him Britain was of no importance. In one mood he was a gambler. He believed that Russia could be destroyed in a Blitzkrieg, as France had been destroyed. That was why the German army had no winter clothing or equipment in 1941–42. But in his most common mood Hitler was a cautious soldier of the First World War, insisting that no inch of conquered territory should be given up voluntarily, even when that gave the best chance of a counter-attack. Except for backing Manstein's plan to drive through the Ardennes in 1940 rather than repeating the great Schlieffen manoeuvre of 1914 ('Only keep the right strong') to wheel through Belgium, Hitler did the obvious and attacked on all fronts. In 1944 he justified his decision not to invade Britain by arguing that he had only enough shipping to get the first wave of an invading army ashore, and not enough to keep them supplied when menaced by the Royal Navy.[2] It was easier, he believed, to crush the Red Army, which had barely been able to defeat Finland, than to risk an improvised Channel crossing. Yet the Chief of Staff of the OKW, the German High Command, General Jodl, took exactly the opposite view: to invade England would be easier than invading Russia.[3]

What would Hitler do next? Would he invade Britain in the spring? Or would he, as Paul Thummel reported, march through Spain to take Gibraltar? Or would he attack Turkey and drive through the Middle East to obtain oil in Iraq? This was the puzzle that MI14 was studying in the winter after the fall of France. Strong argued that Hitler would invade Britain in the spring or summer of 1941. It is easy to see why he took this line. His position was like Jellicoe's: he could lose the war in an afternoon. If he had followed the line of the Admiralty and the Air Ministry and he had been wrong, we would have lost the war. Strong knew how efficient the German army was, and how ramshackle ours was after the losses at Dunkirk. He also knew that the Navy could not operate in strength in the Channel until three or four days after an invasion had been launched, and would then be at the mercy of the Stuka dive-bombers. He could not bring himself to believe that the German High Command would wait until they had destroyed the RAF. The Germans had only to launch their ships and their enormous air superiority would enable them to form a bridgehead somewhere on the south coast. Strong found an ally in the Ministry of Economic Warfare. They had previously stressed Germany's deficiencies in oil, textiles and food, and argued that these alone must make her turn to the east. But by December 1940 they had changed their tune, and dismissed any possibility of German economic collapse.

On 31 January 1941 the JIC agreed with Strong, but the Chiefs of Staff noted that their assessment was based on reasoned argument, not factual intelligence. Churchill – against the advice of the Chiefs – sent two armoured divisions to the Middle East, so certain was he that after the Battle of Britain Hitler would not risk another defeat.[4]

Such was the situation when I joined Sanderson and Earle on New Year's Day, 1941. I was at once taken to meet Lieutenant-Colonel Strong, who welcomed me with a smile, though he was somewhat baffled when I had to admit I knew nothing of railways. But then, I was to learn that very few of the officers in MI14 were technical experts, and indeed that technical knowledge could be a positive embarrassment, since one was rarely in possession of more than a quarter of the facts. Technical knowledge was not the problem. Experts were at hand all over Whitehall to answer conundrums. If I had to calculate the possible build-up of German forces over such-and-such a rail network, or the capacity of a port (i.e. the rate at which ships could discharge their cargo and turn round), there was Colonel Bull of Transportation to help me, or indeed Carl Sherrington. The railways I studied were not those leading to the Channel ports. They were those in Central Europe.

Fashionable as it has been to mock MI6, and contrast the grotesque misinformation of Humint (intelligence provided by human beings) with the authenticity of Sigint (signals intelligence, as provided by Ultra), the humble spies operating in Poland, Norway, Switzerland and Central Europe were sending bits and pieces of news that enabled us to compose a jigsaw puzzle, even if many of the pieces were missing. MI6 had its comic side. The only name listed in the War Office directory under MI6 was a Miss Dunsterville, whom I took to be the daughter or niece of General Dunsterville, Kipling's Stalky. Occasionally it took a more corporeal form, when a Captain Buckingham dropped in to see whether we were satisfied with the material it sent us. These were documents called CXs, the reports of agents given code-names such as 'Crispin' or 'Horatius'. Attached to each report was a sheet on which one was asked to evaluate the worth of the information, if possible by checking it against other relevant material. What did the reports tell me? Many of them came from a network of agents operating in Hungary and Romania, and gave details of the number of trains, the equipment or troops carried in them, and occasionally the insignia of a division or military unit as they passed through a station; they also sent us the code-names of the German rail movements. Within days I was charting their passage through such tongue-twisting stations as Kiskunfelegyhaza and Hodmezovasarhely in Hungary, Timisoara and Turnu-Severin in Romania. As early as November 1940 these agents had warned us that rail traffic to the Balkans was increasing, and during February–March some sixty trains a day were crossing Hungary. Their reports may have been low-level intelligence, but they were high-grade in reliability.

I soon learnt at what pressure one had to work. On 11 February the Director of Military Intelligence, General Davidson, was telephoned just before lunch. The Prime Minister and the Defence Committee wanted a detailed appreciation of the routes and times the Germans would take to advance to Salonika and Athens, and they wanted it by half past five. We gave him an estimate, he delivered it at once to the Chiefs of Staff and then to the Defence Committee that evening. Churchill thought the estimate of advance too rapid: we said they would reach Athens on 21 April – in fact they took six days longer. Davidson then told the CIGS, General Sir John Dill, that top-level intelligence must be reorganised if appreciations were to be properly considered and drafted.[5]

I often wondered who our agents were. I guessed they were

humble railway officials, but where was their control, to whom they reported? And what happened to them after the war? In all probability they were shopped by Kim Philby, who as an officer in MI6 knew their identities. Were they arrested by KGB blue caps and sent to the Gulag archipelago? Or were they shot by the communist regimes of their own countries as imperialist spies?

I did not have to wait long to be introduced to Ultra. In a corner of one room stood a teleprinter which occasionally spoke. If you were night-duty officer, you waited for it to clatter into speech, and at the end of the message you conveyed your thanks to the unseen operator by typing 'OK Tks'. Once, when it had hardly spoken all night and I was reading for the first time Henry James's 'The Turn of the Screw', it suddenly went off at 3 a.m. and I nearly jumped out of my skin. Around six in the morning you had to make a summary of the most important communications, get it typed and ready to present to the Colonel before he arrived at 8.30 – then shave and work through the next day. The messages (sent by 'Source Boniface') for the most part referred to movements of German air force units – the first I was shown revealed the movement of a unit to Bulgaria – and I was told that they were of such secrecy that no word of their existence should be breathed outside MI14 – not even to other MI departments, let alone to any inter-service committee that one attended.

The section which relied most on that teleprinter was MI14(b), responsible for the German order of battle. They were expected to identify the whereabouts of every division and formation of the German army, in particular the number of motorised divisions. Their second-in-command was a genial businessman, Colin Tangye, who married one of the experts in the section, Pooh Malcolm. The most junior officer was the remote and aristocratic Peter Acton, who wore an expression of weary disdain. Then there was someone who seemed to know everyone in London, Paris and Vienna and who did much of the patient, repetitive, boring work, Captain Alan Pryce-Jones, later editor of *The Times Literary Supplement*, a man with a fine touch of fantasy, elegant, emollient and unwearyingly kind to me.

The head of this section was the most impressive man in MI14. Eric Birley was a professor of ancient history who on leaving Oxford held a chair at Newcastle, where he became an expert on the order of battle of the Roman army on Hadrian's Wall, and had identified every cohort that had served there. From May 1939 he used the same methods of card-indexing that he had applied to the Roman legions, and thus built up the German order of battle. When I mentioned his name to the great Oxford don Maurice Bowra, he said, 'Ah, the Regius professor of the obvious,' and it is true that Birley's forte lay in careful, plodding work. During 1939 he had had several brushes with the French over German dispositions, and he was right each time. The invasion of Norway had enabled us to identify large numbers of German divisions, but after July 1940 our sources became fewer and fewer, and Birley had to rely on his art as an ancient historian to make inferences on little evidence. He over-estimated the total number of divisions in the German army: in June 1941 it mustered 208 divisions, while Birley put the total at 250. But he was consistently right about the number of motorised and armoured divisions. When the German army invaded Russia it became apparent that the ten armoured divisions deployed in the French campaign had risen to twenty. General Davidson immediately leapt to the conclusion that we had under-estimated the tank strength of Rommel's divisions in Africa, but Birley remained firm: the Germans could have doubled the number of their armoured divisions only by halving the number of tanks in each – and so it proved.[6] He developed a nose for the reality behind appearance. He showed that many so-called German divisions were merely divisional staffs without troops, or static formations incapable of being transferred to another front, or unreliable formations of foreign mercenaries. In September 1942 the US War Department believed the Germans had 382 active divisions. MI14 put the total at 234: German records later showed that in July the total was 233. MI14's estimate of the number in France was almost exactly right.[7] None of this rested on easy deductions. Neither Ultra nor MI6 nor Special Operations Executive (SOE) agents provided much evidence until 1944, and even then it was often conflicting and confused. The German army was always creating new divisions and letting old ones decline in strength. It was not until early 1943 that a large number of documents captured in North Africa made identifications easier; and that was only the prelude to a prolonged dispute about the ability of the German army to keep up its strength by combing out from industry, civilian establishments, even the German air force, manpower to replace losses.

Birley had his limitations. He was donnish, rude and touchy. So long as our intelligence about the German army was fragmentary he was in his element: an ancient historian is trained to make deductions from minimal evidence and untrustworthy sources. But when evidence began to flow he tended to become immersed in the precise identification of coastal artillery units and sanitary companies. And yet it is from such painstaking routine work that reliable intelligence is often obtained. There were many references, for example, to Field Post numbers – not only by agents and prisoners of war but in the German press and radio. They too enabled MI14 to guess where particular divisions were located.[8] In 1943 the Allies set up in Washington a research unit to analyse the horde of documents obtained when von Arnim surrendered in Tunisia. Among them were the categories of foreigners who had been conscripted to serve in the German army. Nordic and anti-Bolshevist volunteers served on the Russian front; Balts, Ukrainians, and other Soviet ethnic minorities in the Balkans, Italy and the West.

One of the most remarkable intelligence officers in MI14 was the Oxford philosopher John Austin. His brain was unclouded by passion, vanity or caution, and his integrity matched his ability. He smiled rarely, and when he did it resembled the sun in winter. In a remarkably short space of time he worked out the composition of the Afrika Korps from the first lot of captured documents. He soon left Birley's section to become the order of battle chief at GHQ Home Forces where he produced an admirable intelligence report called 'Martian' that covered France and the Low Countries. He and Matthew Pryor in MI14 were alone in taking the flying-bomb threat seriously, and Pryor discovered numbers of launching sites that had been passed out as negative at Medmenham, the centre of air photo intelligence. Later he moved to Eisenhower's Supreme Headquarters Allied Expeditionary Forces (SHAEF). He held most of his fellow workers in pitying contempt. Once a junior officer advocated a certain course of action in a memorandum, saying it would leave the enemy surprised; Austin wrote in the margin 'very surprised'. When Montgomery arrived from Italy to command 21 Army Group, Austin had to contend with his intelligence chiefs Brigadier Bill Williams and Major Anthony Part. He summed them up: 'Williams, a lightweight: Part, a feather brain.' This was unjust to Bill Williams, who was in a class by himself among intelligence officers in the field, and had gifts of a high order that Austin did not possess.* Austin's capacity for work was extraordinary. I suppose at one time some 2000 CX reports a week passed through his tray. No detail escaped him. I remember him discussing flying-bomb sites and suddenly reminding a passing corporal that there was no Lifebuoy soap in the lavatory. But, like all of us in intelligence, he made mistakes. He became hypnotised by some train movements just before D-Day and, despite the fact that all German armoured divisions had been reported beneath strength, he conjured up an alarming estimate of 3000 tanks in or near Normandy.

Another don in MI14 was more eccentric. Michael Holroyd was an elderly ancient historian who had been Eric Birley's tutor. He could never finish any piece of work he was set because he preferred to do everyone else's work, or invent a problem for himself to solve. He worked out the German bomber grid in Libya from two map references and three numbers; no one had any use for this information, but it was a satisfying piece of analysis. More profitably, he calculated the number of German troops and their dispositions in Norway from a return sent by an agent which showed how much beer was shipped from Norwegian breweries, what was the ration per NCO and other ranks, and where it was sent. He had the habit of clearing his mind by bearing down on a colleague hard at work to deliver a lecture on whatever problem was intriguing him at the moment. Cigarette in mouth, he would expatiate on the comparative reliability of different sources. 'Enoch is the Swiss general staff's out-tray, Fridolin is their in-tray,' he would say, as cigarette ash cascaded down his uniform and over yours, his lips bright orange with nicotine. 'I won't be lectured by that dreadful old man,' shouted the Director of Plans, Brigadier Jock Whitefoord, when

---

* It was also unjust to Part, who rose to become Permanent Secretary in the Department of Trade and Industry, where he had the misfortune to draw Tony Benn as his minister when Benn was in his most manic mood.

someone had let Holroyd loose in his room by mistake. You learnt suddenly to remember some pressing engagement in another room when you saw him lumbering towards you. He was the kindliest of men. He used to ask lonely young officers to spend a weekend's leave with him at his home on Boar's Hill in Oxford. No less welcoming was his wife Frieda, who addressed her guests as 'dear lamb'. Peter Earle remembered her hung with glass bangles, love trinkets and rabbit's fur, serving tea on every possible and impossible occasion.[9] Eventually, after months compiling charts, graphs, sketches and drafts, Holroyd was packed off to where all good dons went – Bletchley, where he produced a vast reconstruction of the state of German railways; such a masterpiece, said Patrick Wilkinson, that he would hardly allow it to be used because it could never be completed.

By early spring of 1941 it was clear that Hitler had resolved to destroy the Greek army which had inflicted such humiliating reverses upon the Italians and had driven them back into Albania. But was this an isolated operation to create Fortress Europe and expel the last vestiges of hostile force from the Continent? Or was it the prelude to a drive through Turkey to the Middle East? Or perhaps it was a tidying-up operation before mounting the invasion of Britain in the summer? And why did Hitler require such overwhelming strength to defeat little Greece? A campaign of that size could hardly swallow more than a sixth of his forces. Why were so many of his troops in Romania – indeed, where was the bulk of the German army concentrating? Many of the divisions transported to Eastern Europe were the best in the German army. At any rate, it seemed to Sanderson and myself that the invasion of England had been indefinitely postponed – and Earle, watching the Channel ports, agreed.

Then there began to be signs that Hitler had another objective. I received reports from the Polish network that large numbers of sidings were being built at the frontier stations in Poland, at Malkinic, Lukow, Siedlce and Przemsyl; ammunition dumps were being established at Ostroleka and Ostrow; and a large quantity of shipping put in at Kirkenes in March. Early that month we learnt that the bridges over the Pruth and the Dniester had been surveyed by the Germans. Diplomatic sources were full of rumours that

Germany would attack Russia. I wrote Kenneth Strong a minute drawing his attention to this activity and suggesting that there were signs that Hitler might be about to invade the Soviet Union.

It was then that I learnt how difficult it is to question accepted wisdom. Strong had staked his reputation on the overwhelming probability that sometime in the summer of 1941 Hitler would invade England. To him the Greek campaign was a sideshow. He put a series of questions to me. How long would it take the German army to cross Bulgaria and deploy? I calculated three weeks (in the event they did so in a fortnight, though they used fewer divisions than we thought probable). How long would it take them to occupy Greece? Well then, surely by the end of May their crack divisions could be back at the Channel ports. Why should Hitler attack the Soviet Union? Strong asked me. Hitler was getting practically everything he wanted from Stalin: oil, food and minerals. It would be madness to attack such a compliant neighbour.

The debate about the invasion of England was not an academic question. So long as Wavell, the Commander in Chief Middle East, was confronting a defeated Italian army it could be argued he had all the forces he needed. But once the German army and air force controlled Greece and the Mediterranean, and once Rommel's Afrika Korps had crossed to North Africa, it became all too obvious how important the issue was, particularly since the formations Wavell had sent to Greece returned battered and without their equipment. Wavell needed reinforcements, but how many divisions from the United Kingdom could be sent him? If invasion was imminent, none. But if the threat of invasion was removed indefinitely, some could be spared.

On many matters in the conduct of the war Churchill was wrong. But on the issue of the invasion of Russia he was right from the start. As early as 31 October 1940, at an oral briefing of military commanders, he forecast that Hitler would attack the Soviet Union to get the Baku oil.[10] Churchill could count on only one ally, Stafford Cripps, then Ambassador to the Soviet Union. Cripps said that a senior member of the Nazi Party had told an American diplomat in Moscow that Russia was Hitler's real objective. Such third-hand gossip cut no ice with Anthony Eden, with the CIGS or with the DMI General Davidson and the Military Intelligence directorate. Davidson had exposed a flank a month earlier when he made the silly statement that 'the time will never come when it will be safe to say there will be no invasion': Cavendish-Bentinck, Chairman of the JIC, pointed out that if the German air force was switched to other theatres the threat to Britain must be diminished. In January Davidson took the line that all the activity reported in Slovakia was defensive, and on 6 February he advised that an attack on the Soviet Union was 'unlikely for the present' until 'Germany had disposed of Great Britain'.

Then in March Hitler launched a deception plan. He let it be known that the German forces in Romania were simply to guard against a surprise Soviet attack when he launched his invasion of Britain, and moved twenty-one divisions to the west. Eric Birley pointed out that these were second-grade divisions, but the DMI would have none of it, and even Churchill began to waver. Then on 27 March Ultra reported that three armoured German divisions were to move from the Balkans to Cracow. The order was at once countermanded. The Regent Prince Paul, who had succumbed to Hitler's demand that his troops should be given free passage through Yugoslavia for their attack on Greece, was deposed by a *coup d'état*. The new Yugoslav government repudiated Prince Paul's decision, and Hitler was compelled to attack Yugoslavia as well as Greece. Enlivened by the coup, Churchill regained his confidence and wrote to Stalin on 3 April warning him of the impending attack. Stalin ignored the letter. He regarded it as an imperialist plot to draw him into the war and lure him to make a pre-emptive strike. Imprisoned by Marxist ideology, he gave orders that even if German troops crossed the border the frontier troops should hold their fire so that no suspicion of provocation could fall upon him.

During the next two months we on the staff of MI14 battled in vain to convince Kenneth Strong, Davidson and the Joint Intelligence Committee that Hitler's target was Russia. Strong might have changed his mind, but he left MI14 to take the next step in a regular officer's career, commanding a battalion. He was succeeded first by a weak, and then by a narrow-minded and stupid, officer.

Some information was counter-productive. At the end of March the Polish underground forecast an attack on 15 April, other MI6 sources gave a date in May, while diplomatic gossip mentioned June. Towards the end of April the DMI was arguing that a pincer attack on Suez was more likely and in any case Hitler would not attack Russia until after the harvest. And what evidence was there of any concentration of troops? That argument had force, because Hitler delayed the movement of troops to the east as long as he could. The German army used land lines to transmit orders, so Ultra gave no sign from that quarter. But the German air force began to chatter. On 24 April a signals unit was moved to Cracow to be subordinate to Fliegerkorps V, which had formerly been in France. Fliegerkorps VIII was to move from Greece to Gatow in Berlin, and Luftflotte 4 was to go to Moldavia. Then, on 5 May, and perhaps most decisive of all, a unit designed to set up prisoner of war camps moved from Zagreb to east of Cracow. By 19 May a dozen divisions were identified moving to the Eastern front, many of them veterans of the Greek campaign. The Polish, Czech and Yugoslav sources of MI6 confirmed the stream of troops towards the Russian border. By mid-May Birley's section estimated accurately that 100–120 German divisions faced the USSR.

Yet the sceptics found a new explanation: Hitler was mounting a mammoth threat. He would make new demands of the Soviet Union, and Stalin would give in to them in order to delay the offensive – if indeed there was to be an offensive – until nearer the winter. Even Stafford Cripps took this line. Questioned after his bewildering flight to Scotland in May 1941, Hitler's former deputy Rudolf Hess said no plan to attack Russia existed.

Nevertheless, the evidence from Ultra mounted – to such an extent that the Bletchley analysts declared the attack was imminent. They argued that Hitler was inspired by the concept of Blitzkrieg, and thought his military dispositions would bring the quick success in Russia he had achieved in France the previous year. The Joint Intelligence Committee still havered, and the War Cabinet itself held an indecisive meeting on 12 June. On that very day Bletchley produced a decrypt of a telegram dated 4 June sent to Tokyo by the Japanese Ambassador in Berlin. Hitler had told him, he said, that communist Russia must be eliminated. Romania and Finland would join Germany; if Japan remained neutral Hitler would have no objection. No date was given for the offensive, but it was imminent. The Foreign Office and the DMI still thought an ultimatum might be delivered and Stalin would cave in. Cavendish-Bentinck, who did not always follow his Foreign Office brief, had been unable for months to convince his colleagues on the JIC of the probability of the attack; but at last they were convinced.

The speed of the German advance through Greece and Yugo-slavia in April 1941 had one curious effect upon military intelligence. Yet again the Germans proved masters at moving and fighting more quickly than the best judges thought possible. How long then could the Russian army hold out? Cripps gave them three to four weeks. In early June MI14 were asked how long it would take the Germans to reach Moscow. They replied six weeks. The Russian section MI3(c) was then asked whether the fall of Moscow would lead to the collapse of the USSR. They replied that it would. These were some of the reasons why this bizarre estimate – that Russia would fall in six weeks – found its way into the paper which the Joint Intelligence Committee sent to the Chiefs of Staff.

Despite our warnings to Stalin of the impending attack he deployed his main forces too far forward. Between July and September the flower of his trained army was encircled at Bialystock and Kiev: the Russians lost between half and three quarters of a million men. The loss of the Donetz basin in the autumn was also considered to be grave, as nothing was known of Russia's industry east of the Urals.

Once again Churchill went against his experts. In Whitehall only the Chief of Combined Operations Mountbatten, Cavendish-Bentinck and a White Russian émigré working in the Ministry of Economic Warfare, Munia Postan, believed Russia would survive. Postan, who was the professor of economic history at Cambridge, declared that Russia had always had limitless resources of men and space. Yet even Churchill agreed with the Chiefs of Staff that the army should be ready to meet an invasion by the beginning of September. To their credit the JIC demurred: they said Hitler could not possibly now invade before 1942. Since there were no signs of German armies being redeployed, the Prime Minister can-celled the order on 1 August.

There was only one section of MI3 that could have stood out against official pessimism: the Russian section. Unfortunately

MI3(c) was a subject for rich comedy. It consisted of two brewers. One, a cavalry officer, had lost a packet in the October Revolution. The other had sold stout in Estonia. Both despised the Soviet regime and joked about Russian ineptitude. 'Another army lost,' they would chortle as the Germans encircled vast numbers of Russian soldiers. But the welcome they gave to Russian defeats was not as serious as their incompetence. Neither had a notion of constructive research, and they were incapable of building a sound Russian order of battle. Nor would they exert themselves. One day Leo Long took them a sheaf of Abwehr decrypts that identified many Russian divisions. With three months' work they could have collated the material and checked their own hypotheses, but they refused to look at the decrypts. The section was consistently wrong on every major issue until 1942 when some new blood, notably a Canadian officer, Major Ignatiev, joined them and the moustachioed cavalry officer departed, promoted, of course, to Colonel.

In the first months of 1941 there was little we could do with the information that the German forces were building up in the Balkans except warn the Chiefs of Staff that Greece was the next most likely victim of Hitler's ambition. All we could do was watch, through Ultra, the defeat of our forces in Greece. The Greek dictator Metaxas had given the coldest of welcomes to our proposal to send forces to Greece: who could blame him, with the memory of the disastrous British attempt to rescue Norway in 1940 fresh in his mind? When Metaxas died in January 1941 Churchill, against the advice of the Chiefs of Staff, determined to intervene.[11] His romantic temperament was stirred by the Greek victories when the Italians invaded the Epirus in northern Greece and humiliated the hyena Mussolini. General Wavell stood out against the Prime Minister, for at this very time General O'Connor, fresh from his victory over the Italian army in Cyrenaica, stood poised to advance and take Tripoli. Churchill sent Eden and Dill, the Chief of the Imperial General Staff, to soften up Wavell – though at the last moment he had second thoughts and emphasised that the decision to send an expeditionary force to Greece must rest with Wavell himself. As so often happens when one protagonist weakens, the other becomes accommodating, and Wavell agreed to the Greek venture. The Chiefs of Staff predicted that troops sent to Greece would be lost:

but when the Serbian coup overthrew Prince Paul in Yugoslavia, the War Cabinet refused to back down.

MI14 predicted that the Germans would use five to ten divisions to invade Greece. The estimate proved accurate, and we watched with sinking heart the inevitable retreat of the British forces in April. Three British divisions and an armoured brigade were evacuated but lost all their equipment; they also lost 12,000 prisoners of war. And then our spirits in MI14 rose. Hitler, fearing that caiques carrying troops to invade Crete would be mauled by the Royal Navy, ordered his elite parachute troops to be dropped on the main Cretan airfield at Maleme, where the gliders could land and aircraft could transport heavy equipment and troops. Airborne troops were also to land at Khania, Rethymnon and Heraklion; seaborne troops would follow. On 6 May Ultra revealed the exact places they intended to land and the probable date. Once the German dive-bombers and fighters were established on the airfields, ground troops and supplies would be brought in by sea. Churchill was ecstatic. He imagined our tanks and assault troops destroying the enemy. In fact the British had only two obsolete tanks and few heavy weapons. He authorised Wavell to tell General Freyberg, the courageous New Zealander commander in Crete, the gist of Ultra, and to impress upon him the chance he had to annihilate the invaders even though the German forces would be strong. (We guessed the number of transport aircraft accurately, but over-estimated by half the number of troops.[12]) Even the postponement of the landings by two days was revealed. In MI14 we waited agog.

Everything went as Ultra predicted. The Germans, particularly the parachutists, suffered appalling losses – 4000 were killed and 2500 wounded. Fliegerkorps VII was cut to pieces: hundreds of aircraft were destroyed, and the Germans never reconstituted it. One naval convoy was sunk by the Royal Navy and another was mauled and turned tail. Hitler was never again to use his parachutists in that role, as he might have done later in Malta. But the Germans captured the airfields, and the British forces were routed. Once again, as earlier in Greece, the Navy had to evacuate what troops it could get away, losing three cruisers and four destroyers; two battleships and an aircraft carrier limped home damaged.

What went wrong? Ralph Bennett has re-examined the evidence. Freyberg maintained after the war that he was given Ultra, but forbidden to make use of it. Did Menzies in MI6 modify Churchill's order to give Freyberg Ultra on grounds of security? Possible, but not proven. Did Freyberg pay too great attention to the seaborne landings and leave forces inadequate to deal with the airborne landings? Probable, but forgivable. But Bennett, who recognises Freyberg's plight as a commander, admits that he was wrong in not devising a better defence plan for Maleme airfield, and in authorising his brigade commander to withdraw from the southern side during the first night.[13] The fact remains that on the sole occasion on which intelligence gave our commanders a cast-iron guarantee of success, they had failed. I shall never forget the incredulity and gloom that settled over MI14 when Crete was lost.

It later became received wisdom that the spirited Yugoslav coup and the despatch of British troops to Greece postponed Hitler's attack on Russia by a month, and the postponement saved Moscow. This became Churchill's justification of the disastrous decision to send forces from Libya to Cairo to defend Attica and Crete, instead of allowing General O'Connor to advance and take Tripoli. The justification is dubious. It was lack of transport that held up the German attack in Russia rather than lack of fighting formations: not many had been needed to throw us out of Greece.

I continued to follow the sweeping German advance in Russia, and noted that in the autumn we began to get identifications of German divisions and of the direction of their offensives. I did not know it at the time, but the cryptographers at Bletchley had at last broken into the German army Enigma keys. I was not to occupy myself long on these enemy movements, as I stopped studying railways and set myself to learn about ports after Rommel landed in North Africa in February 1941.

However incompetent the Russian section of Military Intelligence was, intelligence officers who dwell with glee on the shortcomings of their colleagues are always punished for their conceit. Intent on the troop movements to Poland and Eastern Europe, I failed to predict the transit to Libya of Rommel's Afrika Korps. Detachments of the German air force were identified there by Ultra in January 1941, and there were reports of German troops in Italy: but were they bound for Libya or an attack on Malta? On 22 February that young Oxford don Lieutenant Bill Williams (who was later to become Montgomery's chief intelligence officer), on patrol with a detachment of the King's Dragoon Guards at El Agheila, exchanged fire with German motorised units. Rommel's forces had arrived. Within weeks Rommel had driven the depleted British forces back to the Egyptian frontier and had invested Tobruk.

Each military intelligence section exhaled its own aroma. The Iranian and Iraqi section had an air of languor. It was there that I met James Pope-Hennessy bubbling like a hookah with the hottest gossip – not of the war, but of the *beau monde* and Lady Cunard's latest *soirée* at the Dorchester. The Italian section, MI3(b), was, as might be expected, manned in part by art historians. Its chief was David Talbot Rice, a professor at Edinburgh, and Terence Hodgkinson, later curator at the Victoria and Albert Museum and Director of the Wallace Collection, was on his staff.

I had imagined that they would have been monitoring the movement of troops in North Africa by rail and through the ports, but they had discounted CX messages from agents that German troops were moving through Italy. No one had been watching shipping movements in the Mediterranean. I was therefore summoned to calculate how much shipping had crossed to Tripoli, and my preliminary study revealed that a staggering amount – enough to take two whole divisions – might have crossed; though the guesses by RAF pilots stationed on Malta of the size of the ships they spotted were so inaccurate and incomplete that the margin of error in any assessment was considerable.

From then on Rommel's Afrika Korps became my concern to the exclusion of almost everything else. After Rommel reached the Egyptian frontier he settled down to build up his supplies. General Davidson laid down that the Afrika Korps would be unlikely to advance until they had built up thirty days' supplies, and it became my job to estimate when they would have done so. First I had to calculate the gross registered tonnage (GRT) of shipping going to

Tripoli and Benghazi; then I had to convert that into space for personnel, vehicles and stores. Next an estimate had to be made of how much motor transport the German and Italian forces possessed to carry the supplies to the forward areas – our Long Range Desert Group watched the roads and reported. Finally I needed to calculate how much the enemy forces consumed while sitting still, and how much they could accumulate, to reach the magic figure of thirty days' supplies.

Much of the credit for such calculations went to Colonel Keble in Cairo, and telegrams shot back and forward between us. I judged that our assessment of the requirement of a German division in action – 280 tons a day plus an additional 140 tons for corps and army requirements – was sounder than the Middle East estimate; and I got caught in cross-fire between Wavell's DMI Brigadier Shearer in the Middle East, and the Joint Intelligence Staff in the War Cabinet Office, for insisting that a ship of 5000 GRT could carry on average 120–150 vehicles, 500 men and 2000 tons of stores. Unfortunately Middle East intelligence underestimated enemy losses and capability, and Shearer was sacked.

Those losses were soon sensational. Bletchley was breaking the German air force Enigma every day, and by July 1941 British submarines and attacks on coastal shipping had cut Rommel's fuel supplies so severely that he had petrol only for two days' operations. He could not even attack Tobruk. Four Italian liners were transporting Italian reinforcements, and Ultra revealed in August that a new German division, 90th Light, was in Libya. Another intelligence triumph was in the making. The Germans had accused the Italian navy of using vulnerable cyphers, and bullied them into using a new machine cypher for directing the movement of shipping across to Africa. Bletchley broke this cypher almost at once, and from mid-summer onwards our commanders knew in advance of almost every convoy and ship that was to sail for Libya. We knew what even the tiniest vessels carried. On 15 September, for example, we learned the exact route two liners, the *Neptunia* and the *Oceania*, would take for Tripoli. On 18 September they sailed: both were sunk. Out of a convoy of ships of 6000 GRT only two would survive. I calculated that by the beginning of October Rommel could not mount a campaign that would last more than a fortnight.

Of course some ships got through; but in late October the Royal Navy sent two cruisers and two destroyers to Malta and their successes compelled Rommel once again to postpone his attack on Tobruk.

We now had reports of the number of serviceable tanks in each of Rommel's armoured divisions. Another cypher, which carried German High Command appreciations of the situation in North Africa and was used between the main supply bases, was broken in the autumn of 1941. This enabled Birley's order of battle section to sort out the formations in Rommel's forces which had been renamed, and which were in danger of causing confusion until it became clear that the new names were not additional divisions but merely old units under a different name.

Ultra was not the only source of Sigint available to Eighth Army. The Long Range Desert Group reported the numbers and types of German vehicles moving eastwards. In the desert sat other radio operators, the Y service, listening in to the exchange of messages between divisions and regiments, which were conducted in low-grade cyphers. But what one side in war can do, the other side can do also; and Rommel's intelligence service was so efficient, and radio battlefield security in Eighth Army so lax, that he was as well informed of our movements and intentions as we were of his. His tanks were superior to ours, better armoured and better handled technically, and the famous 88mm dual-purpose anti-tank and anti-aircraft gun destroyed British armoured formations. The German battle drill and desert tactics gave them mastery over the brave but inexperienced British cavalry regiments, which charged as if they were at Waterloo or Balaclava and allowed the Germans, their own guns and tanks hull down, to pick off ours one by one.

Nevertheless, in November 1941, just as Rommel was about to assault Tobruk, the Eighth Army forestalled him. We watched the ding-dong battle through Ultra; despite Rommel's early success the war of attrition against his supply lines paid off, and on the night of 16–17 December he pulled out of Cyrenaica, evading the British attempts to trap him. For the first time in the war a British army had defeated a German army. The Germans and Italians suffered 40,000 casualties. Moreover, they shifted their 2nd Air Fleet from the Russian front to reinforce Fliegerkorps X.[14] At the turn of the year the two armies sat watching each other on the Tripolitanian border.

But the tide turned. At last the German High Command took action to prevent the Italian navy and the convoys being driven from the seas. Field Marshal Kesselring was appointed to command the whole area, and he judged that the key to the British success was Malta. He reinforced the German air force in Italy and began to bomb Malta and attack every convoy that left Gibraltar to bring supplies to the island. Ship after ship – cruisers, destroyers and cargo carriers – was sunk, and the Navy lost further ships when they struck a minefield off Tripoli. U-boats were sent through the Straits of Gibraltar and sank the *Ark Royal* and a battleship. Now it was our convoys and not theirs that were being sunk. Even when Rommel was still on the retreat a convoy containing tanks got through to replace his losses, and others carrying supplies entered Tripoli. He found the British unprepared, attacked and surprised them. By the end of January 1942 he was in Benghazi, and by February back at Gazala. There had hardly been any warning from Ultra of the attack, but that was not the only reason for our failure.

MI14 and Middle East intelligence were at loggerheads about the strength of the Axis forces. We advised the JIC that the losses suffered by Rommel in 1941 were not as severe as Auchinleck's headquarters in Cairo calculated. Today it appears that Cairo underestimated the original strength of the Axis forces and overesti-mated the casualties they suffered. As a result Rommel had 100 per cent more forces at his disposal than Cairo thought. One large convoy of nine ships had got through, carrying a considerable number of tanks, transport and 88mm ammunition. Although Ultra gave no indication of its cargo we should have pressed Middle East on the matter. Auchinleck's staff, however, kept on repeating that Rommel was in acute need of supplies, even though his advisers knew the contents of the convoy. The CIGS – now General Sir Alan Brooke – wrote to Auchinleck: 'over-optimistic intelligence played a large part in accounting for your troubles'. Auchinleck sacked his intelligence chief and installed in his place General de Guingand (soon to become Montgomery's chief of staff).

By the spring of 1942 Churchill was urging Auchinleck to fore-stall Rommel's offensive before even more supplies got through.

Auchinleck pleaded that he had to detach forces to safeguard his northern frontier in case the German army marched through Turkey and burst through the Caucasus. Then again, he argued that Rommel was now so superior in tanks that to attack him would be foolhardy. These were not convincing arguments to the Prime Minister, who now entered the controversy about the number of Rommel's tanks. Eventually an Ultra decrypt settled the matter in Cairo's favour. Churchill grumbled and continued to urge Auchinleck to attack in May, and in the process to save Malta.

Once again, as in Crete, it became agonising to watch through Ultra – that is to say from the German side – the progress of the battles in North Africa. In the end Rommel forestalled our offensive with a long night march round Bir Hakeim on 29/30 May. He overran an Indian brigade and scattered 7th Armoured Division's headquarters. Then the British counterattacked, and Ultra showed that Rommel was in a mess. The Free French had beaten off an Italian attack on Bir Hakeim, and his supply line round it was far too long. He retired onto our minefields and began to cut a lane through them for his supplies. He could not get his anti-tank defence ready, he said, until 2 June. In London we expected a further attack by our forces on 31 May or early on 1 June. It failed with heavy losses. Eighth Army impaled itself on an anti-tank screen improvised by Rommel's genius. The intelligence staff did not appreciate Rommel's plan of attack; during the battles Ultra decrypts arrived too late; and the commanders of corps and divisions rarely guessed when and where the Germans would attack.

And then, once again, the tide turned. In the first week of August Churchill and Brooke were in Cairo. Auchinleck was sacked, Alexander put in charge of the Middle East theatre, and Montgomery given command of Eighth Army. On 17 August Ultra decrypted the German army appreciation of the situation and revealed Rommel's plan for capturing Alam Halfa which, he believed, would open the road to the Nile Delta. It also told us the very date, 26 August, when he would attack. The new commander of Eighth Army had a new style of command. Montgomery told his troops exactly what Rommel would do, and why he would be defeated. The security service was distraught and the Prime Minister himself was critical of this indiscretion. Although it was a few days late, the attack proceeded exactly as Ultra had forecast, and Rommel was seen off. Morale soared in the Eighth Army. The wilting offensive against the German convoys perked up. Our submarines were again able to operate intermittently from the besieged Malta, but the most striking successes were made by the RAF. Tanker after tanker was sunk, freighters too. By December over 50 per cent of the enemy ships sent to Libya were sunk. Precisely because of the continual German anguish over lost supplies, the decrypts also revealed what difficulties in manpower and materials Rommel was suffering. The rations were so low that more men fell sick than could be replaced.

Inspiring and mettlesome as Rommel was, he had his faults as a commander. Just as the British dissipated their forces by fighting in battle groups, 'Jock Columns', instead of in full-blown divisions, so the Germans dissipated their shipping and oil supplies all over the Mediterranean. Although our Admiralty and the Ministry of Economic Warfare would not concede that the Afrika Korps were short of ships, shipping was their bottleneck. Only the *Wachtfels* and two other ships survived the 1941 crossings. By 1942 the ships crossing were seldom to be found in the pre-war Lloyds Register. They had all been newly built. In September 1942 Count Ciano, Mussolini's son-in-law and Foreign Secretary, said: 'At this rate the African problem will automatically end because we shall have no more ships with which to supply Libya'.[15]

The German and the Italian high commands were often at loggerheads. The Germans fumed at Italian inefficiency, Italian naval pusillanimity, and Italian postponements of convoys. The port facilities improved, but so slowly that fresh recriminations erupted. Nor were the German commanders better pleased with each other. Rommel got across his boss Kesselring, bickered with Fliegerführer Afrika (the air force commander) General von Waldau, and all three rounded on the Quartermaster General and the loading staff at Naples. High-ranking officials flew over to Tripoli, ordering and countermanding. Hitler and Goering themselves took a hand. But Rommel would never listen to objections. He relied on dash and luck, and so long as his enemy was not as well-trained as his troops, that was good enough. But he never put his supply side in order; he never got Tobruk working well as a port; and his shipping suffered the same toll as ours to Malta. In June he captured ninety days' supplies at Tobruk, and one of my last telegrams to Cairo said that Rommel was bound now to drive to the Nile Delta. Even so, he neglected the need to get his water and petrol forward. A great commander knows how far to trust his staff. They will always put the difficulties attending on any course of action before him, but he will know when to override them, minimise the difficulties and go ahead regardless of the fact that his preparations are not complete. Equally he will know when not to do so. Rommel, like Hitler, never trusted his staff.

Ultra was one of the most valuable weapons that civilians fashioned during the war. But it could cause self-inflicted wounds. Here, so it appeared, was the naked truth. What could be more authentic than a signal sent by some German officer to the higher command giving the facts about a situation? But all intelligence must be interpreted, and only the intelligence staff is fitted to do so. Montgomery never asked to be shown Ultra. He relied on Bill Williams to tell him about the enemy dispositions and intentions; and that appreciation was based not only on Ultra, field Sigint, air recce, prisoner of war interrogation and numbers of other sources, but also on Williams's assessment of how Rommel, being the man he was, would react to the situation. Even before Alam Halfa Eighth Army intelligence staff were mastering their job. General Anderson's intelligence staff in Algiers had to learn the hard way, and as a result he was less well served.

There was, of course, the old rogue elephant in Whitehall who interpreted Ultra as he saw fit. Churchill would challenge one or other of the Chiefs of Staff demanding to know why, if the U-boats were in such difficulties, or the German air force so overstretched in Russia, or Rommel's tank strength so low, our forces were unable to exploit these advantages. MI14 could not influence the battles in North Africa. But it could provide a second opinion on the conclusions that the intelligence staff at GHQ Cairo had reached. Similarly, it could act as a lightning conductor to protect the CIGS and DMI from the conclusions that the Prime Minister drew from Ultra.

An Ultra message was not necessarily true. How could the junior German officer who sent it know the whole strategic and tactical picture? Every commander is tempted to exaggerate his need for supplies, for reinforcements, for air support. A bare figure of the number of runners among the tanks of an armoured division conceals the number of tanks in the workshops, some of which are ready to go. Brilliant as the staff at Bletchley were in decyphering, translating, processing and transmitting messages at top speed, much of Ultra at that time referred to events that had taken place yesterday, or as long as a fortnight or more ago. Bill Williams used to say that he and his staff were not doing their job properly at Eighth Army unless his appreciation had anticipated Ultra.[16] Where strategy was concerned, an Ultra message might raise more questions than it solved.

In tactics, too. When Ultra fell silent, trouble could be brewing. Ultra reported the disagreements between Rommel and Kesselring as the Afrika Korps retreated in Tunisia. The Y service at army and corps level gave better information, but when both went off the air, wrong deductions were made and Rommel routed American troops at the Kasserine Pass in February 1943. Ralph Bennett judges that the evidence was conflicting and could have been interpreted in several ways, but as a result Eisenhower sacked his intelligence chief Mockler-Ferryman and replaced him with Kenneth Strong. When, however, Rommel turned east and attacked Montgomery at Medenine, Ultra told us his plan: six hundred anti-tank guns were massed to meet his point of attack and he lost fifty tanks in a few hours. Rommel left Africa three days later.[17]

In June 1942 my days at MI14 were drawing to a close. General Davidson decided that I should be sent to the Staff College at Camberley, and before going seconded to an infantry brigade; on one exercise I actually commanded a platoon, and was rightly reprimanded for leading it into attack from the front. At the Staff College, surrounded by regimental and staff officers who had been serving in field formations, I learned how ignorant I was.

After the four-month course at Camberley I became the Intelligence Officer of 9th Armoured Division and had hopes of seeing action. It was not to be. I applied to serve in SOE, but that too was turned down. I suppose that as an Ultra-user my destiny was staff work, and not the front line. The division was in the end cannibalised to provide reinforcements for existing armoured divisions. Before it was disbanded we took part in a grand exercise in the south of England, a training for the Normandy landings in which we played the role of the German defenders and were steadily rolled northwards. One morning, outside my caravan somewhere in Buckinghamshire, I was explaining the situation to a group of generals who had come to see my map when I recognised my old chief. 'We're bringing you back to us, my boy,' said General Davidson, and on 15 March 1943 I found myself back in Whitehall. But this time not at the War Office. I became the War Office's representative on one of the two teams of the Joint Intelligence Staff at the War Cabinet Office.

CHAPTER THREE

Grand Strategy in the War Cabinet Offices

I joined the Joint Intelligence Staff just after the turning point in the war. With the annihilation of the German Sixth Army at Stalingrad and Montgomery's victory at El Alamein the strategic initiative at last passed into the hands of the Allies. From now on, instead of us reacting to Hitler's offensives, he had to react to ours. I spent the first few days in my new post reading past strategic appreciations that my colleagues-to-be had drafted.

No one who worked in the War Cabinet Offices could doubt who was head of it. For Winston Churchill the war fulfilled a lifetime's ambition. He regarded war as the most enthralling part of the historical drama into which he had been born to play a part. He remained at heart the lieutenant in the Hussars who in 1898 had charged the Dervish army at the battle of Omdurman, and the newspaper correspondent who had been captured by and escaped from the Boers. As First Lord of the Admiralty in 1915, having failed to convince his Cabinet colleagues to launch an assault on the island of Borkum off the north German coast, he took up the plan to send an expedition to the Dardanelles, knock Turkey out of the war and end the stalemate on the Western front. It ended in disaster. He lost his post in the Cabinet and his reputation as a strategist.

Yet when he came to write the life of his illustrious ancestor Marlborough he found a justification for the Dardanelles campaign. Marlborough had refused to fight a war of attrition in Flanders; instead he marched to Bavaria and fought a war of manoeuvre. What else, Churchill argued, was the Dardanelles but an attempt (bungled by incompetent admirals and generals) to break the nightmare war of attrition on the Western front? Had he but had plenary powers it could have succeeded. How well he knew the contempt generals had for politicians, whom they referred to as 'the frocks' (i.e. men in frock coats – as people today say 'the suits'). Not even Lloyd George had been able to prevent them from decimating a generation on the Western front. That was why, when he became Prime Minister in 1940, Churchill also gave himself the portfolio of Minister of Defence. Now at last he had those plenary powers he so longed for in the Dardanelles. At last he had the chance to devise a grand strategy.

Churchill did not exercise his plenary powers through the War Cabinet. That was hardly more than his mouthpiece. He exercised them by convening a kitchen cabinet of experts in the War Cabinet Offices: men who were numerate, could juggle with figures and confound the conventional views expressed by the various ministries, especially the armed service ministries. When he wished to push a policy of his own, he would summon after dinner the Chiefs of Staff, or their chairman General Sir Alan Brooke alone. Or he would call a meeting attended by his experts, 'the Prof' (Cherwell) on his right, slide-rule in hand, to arraign those who were thwarting his plans. At first the tone was genial and bantering; but as the night drew on Churchill would become menacing, truculent and harsh. If he could not overbear the opposition, he would adjourn the meeting in the early hours of the morning and reconvene it later in the week in the hope that he could wear down his opponents. At that next meeting he might bring in Attlee, Eden and his old friend Oliver Lyttelton and other members of the War Cabinet who often had not read their brief, if indeed they had been sent one. They would chip in to say that they agreed with the Prime Minister; the opposition would be browbeaten for producing new, and therefore false, figures; and the Army and its commanders would be pilloried as pusillanimous and lacking the imagination to seize the 'glittering prizes' that fortune had put in our way.

His goading and prodding of ministers and service chiefs was not confined to strategy. No plan could be advanced without the Prime Minister mounting his favourite hobby-horse, 'teeth and tail': why was there always so vast a number of troops to support so small a number of fighting soldiers? In 1940, when General Nye, later Vice-Chief of the Imperial General Staff, was Director of Staff Duties, Churchill turned on him: 'How a man in your position can

45

be put upon to this extent by technical experts that you should really think it necessary to send to the Middle East a further 2000 signallers when you have already decided to embark 19,000 and 12,000 are already there. Why, when I was at Omdurman, we had flags at the fort . . .' To which Nye could only reply: 'Well, sir, if you really think that, then all I can do is to try to give you a few simple headings under which you could begin to study the problem of modern signals communications.'[1] In July 1942 Churchill was asking why the ration strength in the Middle East was 750,000 whereas the fighting strength was only 100,000, and would not comprehend that the Middle East was a vast base for operations in no fewer than nine theatres of war.[2] Nor did he scruple to send commanders in the field telegrams through MI6 channels behind the back of the CIGS urging a particular course of action with which he knew Brooke disagreed. When Brooke let him know he had been detected, he showed surprise that he had been caught out, but not the faintest sense of shame.[3] What was one to do with a Prime Minister who intended sending a telegram to Auchinleck outlining a plan based on the battle of Austerlitz?[4] After such an intervention it could take as much as ten days, with telegrams flying to and from the Middle East, before confusions could be resolved and the course of action as originally envisaged by the Chiefs of Staff approved.

Yet the greatest gift that Churchill brought to war was his personality. You could not work in the War Cabinet Office without it impinging on you. His energy at the age of nearly seventy was prodigious. During the war he travelled over a hundred thousand miles, and spent over a thousand hours on the sea or in the air doing so. In his bath or in his bed he dictated memoranda cajoling, encouraging, bullying his ministers, generals, advisers and civil servants, maddening them and yet inspiring them with commands that might vary from telling them to watch their grammar to seeing that the troops in Italy had beer to drink. Whatever his mood – anger, resentment, pique or exasperation – it was succeeded by magnanimity made all the more enchanting by flashes of humour. He saw life as a comedy as well as an epic.

Even Churchill's most irritating or hare-brained military schemes, no one could ever doubt, sprang from his determination to grasp the enemy's throat and further the cause of our country and of the British Empire. Small wonder that he had the Empire in mind when the dominions, India and the colonies provided so many troops for his campaigns – they were in the majority at El Alamein. It is true that he was inconsistent, blew hot and cold and promoted mutually exclusive policies. But he differed from other all-powerful leaders in one respect. Napoleon refused to take counsel: his marshals were his servants. Hitler overruled his generals: no battalion, let alone army group, could be moved without his permission. But Churchill, though he drove Brooke to desperation, gave way to his Chiefs of Staff provided they were united and stood firm.

The Prime Minister was by nature bellicose. Long ago, in October 1914, when he was first lord of the Admiralty, he told an astonished Prime Minister that he would resign from the Cabinet if he could be given senior military rank and the full powers of a commander of a detached force in the field so that he could reinforce Antwerp, where the Belgian army was still holding out. (He formed a naval division and sent it to Antwerp, which fell five days later.) That indomitable spirit that had defied defeat in 1940, that restless mind firing off instructions for 'action this day', bred military schemes like rabbits. Much of the time of the Joint Planning and Intelligence Staffs was spent in examining the anatomy of the particular rabbit that had jumped out of the hat during the night. Churchill was always urging troops to be landed somewhere – at Trondheim or Petsamo in Norway, at Spitzbergen, at Bordeaux or Brittany, in Sardinia or the Dodecanese, in Rangoon or on the tip of Sumatra. What such expeditions were meant to achieve, where they were to advance, and how they could escape annihilation by superior enemy forces moving on interior lines, was never clear.*

It was all too easy for someone such as myself who spent hours countering many of Churchill's proposals to forget that not all his

* The distinguished American historian of the Second World War, Gerhard Weinberg, considers Brooke to have been wrong to oppose Churchill's plan to land in Norway in 1942. The sea route to the Soviet Union would have been protected; Swedish iron ore exports would have been interrupted in winter; and the very fact that Hitler concentrated his battleships and cruisers in the Baltic showed how much he feared such a move. But what would a British force at Hammerfest or Trondheim have done? Lacking air cover, unable to stop German reinforcements, they would once again have been flung into the sea.[5]

strategic decisions were wrong. It went against his romantic love of France to refuse to send Spitfire squadrons there in June 1940: but he did so. Nor did he shrink from destroying the French fleet at Oran after the fall of France, to prevent it from being pressed into service against us. To the misgivings of the Chiefs of Staff when Britain was facing invasion, he sent troops to the Middle East. It was Churchill, not Brooke, who first saw the advantages of a landing in North Africa, and it was he who brushed aside the quaking officers on Eisenhower's staff who feared that the presence of two German divisions on Sicily might defeat the Allied invaders. Churchill was one of the few who did not succumb to euphoria after the collapse of the German front in Normandy in August 1944 and believe the war was virtually over, and he saw quicker than his military advisers the significance of the atom bomb. Nevertheless, he never understood how logistics determine strategy. Time and time again the Chiefs of Staff advised him that no amphibious expedition could succeed without superiority in the air: it was as if they had not spoken. Had Churchill always had his way the list of British defeats would have been even longer.

But he did not always have his way. The man who saw to it that he did not had succeeded Dill as CIGS in October 1941. General Sir Alan Brooke's relaxation was bird-watching; and with his small-boned face and dark shining eyes he looked like a night-owl with a beak ready to peck any predator on his territory. He was the only man to stand up to Churchill, tell him to his face that what he was proposing would be disastrous and would dissipate the Allied forces, and endure night after night countering his schemes until two in the morning. To read Brooke's wartime diary – or that of his military assistant – is to be astonished at the relentless demands Churchill made on his time. One day in July 1944 Brooke went to a Cabinet meeting on Greece at 3 p.m. ('Complete waste of time, not a decision made'). At 5.30 No 10 asked if he would come over for another Cabinet meeting on Greece. Knowing he had to attend the Defence Committee with Eisenhower present at 6.30, Brooke exploded: 'No, I won't go. I have sat in his bloody Cabinet all day: tell him to wind it up with my compliments.'[6] He would remind Churchill of the Allies' overall strategy. 'I do not want any of your long-term projects, they cripple our initiative,' Churchill growled.

'I told him,' said Brooke, 'that he must know where he was going, to which he replied he did not want to know.'[7]

In his diaries, written late at night, Brooke spilt his wrath over Churchill's inconsistencies and, as he saw it, imbecilities. One morning Brooke arrived to find that the first item on his brief for a meeting of the War Cabinet – which his planning staff had sat up all night to prepare – was the Prime Minister's new proposal to substitute for the Normandy landings a landing at Lisbon and an advance across the Pyrenees. Brooke, who had been brought up as a boy on the French side of the Pyrenees, told Churchill that he knew more about those mountains than Churchill did, and then what he thought of his plan. The time of his staff, he said, should not be wasted on such proposals.

After one such encounter Churchill told General Ismay, his chief of staff, that he did not think he could continue to work any longer with Brooke because 'he hates me. I can see hatred looking from his eyes.' 'Hate him?' Brooke told Ismay, 'I don't hate him. I love him. But the first time I tell him that I agree with him when I don't will be the time to get rid of me, for then I can be no more use to him.' When Churchill was told of this response, tears filled his eyes and he murmured, '*Dear* Brooke.'[8]

Alan Brooke had a brusque manner and a mind that held all the facts and figures that govern strategy – about shipping, landing craft, transport and reinforcements. Old Admiral Pound, who was dying and often fell asleep in meetings, ceded the chairmanship of the Chiefs of Staff to him with no hint of resentment, and Air Chief Marshal Portal, whose brain matched Brooke's, accepted his leadership without question. So did every general in the army, all of whom, Montgomery included, stood in awe of that sharp tongue and the instant reproofs for inefficiency or slack thinking. 'I flatly disagree!' he would bark not just at his subordinates but at meetings with the American Chiefs of Staff.

Brooke took over command of British strategy at the blackest period of the war. First Malaya and Singapore then, in February 1942, Burma and Java were lost. By April the Japanese had seized the Andaman islands and the British fleet had to retire to the coast of East Africa. The first British request for American troops was not for the war against Germany, but to protect Australia from the advancing

Japanese. And the first American request for aid was for a British air-craft carrier to leave the Indian Ocean and join the hard-pressed American fleet in the Coral Sea. Admiral King, the Commander in Chief of the US fleet, never forgave the British for refusing to order it to sail there. Meanwhile the German army was driving towards the Caucasus and threatening the British supplies of oil in Iraq. When the Americans and British conferred to make plans, they first asked themselves what they could do to prevent Russia from being knocked out of the war, and what they must do were that to happen.

So when in April 1942 the American Chief of Staff General George Marshall, and Harry Hopkins, President Roosevelt's friend and trouble-shooter, arrived in London, they brought with them an operation put forward by the American planners under General Eisenhower. Their plan was to establish a cross-Channel bridge-head between Calais and Dieppe that very summer. Then in 1943 the Anglo-American armies would break out of it.

'Do we go east, south or west after landing?' asked Brooke. General Marshall said that the plan envisaged a drive towards Paris. Brooke was appalled. The Americans could contribute only two and a half divisions. To expect a force even of ten divisions to survive in a bridgehead, the ports exposed to air attack all winter, and then to expose one's left flank to a German counterattack seemed senseless.[9]* It should be remembered that both Marshall and Brooke were under pressure from the President and the Prime Minister to do something to relieve the Russians, who continued to give ground under the new German offensives. Churchill in particular was embarrassed by the press campaign for 'A Second Front Now', orchestrated by a rum alliance of the Beaverbrook press and the Communist Party. Brooke, however, had to explain

* Weinberg states that, in order to present Brooke as a consistent opponent of a landing in 1942, the historian Arthur Bryant who edited his diaries suppressed an entry which described a Chief of Staff meeting at which Brooke advocated landing in the Calais-Boulogne area, whereas Mountbatten favoured Cherbourg. But in fact the passage refers to a very different kind of operation, such as the raid on Dieppe: 'I had propounded a theory that a western front to be of use must entail withdrawal of forces from Russia. That it was impossible with the land forces at our disposal to force the Germans to withdraw land forces from Russia: but that it might induce them to withdraw air forces. But to do this a landing must take place within our own umbrella namely in the vicinity of Calais and Boulogne.'[10]

that operations in 1942 were virtually impossible. All available British shipping had gone to the Indian Ocean and the Middle East. In the end they agreed to mount a major cross-Channel operation in 1943; and when Churchill and Brooke visited Washington in June 1942 Brooke confirmed that the British Chiefs accepted that France should be invaded the following year.

They then found that their Generalissimos had other ideas. When Churchill had set sail for Washington in December 1941 he had taken with him a plan for an Anglo-American landing in Africa, and Roosevelt had approved. It was not a case of the President bowing to Churchill's pressure. Roosevelt was anxious that American troops should be in action against the Axis forces somewhere in 1942. He feared that if they were not, public opinion would demand that the main American effort be transferred to the Pacific. The force was to land at Casablanca, but the scheme was shelved for lack of shipping and because an advance north would depend on a rickety wood-burning railway with insufficient capacity to supply an adequate force. The Joint Planning and Intelligence Staffs regarded a North African landing as one of the variants open to the Anglo-Americans, but Brooke had still not warmed to it in June 1942. All British and American forces should be concentrated in Britain; and Henry Stimson, the American Secretary for War, warned Roosevelt against letting the British sirens entice him into their Mediterranean lair. But when Churchill again suggested in private in Hyde Park, with no military advisers in sight, the advantages of a landing not on the west, but on the north coast of Africa, Roosevelt got the Combined Chiefs of Staff to agree to produce such a scheme as an alternative if further study showed that a cross-Channel operation in 1942 was impossible. It became impossible as they were conferring. On 21 June, while Churchill was talking with Roosevelt in his study, Marshall handed them a message that Tobruk had surrendered. Roosevelt expressed his sympathy exquisitely; Marshall diverted 300 tanks, 100 guns and later General Brereton's bomber force to Cairo; and when Brooke returned to London he at last saw the direction Allied strategy should take.

Brooke appreciated that the Germans had the immense advantage of interior lines of communication. They could always move troops quicker than the Allies to any part of the Continent. If, therefore, the Allies were to invade anywhere, they would have to build up their forces very quickly to avoid being driven into the sea by the finest professional army in the world. The Allies would never achieve that build-up unless they had command of the air and a vast fleet of landing craft and supply ships. *Per contra*, the Germans laboured under one enormous disadvantage: they were outnumbered by the combined Soviet and Anglo-American forces, and they could not compete with the American production lines that turned out ships, aircraft, tanks and above all motor transport of every kind, including the famous Jeep.

From these premises sprang the concept that Brooke argued should guide Allied strategy. That was the concept of *stretch*. The German forces must be stretched so that they were strung out virtually the whole length of occupied Europe, from north of Narvik to the Spanish frontier, and from the south of France to the Balkans and Greece. Every part of the coast must be threatened by ruse, by disinformation and by guerrilla forces, *maquis* and partisans, so that when the time came to invade Europe the Germans would be unable to bring an overwhelming force to bear that could destroy the invader's bridgehead.

Brooke never forgot that shipping was the crux. Not simply shipping needed for the combined operations, but shipping to transport American divisions and supplies across the Atlantic and to move British divisions and supplies to Egypt – and also to India to counter the Japanese. Reopen the Mediterranean, and the long haul round the Cape of Good Hope to the Middle East would be ended. A million tons of shipping would be released.

As Brooke was coming to these conclusions, the Battle of the Atlantic had taken an ominous turn. In 1941 Ultra had enabled the Navy almost to drive the U-boats back to their bases, such were their losses. But then in 1942 the Germans added a fourth wheel to the Enigma machine installed in U-boats. Ultra dried up, the cryptanalysts were baffled, and the Germans in their turn cracked the Royal Navy's cypher and therefore knew which routes our convoys would take. The U-boats first made a killing off the American east coast, where shipping was unprotected, and next attacked the convoys. Eight million tons of shipping were lost in 1942, of which six and a quarter were sunk by U-boats. In July alone 400,000 tons were lost, and until well into 1943 sinkings exceeded the building of new tonnage. Brooke considered our immediate objective must be to hang on as best we could. The Allies might find shipping for a limited operation in North Africa, and a little more to reinforce India. But to imagine that American divisions and equipment could be sent to Britain in sufficient quantity for an autumn landing in 1942 was madness, and even for a spring landing in 1943 problematic. So he now threw his weight behind the North African campaign.

Sensing that this was so, General Marshall, Admiral King and Harry Hopkins visited London in July 1942, in considerable alarm. Marshall was perturbed that the British were going back on their agreement to mount a cross-Channel operation in the summer of 1943. This time Marshall suggested landing six divisions on the Cherbourg peninsula and establishing a bridgehead which would be reinforced in 1943. In the end the American Chiefs were persuaded that, while preparations to invade Europe in 1943 should continue, the situation on the Russian front might become so grave that such an invasion would be impossible. The Allies should therefore launch a combined operation on the north coast of Africa. They also agreed that a small cross-Channel diversionary operation was not feasible. Ill-conceived though it was, the Dieppe raid of August 1942, in which the Canadians endured such fearsome losses, showed that to be self-evident.

It was from these beginnings that the celebrated division arose between the American and the British Chiefs of Staff on the issue of a Mediterranean strategy as opposed to a cross-Channel strategy. Brooke believed that Marshall never understood his point that the Germans would be able to build up their forces quicker than the Allies in an opposed landing in Europe. That was why the British Planning and Intelligence Staffs stipulated that Overlord, the Normandy invasion, could not be launched until three conditions obtained. The Allies must have air supremacy; they must not have to face more than twelve mobile divisions in France; and no more than fifteen divisions could be withdrawn by the Germans from other fronts. Marshall felt he had been – not outsmarted, because he was too high-minded to accuse his ally of duplicity – but outmanoeuvred. In his heart he believed that the British were putting first the defence of their Empire, in the Middle East, in India and in the Pacific; and for that reason they had gone back on their agreement in April to put the invasion of France first. Nor was this belief absurd. The words 'British Empire' were often on Brooke's lips, and never out of Churchill's mind. (The pre-war Chiefs of Staff approved Chamberlain's Munich Settlement on the grounds that the Empire was not endangered.) Very rightly, Marshall held that the war in the West could be won only by a cross-Channel invasion. Very rightly, he feared that if too many forces were committed in the Mediterranean Overlord might be indefinitely postponed. The Americans also suspected Churchill of attempting to justify his Dardanelles policy of thirty years ago. Nor did they fail to comment that the Prime Minister's plan to attack 'the soft underbelly of the crocodile' was not a felicitous description of the mountainous spine of Italy.

The Americans had further ground for concern. The British could not afford to incur casualties. When they finally invaded Europe in June 1944 they had five million men, the Americans eleven million, under arms. By September 1944 British divisions in Europe were being cannibalised to provide reinforcements. Both Churchill and Brooke feared a massacre on the Normandy beaches. Henry Stimson considered that 'The shadows of Passchendaele and Dunkerque still hang heavy on the imagination of those leaders.'[11]

Montgomery knew that the imagination of the citizen army he commanded was also at work on those losses: that was why he reassured his troops that he would never commit them to battle unless the plan he had formed was 'teed up' and they would be supported by overwhelming air cover and artillery fire. I remember when Tobruk fell in June 1942 the young New Zealand officer who was working with me in MI14 said, 'Christ, the buggers can't have fought'; and this disaster, coming so soon after the ignominious surrender of Singapore, made Churchill fear that the morale of the Army had crumbled. 'Get you the sons your fathers got, And God will save the Queen', ran the last lines of the first poem in *A Shropshire Lad*. But were we the sons of our fathers who had endured the horrors in the trenches and died there in their thousands?

The Army's morale did not crumble. The fighting spirit of certain formations – the Brigade of Guards, the Commandos and other elite units such as General Roberts' 11th Armoured and the 15th Scottish Division – was beyond question, but some of the divisions back from North Africa, such as the famous 7th Armoured Division, the Desert Rats, were battle-weary and disinclined to put their lives on the line again in the unfamiliar *bocage* dissected by sunken roads and hedgerows. Both American and British tanks were inferior to the enemy's, as were their anti-tank guns. In Normandy the Germans were to inflict upon the Allies 50 per cent more casualties than they suffered because they were better trained – trained in two years of fighting on the Russian front, trained to exploit any advantage that appeared on the field of battle. The German non-commissioned officer was trained to take over if his commander was killed. There was more *Kameradschaft* in the German ranks. Soldiers understood that they were expected to do more than they were actually ordered to do. Perhaps Churchill's remark about 'teeth and tail' was not so wide of the mark: the Germans had 25 per cent more of their troops in combat units than the British. The Prime Minister was right to press for our forces in Italy to be redeployed to reinforce the fighting strength in Normandy.[12]

In the higher ranks, our failings went back to the standing of the peacetime army. The British officer between the wars was not the professional he is today. The Army provided him with a life in which hunting, shooting and playing games were almost considered to be part of his work. They were meant to give him an eye for country and the spirit of teamwork and comradeship so that 'the men would follow him anywhere'. He knew the points of a horse, not of a tank. He cared for his men, but his horizon rarely rose above the regimental mess. The top brass stamped on originality, ignored air power and despised intelligence, and the Staff College still taught the tactics of the First World War. A few good brains stood out – Wavell being the best of them – but much dead wood had to be cleared away in the first two years of the war. The nation got what it deserved. Public opinion had been hostile to military expenditure and was in general pacifist – in the sense that the majority wanted to believe that never again would European nations go to war. A few pacifists vowed never to fight again whatever the cause.

As a result there was no cadre of regular officers fit to command formations above a battalion. Brooke wrote in his diary in March 1942: 'Half our Corps and Divisional Commanders are totally unfit for their appointments; and yet if I were to sack them I could find no better. They lack character, imagination, drive and power of leadership.'[13] Wellington had made the same complaint in the Peninsular War: 'When I reflect upon the characters and attainments of some of the general officers of this army, and consider that these are the persons on whom I am to rely to lead columns against the French, I tremble . . .'[14] Brooke blamed the First World War for decimating the country's leaders; but Germany had suffered even worse losses. The difference was that Germany had a professional officer class, a General Staff and a long tradition of conscription.

The British and Americans doubted each other's military ability. The British, who had been fighting for two years, thought American commanders lacked battle experience: their soldiers were fine fellows, but Brooke, watching them training in Northern Ireland in 1943 for the Algerian landings, was unimpressed by their staff work; and the bloody nose Rommel gave them in the Kasserine Pass in February 1943 confirmed him in his opinion. He forgot how well the Americans had fought at Guadalcanal and in the Philippines. He was dismayed that Marshall and Eisenhower would ask their planning staff for a brief, which they would usually accept; the British practice was for the commander himself to decide what to do and where to go, and the staff's job was to make that feasible or tell him it was not. The British, Brooke included, never understood the strength of American manpower and industry, how prodigal Americans could afford to be with equipment and transport.

For their part, the Americans did not feel obliged to take advice from an ally who had been defeated in Europe, Africa and Asia. To them the British were over-cautious and obsessed with tidy staff-work, tidy battles. Their ideal commander was the flamboyant General George Patton, their model for a battle was American football, in which you hurled yourself at the foe and grappled him to the earth. Their elite troops – the Marines, the Airborne and other picked divisions – they regarded as a match for any Allied or enemy formation. Stimson believed that American troops would storm ashore in Normandy uninhibited by memories of the Somme. As the greatest manufacturing nation in the world, the civilian recruits were often skilled mechanics and tough managers. The Americans knew they had much to learn, and they learnt faster than the British.

As a result of these differences, every proposal to press on with other operations in the Mediterranean – to take Sicily, invade Italy, attack the Balkans – was regarded with apprehension and suspicion by the Americans. Brooke's first difficulty, however, was to get his own team together. At the beginning of December 1942, soon after Eisenhower's forces landed in North Africa, Churchill swung towards a cross-Channel invasion in 1943. Then the combined operations department put forward a plan endorsed by Eisenhower to invade Sardinia; once again the plan did not envisage going anywhere after the beaches were gained. In mid-January Brooke got the Americans to agree that Sicily and not Sardinia should be the next target, only to find a week later that his own planners in the War Cabinet Offices considered Sardinia the better bet. The Americans would have been surprised to learn that Churchill was now urging a cross-Channel invasion. In July 1943, on the day Sicily was invaded, he was saying to Brooke: 'If you think you are going to get off with your Sardines this year, you are mistaken – we shall go across the Channel.'[15] When the Italians showed signs of suing for peace, it was almost impossible to refuse to take the next step in the Mediterranean strategy and invade Italy. This time Brooke was supported by the American air commanders, who wanted the Foggia airfields from which to bomb south Germany.

But Marshall was again alarmed, and was determined to hog-tie the British to Overlord. Brooke was to complain that at the Casablanca (January 1943) and Quebec (August 1943) conferences the Americans demanded lawyers' agreements which 'once signed could never be departed from'.[16] (But were not his three conditions for Overlord no less a legal agreement?) The British Chiefs of Staff understandably pleaded for flexibility, so that if the Allies broke through in Italy they could exploit their victory. When Mussolini fell in July 1943 General Alexander ordered a standstill on the seven divisions and landing craft that were to be transferred from the

Mediterranean to become the spearhead of Overlord. The Americans interpreted this as further evidence that the British intended to cop out from the cross-Channel invasion, and the British suffered a reverse at the Quebec conference when they had to agree, with reluctance, to the invasion of the south of France by an American-French force to relieve pressure on Overlord.

The spectacle of Churchill grasping at every opportunity to go off in some new direction hardened the American strategists. Why should they be beguiled by this Atalanta who, every time the goddess of love bowled a golden apple across her path, stooped to gather it and was deflected from her true goal? They sensed too that Brooke was apprehensive each time the Allies launched an amphibious operation. He feared that the Salerno landings would fail, and castigated the JIC for vagueness about enemy reaction when the operation was being planned. In his heart he feared Overlord. But in his mind he recognised it was inevitable. His resolution was to be tested. On 19 October 1943 Churchill ordered plans to be made were Overlord to be cancelled. Brooke knew that immediate opposition only made the Prime Minister more obstinate and intent to get his own way, so he saw to it that the Chiefs of Staff duly clucked in sympathy. But he had no intention of cancelling Overlord, and on 11 November the Chiefs reaffirmed their commitment to it.

Such was the panorama that I had to survey and in part memorise when I began to work in the War Cabinet Offices. What role did we, the intelligence staff there, play in the debate about grand strategy? How did we work, and what were our disputes? They were as intense during the war as the disputes of the military historians have been after it.

CHAPTER FOUR

❖

The Joint Intelligence Staff

The military branch of the War Cabinet was organised on one cardinal principle: the Chiefs of Staff must be given a unanimous view by their planning and intelligence staffs. Their conclusions might include qualifications, but they must be as definite as possible. The Chiefs of Staff might reject the advice and tell their staffs to think again on different assumptions. Or, more often, the staffs would be faced by questions and criticisms put to them by the Prime Minister briefed by his kitchen cabinet. The War Cabinet secretariat under General Hollis was there to help them; and he in turn was wired to General Ismay, Churchill's military troubleshooter.

It was also obvious that the planners and intelligence must express a unanimous view to the Americans. In one sense life was made easier for the British because, unlike the Prime Minister, who was always liable to resurrect some idea that his Chiefs of Staff thought they had buried long ago, President Roosevelt, though Commander in Chief of the American armed forces, had no pretensions to be a strategist. He relied on the massive integrity of General Marshall, and what Marshall said was the unanimous American view. But in another sense things were not so easy. Admiral King, the Commander in Chief of the US Fleet, was determined to pursue his own war – the war in the Pacific; and whenever possible he would try to divert landing craft and troops there rather than across the Atlantic. But there was less divergence between Washington and London on the details of planning and intelligence than might have been expected. The work spent studying Churchill's schemes, however unrealistic, paid off. The British had already examined the options available, and could put before their American allies all the pros and cons. It was this that gave the British an advantage in argument at the Casablanca and Washington conferences in 1943.

The Joint Intelligence Staff owed their existence to the Director of Naval Intelligence, Admiral Godfrey. Godfrey was a sea-dog with the customary Naval disdain for the 'Royal Advertising Force' and, after fishing our troops out of the sea off Dunkirk, Greece and Crete, for what he called 'the Evacuees'. In 1941 he recognised that the JIC could not find time to draft papers for the Chiefs of Staff and the Joint Planners, when often the Prime Minister expected answers within twenty-four hours. The JIC had too many other duties, not least of which was supervising all the other inter-service intelligence bodies. So he and Cavendish-Bentinck persuaded their colleagues to create in their mirror image two teams called the Joint Intelligence Staff to do the work for them, and produce drafts for their approval. Each member of the team would take the draft to his own ministry and try to get his Director of Intelligence to agree to sign it. In my case the Director of Military Intelligence (who would have circulated the draft to the sections under him – primarily MI14 – to check the figures and criticise the argument) would then go through the draft with me and urge me to change this, or modify that, or on no account to agree with some other contention. The Joint Intelligence Staff would then meet, each of us with the list of amendments that his Director of Intelligence had proposed, and try to reach agreement. The agreed paper would then go to the JIC, where one's own Director might be indignant that his strictures on the draft had not been accepted.

Each of us on the JIS, when the paper we were drafting concerned most vitally his own ministry, would find his colleagues curiously critical and insensitive; but when one's own ministry was only marginally concerned how odd it was that the main protagonist, so sensible and receptive at other times, seemed hide-bound and crippled in argument by the ridiculous brief his ministry had given him! The War Office was nearly always at the centre of the problems we considered, so I found the going rough.

The final resolution of these difficulties rested with the chairman of the JIC. William Cavendish-Bentinck may have been the youngest member of that body, but he did not stand in awe of admirals, generals or air marshals. No aristocrat ever looked more aristocratic. The black coat, striped trousers and spongebag tie were surmounted by the delicate peaches-and-cream complexion of a face which might have been in the mind of Dorothy Sayers when she created Lord Peter Wimsey (he did in fact end his days as the Duke of Portland). Bill Bentinck sometimes dropped into our mess before dinner to pick our brains and get a premonition of likely disagreements on the JIC. He held informal meetings to discuss enemy intentions, and encouraged junior as well as senior officers to speak their minds. No one was better informed about every intrigue in the War Cabinet Offices, and he never disclosed his sources. 'My dog Angus tells me . . .' he would begin; and you listened.

It was he who convinced the service chiefs that obsessive secrecy about plans could bring disaster. When in 1940 the British decided to land troops in Norway, the planners operated in such secrecy that they never consulted the intelligence staff, nor asked them how many divisions and aircraft might oppose us and when they might arrive on the scene if we landed. Bentinck got the planning and intelligence staffs to work together in adjacent rooms.

He was both astute and prescient. Against the view of the War Office he maintained in 1940 that the Germans would not invade unless they won air superiority, and when the Director of Military Intelligence, Beaumont-Nesbit, insisted in a JIC paper of 7 September 1940 that they would, Bentinck and Godfrey refused to sign the paper.[1] He was the first on the JIC to discount the danger of a German invasion of Britain in 1941; he refused to believe reports that the Germans would persuade Franco to give them free passage through Spain to attack Gibraltar; and he was among those who declared that Hitler was about to attack Russia. Later he admitted that it was instinct rather than evidence that made him so sure of this last: 'I had at the back of my mind the French saying "*On revient toujours à ses premiers amours et aussi à ses premières haines.*" '
For Bentinck Britain's interests were paramount, but he could carry *Realpolitik* too far. In an indiscreet memo of February 1943, opposing one of the many phantom invasions of Europe intended to deceive the Germans, he wrote that since Stalingrad our immediate strategic objective had changed. Until then it had been in our interest to do all we could to take pressure off Russia. Now that the tide had turned, it was in our interest to let Germany and Russia

bleed each other white. We would find it easier to effect a landing in Europe, and Russia, however sentimental the British people might be about her, was likely to be a troublesome customer at the end of the war. Quick as some have been to take this as conclusive evidence that Britain did not intend to open a second front in 1943, it did not deter us from landing in Italy, and this off-the-cuff whiff of prescience about the post-war world did not affect the strategic assessments of the Joint Intelligence Committee.

Although Bentinck prompted the newly formed Joint Intelligence Staff to draft a paper predicting the attack, it was months before he could persuade his colleagues to sign it. Yet he had the gift of producing harmony among the service intelligence chiefs. He would listen, his long fingers touching his chin, looking relaxed and cunning, defusing disagreement with banter. An intelligence officer who argues that the worst case is the most likely is a menace: he paralyses his commander's initiative. Bentinck would try – not always successfully – to deflect any of the armed services from inserting a cover-up clause in case their estimate of the Germans' capability proved to be wrong. He was adamant in backing the Joint Intelligence Staff view that the German army would be unable to transfer any significant number of divisions from the Russian front when the Allies landed on the Normandy beaches. He could not, of course, overrule his colleagues from the armed forces: 'I always had,' he said, 'to produce overwhelming evidence in arguments with my service colleagues.'[2] He was a shrewd judge of people, and spotted Kim Philby as an odd fish when he once appeared at a JIC meeting.*

But like all of us he could make misjudgements, and occasionally he allowed his diplomatic training to form his preferences. He preferred General Dill to Brooke as CIGS – he thought Brooke too much of a bully – and Air Chief Marshal Portal to both. He had his reasons for holding these views.

Brooke challenged the considered verdict of the Joint Intelligence Committee. Against the evidence he maintained that the

---

* 'I suppose that accounts for it,' he said when told that Philby was the son of St John Philby, whose defeatism and praise for Hitler in 1939 made Bentinck exclaim that his Indian government pension should be cut off. The elder Philby was detained in Britain on similar grounds to Oswald Mosley.[3]

German High Command must have retained a central reserve of some twenty divisions in Italy to thwart any Anglo-American landing or initiative. He was also convinced that the Germans must try to capture the Baku oilfields in the Caucasus; and what easier way to do so than to persuade Turkey to give their armies passage? For months he scouted the plan to land in North Africa for a similar reason: Hitler would blackguard France into letting him cross Spain and take Gibraltar. On the JIC Admiral Godfrey would have none of this: he was his own master and argued from the evidence. On the other side of the table General Davidson reflected Brooke's fears. Unfortunately Godfrey not only slighted Davidson: he was no less scathing about the ineffectiveness of the RAF in bombing U-boat pens and naval installations (in which inevitably air crew lost their lives). Davidson and his Air Force colleague got Brooke and Portal to ask old Admiral Pound to give them a more amenable naval representative. Bentinck admired Godfrey, but when he was asked point-blank by Pound's deputy whether Godfrey was difficult to get on with, he had to say that meetings of the JIC at which Godfrey was not present went a good deal more smoothly than those at which he was. In September 1942 Godfrey was promoted to vice-admiral and replaced on the JIC the same day, by a curt memo from Pound, with someone not of his calibre.[4]

This lamentable intrigue took place before I joined the JIS. Our masters in the JIC were not an impressive team: in Bentinck's view much inferior to the Joint Planners where the naval and air representatives always went to the top of their profession. Geoffrey Vickers from the Ministry of Economic Warfare, a First World War holder of the Victoria Cross, was able enough, but both the Air Force and the War Office insisted that their representative on the Joint Intelligence Staff should argue from the brief prepared by their ministries. We had read the evidence, but it was the job of those who briefed us to analyse it. Each of us brought to the table our own service's interpretation of the evidence. Then the battle began.

The Joint Intelligence Staff worked underground in bomb-proof offices next to the War Cabinet itself in Great George Street, just off Parliament Square. I can still remember the dull thump and a faint tremor when we were working on a Sunday morning and the Guards Chapel in Birdcage Walk 200 yards away was hit by a bomb. We rarely encountered Churchill himself. Once, however, I saw him come rolling down the passage in his boiler suit. As he was about to pass our diminutive mess, where Marine sergeants served us stupefying whiskies before we resumed our labours deep into the night, he put his head around the door and said with a seraphic smile: 'Working hard, I see, gentlemen.'

I would arrive in the morning hoping not to be greeted by the news that the Prime Minister wanted us once again to study the merits of taking Trondheim, and after a word with my Colonel, would walk across the Horse Guards to the War Office to see old friends in MI14 and ask them for a brief on the likely opposition and build-up of German forces were we to do anything so foolish as again to land in Norway. There I read the Ultra decrypts and moved to other departments whose views I wanted for our work. If a JIS draft were ready, the most disturbing duty was to go through it with the Deputy Director of Military Intelligence – sometimes with General Davidson himself.

Davidson was a trim, compact figure with twinkling eyes – a genial uncle who was courteous to his staff, solicitous to the elderly and encouraging to the young. His deputy, Brigadier Kirkman (whose brother rose to be Corps Commander under Montgomery), was the counterbalance: sly, sarcastic, disapproving but meticulous. If you took your draft to Davidson you knew what its fate would be. He would not challenge the main premises, but would inflict death by a thousand cuts. He had signed JIC papers which maintained, even before Stalingrad, that if the Allies invaded Europe, the Germans would be unable to send any sizeable force to the west from the Russian front. But he never assented in his heart to this proposition as an act of what theologians called 'unformed faith'. So if, after hours of arguing, I was able to get my colleague to agree to insert in the draft that in certain dire circumstances, the Germans 'might conceivably send two or even three divisions to the West', General Davidson would amend the section to 'may well send four to six divisions to the West'. He did this to humour the CIGS – for Brooke was reluctant to accept the advice of his intelligence staff, and clung to the notion that somewhere in Germany Hitler had a strategic reserve; as indeed Hitler should have done.

Davidson would emerge from his office en route to brief the CIGS with a stack of files under his arm in which a dozen or so pages had been flagged, some of the flags fluttering to the floor as he walked. His opposite number General John Kennedy, Director of Plans, would emerge from his office with a slip of paper in his hand – all that he required to brief Brooke. Cavendish-Bentinck regarded Davidson as a 'very mediocre officer with a permanent desire to make our reports fit in with the view of the CIGS'.[5] Peter Earle told me that when he became military assistant to Brooke, the Vice-Chief of the General Staff, General Nye, used to urge Brooke to get rid of Davidson; but Brooke liked to see familiar faces, and took no action until Davidson's passion for detail and long-winded exposition exasperated him and he finally gave the word. A month later he turned to Nye and said, 'Why didn't you tell me to sack that fellow before now?' Most of us who worked for Davidson were fond of him, but we saw his failings. He was succeeded in 1943 by General Sinbad Sinclair, who after the war took over from Stewart Menzies as head of MI6.*

After I emerged from Davidson's or Kirkman's room, the draft in tatters (the Military Intelligence departments and MI14 sections concerned each having had a bite at it), I would return to the War Cabinet Offices. There I found my colleagues assembling to go through the draft and if possible finalise it.

We on the Joint Intelligence Staff, who wrote the papers for the JIC to sign (or reject), were all civilians dressed in uniform – with the exception of Captain Charles Drake RN, who had retired to become a stockbroker. My Colonel, Larry Kirwan, later the Director of the Royal Geographical Society, was the easiest of men to work for, and left me in charge when he went off in attendance at Quebec and other major conferences. He compared Cavendish-Bentinck to a Greek Archimandrite, and noted that he often took a line quite different from the brief his subordinates in the Foreign

---

* Sinclair's time there was a disaster, a tale of failed attempts at the assassination of foreign troublemakers such as Nasser. It culminated in the fiasco of the wretched frogman Commander 'Buster' Crabbe, who was killed trying to inspect the hull of a Soviet cruiser on a goodwill visit to Portsmouth.[6]

Office had given. Sir Andrew Noble, a baronet, was the senior Foreign Office member; as a joke he could reel off paragraph after paragraph of the official opening of a despatch (which when encyphered was reduced to one group of figures). His own contributions seemed to have much the same degree of originality, but he was always willing to be the one ready, as he put it, to 'hatch out a draft'. As a Naval colleague I had my near-contemporary Charles Fletcher-Cooke, impersonating a Naval Lieutenant-Commander. At Cambridge he had been President of the Union, editor of *Granta* and much else besides. He returned in 1944 from a short trip to Washington with the usual parcel of goodies from that unrationed land and also with the gramophone records of *Oklahoma!*, to which he gave spirited imitations of the dances.

My Air Force colleague was a far older Cambridge graduate. Francis Ogilvy, dressed as an RAF Squadron Leader, was by that time at the top of the advertising agency Mather & Crowther. Fair, red-faced, stout, he would rap on the counter at his club for three double whiskies before he felt ready to dine; but, skilled as a copywriter and adept at presentations to clients, he was a master at drafting. He demanded a strict, logical argument before he would endorse a particular view. He would cut out the epigrammatic reviews that I wrote in the evenings for the *New Statesman* and hand them to me covered with corrections and satirical comments; and he taught me how to draft less badly than I did. He used to say that the best advertising agencies were not nefarious persuaders but business doctors, who told a potential client that his product cost more and was less well designed than that of his competitors. If after that he still gave you his account, you could do business.

Indeed, the Air Ministry had beyond question the most impressive team, and its senior representative came to dominate the JIS. Howard Millis wore Air Force uniform, but it was covered with decorations (DSO and MC with bar) won during his days as an Infantry officer in the First World War. Medium height, dark hair, spruce, his cheek was furrowed by a scar: he had been shot through the face on the Somme, was gassed and wounded again at Passchendaele, and survived the German offensive in 1918. By now he had become a senior partner of Barings and was Vice-Chairman of the Governors of the BBC. That in itself demanded good judgement.

The demands of war censorship conflicted with the reputation for accurate reporting of war news the BBC was determined to acquire, and which won admiration throughout occupied Europe. At Barings Millis had the reputation of being short-tempered, but he was invariably polite, intelligent and unshakeably tenacious in argument. Yet he had a way of conveying by a look, a steady unforgiving gaze, that to disagree with him was to be specious and probably devious. I was told on my arrival that in 1941 he had kept putting to the Planners the advantages of landing in North Africa, and conquered the doubts of Alan Brooke and the Americans. As late as 1943 Admiral King was still maintaining that Hitler might suddenly drive through Spain, take Gibraltar and imprison the Allied forces in the Mediterranean. Millis persuaded the JIS that this was beyond the capability of the German army, and the Foreign Office backed him, saying that Franco would resist. The Foreign Office was again right in forecasting that the French army would not for long oppose an Allied landing in Algeria – though the French Admiral Esteva allowed the Germans to land on the Tunisian airfields.[7]

The papers we wrote ranged over the globe. How important are the Balkans to Germany and what problems do they face there? What will be the strength of the Japanese forces in the Andaman islands if we decide to retake them? Will Bulgaria revolt? What is happening in Greece? What principles should dictate our bombing policy – and what is its effect? It was, of course, difficult to arrive at a unanimous view. The Royal Navy was neutral. After all, the likely opposition to any combined operation by the German navy would amount to only a few torpedo boats. Their own private war against the U-boats in the Atlantic rarely concerned us, except when the Prime Minister directed that if Portugal refused to give us bases in the Azores for our long-range anti-U-boat aircraft we should take the islands by force. The Foreign Office, alarmed by this treatment of Britain's oldest ally, wanted to put the disadvantages of such Hitlerian treatment before the Chiefs of Staff. But on most issues the Foreign Office took a somewhat *dégagé* pose. If a diplomatic issue, such as Turkey's neutrality, was on the agenda, they would announce with solemnity that Turkey would be governed by its own self-interest. What country is not?

The real battle was joined between the Air Ministry and the War

Office. The Royal Air Force were consistent optimists. They took the line that there was hardly any need for Overlord. A few more thousand-bomber air raids would finish the war. This was, of course, music to Churchill's ears, and the RAF hoped to get industrial priorities rearranged so that more resources would be made available for Bomber Command and less for tiresome support operations for the land forces or for the Navy and Coastal Command in the Battle of the Atlantic. The Ministry of Economic Warfare blew hot and cold, dubious when asked to endorse Air Marshal 'Bomber' Harris's strategy of flattening German cities to break German morale, encouraging if the bombers went for ball-bearing or synthetic-rubber factories.

The War Office, however, was a consistent pessimist. Such had been the reverses suffered by the Army that the War Office – so my colleagues thought – tended to exaggerate the scale of German resistance to any Allied initiative. Nor were they so wrong to do so. In North Africa, at Salerno and at Anzio, and especially in the Balkans, the German army conjured reserves seemingly out of thin air. My chiefs in the War Office had good reason to be cautious, but they found difficulty in marshalling convincing reasons for this caution. Its true cause, which they did not think politic to admit – and were reluctant even to admit to themselves – was that the German army was superior in equipment, training, tactics and battle drill. The Air Ministry representatives on the Joint Intelligence Staff were justly proud of the courage of our fighter pilots in the Battle of Britain and our bomber crews over Germany. It was difficult to convince them how bloody and harsh an affair infantry warfare is. Francis Ogilvy teased me by declaring: 'Major Annan is working on a new and revolutionary theory. He hopes shortly to be able to show that the strength of an army is increased by exercise, provided that the exercise is taken in retreat. Thus the further the German army withdraws, the stronger it will become.'[8]

Nothing produced more hyperactivity on the Joint Intelligence Staff than the preparation for an Anglo-American conference. The early conferences at Washington and Casablanca had gone much as the British wanted. There had been no agenda. Discussion ranged over every aspect of policy, and the American and British Chiefs of Staff got lost in a maze of telegrams to and from their staffs at home in search of facts and forecasts. Churchill had been well satisfied with the Casablanca conference. He had got provisional agreement to assault Sicily and, at the Washington conference, to invade Italy. The American Chiefs of Staff were troubled. Surely the Allies were in danger of forgetting their commitment to Overlord, the cross-Channel invasion. They sent a telegram in June 1943 saying that 'there is danger of us exploiting success after success in the Mediterranean'; and their unease was heightened when General Alexander issued the standstill order countermanding the movement of troops and landing craft for Overlord. To sort these matters out a conference was arranged in Quebec in August.

The Prime Minister set out in a determined frame of mind. Not without cunning, he agreed that the agenda should be short, strictly adhered to, and deal mainly with the Far East. At first all seemed to go well. The Americans agreed that the Italian campaign should continue on the understanding that the stand-still order was revoked; and Churchill agreed that no substantial operation could be undertaken in the eastern Mediterranean. But the Prime Minister had been hoist with his own petard. Not only was his pet amphibious operation in the Indian Ocean turned down by his own Chiefs of Staff, but the operation there that had been approved, namely retaking the Andaman islands, took landing craft away from the Mediterranean. When Italy collapsed in September 1943, only two brigade groups were in reserve for ancillary operations.

Churchill used to call the Joint Planners 'psalm-singing defeatists' for puncturing so many of his schemes. As soon as he put a lump of sugar on the table these disgusting bluebottles would settle on it. The intelligence staff were less inhibited. They tried to detect Germany's weaknesses or, at least, the limitations of her power. In 1942 the Joint Intelligence Staff under Millis's inspiration provided a list of impossibilities. We maintained that the Germans were not strong enough to invade Iran, or to drive through Turkey to Syria. In 1943 we declared that from now on the German army would be on the defensive, unable to mount a major operation in Russia. Loud were the jeers when von Manstein launched his 'Citadel' attack at Kursk, but in the event the JIS were proved right: the German army lacked the reserves to sustain their attack and the Russians passed to the counter-offensive.

And yet it must be admitted that some of the most ill-judged JIC papers were written under Millis's influence, particularly at the time when the Allies were pondering what should be their next move after the German defeat in North Africa. In March 1943 the JIS flew a kite. Instead of landing in Sicily, why not mount the cross-Channel invasion? The Russians were driving the Germans back, therefore the Germans would have to deplete their forces in the west. The Chiefs of Staff were not impressed. So the JIS tried again. What would the Germans regard as their vital interests in the Mediterranean? Martin Watson, a fastidious analyst representing the Ministry of Economic Warfare, came into his own. He argued that the Balkans, in particular the bauxite at Mostar, were vital to Germany's economy: they were more important to them than Italy. Inspired by this, Millis declared that the German garrisons in the Balkans were 'even now barely sufficient to retain control';[9] and he got the JIC to sign a paper to the Chiefs of Staff arguing that in order to provide more troops to hold the Balkans, Hitler might withdraw his forces to northern Italy. The Chiefs were again unimpressed. A month later, in April 1943, the JIS again argued that if Italy collapsed the Germans would have to retreat to a line in the Appenines from Pisa to Rimini, and also gave a cheerful estimate of German resistance in France were the Allies to land there in 1943.

The month of August saw the consequences of Roosevelt's throwaway line at Casablanca about unconditional surrender. When the Italians put out feelers for peace it took over four weeks of comings and goings involving three Italian emissaries while the Allies tried (and failed) to impose their policy. That gave the Germans time to scrape up reserves and issue orders for disarming the Italian forces. They expected the Allies to make an airborne landing near Rome, so they did not move their newly arrived divisions in north Italy to the south. Rommel took command of them.

Over a hot weekend we drafted a paper on German plans and intentions. We rightly argued that Hitler would not make a strategic withdrawal in Russia. If he did so, where was he to find the forces to fight in Italy? At 2.30 a.m. on Sunday morning we got out a draft for the directors to sign. They rejected it. On Monday afternoon we began again. By now the Director of Military Intelligence was on record as saying that the Germans could provide only twelve 'offensive' divisions. If, argued Martin Watson, the Germans had to hold the Balkans for economic reasons and Italy required a million tons of oil a year and coal, and if, argued Millis, to hold the Balkans meant that the Germans could provide only four extra divisions for Italy, how could they hold on? I kept on arguing that the Germans would oppose us tooth and nail if we landed at Salerno, and stuck to our figures (which proved accurate) of the build-up of their forces when we landed.

Then unexpectedly the door opened. Denis Capel Dunn, the Secretary of the Joint Intelligence Committee itself, appeared bearing a decrypt. The decrypt described a conference between Hitler and his supreme commander in Italy, Field Marshal Kesselring. Hitler said he had no intention of holding the soles of the boot of Italy, and 'drawing with his finger upon the map' indicated the three lines where he would stand.

What were the three lines? Were they south of Rome? Or the Pisa–Rimini line of the Appenines? The river Po? The Alps? I had been arguing that Hitler would not yield ground, but the dramatic decrypt swung my colleagues to a man against me: Hitler could hardly have drawn three lines on the map between Rome and Salerno. We tore up our draft, opted for the north and finished at 3.30 a.m. on Tuesday morning.

Nor were we wrong. After the war it was discovered that Hitler did intend to make such a strategic withdrawal. All during September a flood of decrypts confirmed that Hitler planned to withdraw to north Italy to organise the defences there. Sardinia and Corsica were to be evacuated, and the Japanese ambassador in Berlin was told that Hitler had no intention of holding on in the south if the Salerno landings could not be defeated: nor would he attempt to hold Rome.

The JIS were elated. On 14 August we had forecast that the Germans would try to hold the Balkans, and discounted the possibility that Hungary or Romania would capitulate – though we were wrong to hint that the Germans might have to abandon Greece.

On 14 September we declared that it was the 'German intention eventually to withdraw to the north'.[10] Once again Millis got the bit between his teeth, and on 29 September he persuaded his colleagues that Hitler would be mad not to retreat to the Alps, holding only Venezia in order to deny us the airfields there, from which Vienna could be bombed. Indeed, if support for Tito in Yugoslavia could be stepped up and 'Allied action' increased, Germany might be forced out of the Balkans, or at the very worst be compelled to send further reinforcements there.[11] This was too much for Charles Fletcher-Cooke and myself. We christened that paper 'Roaring Through the Balkans'.

And then Hitler changed his mind. Kesselring was an abrasive character, and enjoyed putting Rommel in his place. Why, he asked, retreat so far north when the Allies were advancing so slowly? The fact that they were withdrawing landing craft from the Mediterranean suggested that Italy was a subsidiary front and would not need much reinforcement. Above all, why expose the Balkans to an Allied invasion: was not this the most dangerous threat of all? So on 2 October Hitler ordered his forces to give as little ground as possible, and to stand south of Naples.

Intelligence officers in the field began to re-examine the evidence. From optimism they plunged to pessimism. General Alexander now pointed out that the Germans had twenty-four divisions in Italy – might they not find sixty divisions in all, take the offensive and throw him out of the country? The JIC said there was no strategic reserve to produce sixty divisions; in any case, five or six of those twenty-four divisions were in Istria and Slovenia counter-attacking Tito's partisans. (By this time the cryptologists at Bletchley had broken by brainpower the 'Fish' cypher on which German strategic communications were processed. Unfortunately, most messages of this kind were sent by land line.) What we learnt from Ultra was disheartening. It revealed that the Germans were withdrawing crack divisions from Italy back to the Russian front.[12]

The CIGS was exceedingly displeased with his Intelligence advisers. At the Quebec conference Brooke had been unconvinced when he was told the JIC's contention that Hitler would retreat to the Pisa–Rimini line: all the more so since at the Washington conference in May the Americans had criticised the British for underestimating Germany's capacity to rise to emergencies. So on 2 November he told the JIC that they were complacent and over-optimistic:[13] 'There has been a tendency in the last two years,' he said, 'to underestimate the forces which the enemy can bring to bear in any particular theatre.'[14]

No wonder Brooke felt that Intelligence was once again wrong. We could not prove that Hitler had changed his mind. Neverthe-less, we were determined not to display the panic that seemed to have gripped Alexander's headquarters. We stuck to our guns and told the Chiefs of Staff that Alexander's fears were groundless and a German counter-offensive was not on; and they accepted this verdict.

Hitler's change of plan damaged the reputation of the JIC and JIS. Millis had deployed an argument that was difficult to counter. Surely the duty of an intelligence staff is to assume that the enemy will act with the utmost strategic wisdom. Manstein, the finest strategist among the German generals, was convinced that Hitler should have withdrawn to the Alps and created a strategic reserve. Manstein had already been the victim of Hitler's strategic inepti-tude: he had planned to attack the Russian salient at Kursk from the south while Army Group Centre battered the other flank of the salient from the north. Hitler wrecked his plan, postponing the attack month after month. When Manstein finally attacked in July 1943 the Soviet High Command were ready for him. They had been informed of the strength and direction of the German offen-sive by the Soviet spy John Cairncross at Bletchley, who relayed to his control the contents of the Ultra decrypts relating to the Russian front. (They were being sent, suitably disguised, to Stalin through our Embassy in Moscow.)

And then Hitler threw away any chance of holding the Russian counterattack by withdrawing divisions from Manstein's army group and telling his generals in Italy to hold every inch of ground south of Naples. It may well be said that after Stalingrad we in Intelligence should have appreciated Hitler's determination to hold to the last man and the last round every inch of territory that he had conquered. To retreat was to give up *Lebensraum*, that dream of settling the Ukraine with Nordic stock, for which he had started the war. Were we to predict that he would follow this policy when it meant the encirclement and destruction of his forces? Indeed, this happened. Army Group Centre in Russia was almost destroyed, and Army Group South would also have been destroyed, had not Manstein in the end disobeyed Hitler's orders and saved his troops. Hitler sacked him for doing so. The extent of Hitler's obsession was not known to us at the time. But even if it had been, an intelligence officer who tells his chief that the enemy will follow a line that is strategic folly will be disbelieved and discredited unless he can produce cast-iron factual corroboration.

There were two other reasons why the CIGS was so irritated. The first was that our generals in the field could have read the initial battle differently. Why mount all-out assaults and incur casualties unnecessarily if the enemy is going to withdraw? There is no evidence that Alexander, Mark Clark or Montgomery was so influenced (though Montgomery's advance was snail-like); but they could have been. The second reason was more serious. We failed to appreciate the German ability to improvise. We counted divisions and guessed how many could be moved from one front to another. We forgot that in any army there are always odds and sods, independent units, some combat formations refitting, some auxiliaries, some service troops that can be cobbled together and under a keen commander hold a line. The Germans reinforced the Balkans, but with *ersatz* units of Croats and Albanians. They upgraded divisions hitherto engaged in guarding lines of communication. Divisions from France and Norway arrived. At the height of the battle the Germans mustered not twelve but nineteen equivalent divisions. These figures pronounce a melancholy verdict on our predictions.

On another major appreciation of German intentions the JIS was correct. We predicted that they would hold the Balkans at all costs. No tactical withdrawal there. Nor were we wrong to refer to the opportunities if we intervened. Like Churchill, Millis was convinced that if we were held up in Italy we should hot up our Balkan threat through commando raids. How much was our judgement affected by a romantic notion of guerrilla warfare? Did we picture continual ambushes, daring sabotage of bridges and transport, demoralised

German units and lightning raids night after night on vulnerable mountain roads? There was some self-delusion here. If insurrection in Yugoslavia flared up, it soon subsided. In September 1943 Gorizia was aflame; in December, after four German divisions there and in Istria had been at work, no spark could be seen. General von Weichs, the German commander in chief in the Balkans, might report that Tito was their most dangerous enemy; but though the German forces, much of which were scratch units, were kept on the hop, the partisans were not a strategic threat until November 1944 when they were equipped with mortars and automatic weapons. When Italy collapsed we learnt that Mihailovic's Chetniks had attacked Tito's Partisans. We then read decrypts disclosing that Chetnik units were collaborating with the Germans, and the Foreign Office reluctantly agreed that supplies to Mihailovic should cease.[15]

On the issue of the Balkans our Foreign Office colleagues on the JIS became as optimistic as Millis. Hungary would turn against the Germans, they said. There were indeed two revolts: both of them botched. Or again they declared that the Germans would have to send massive forces to Romania and Bulgaria to restore order if they followed suit. They never did – until the Russians were at their gates. Pundits overestimated what guerrillas could achieve. They were misled by successes like the destruction of the Gorgopotamos bridge in Greece. It took months for our liaison officers to persuade the Communist guerrilla group ELAS to blow up the bridge. Had it been destroyed earlier it would have cut one of Rommel's supply lines when he stood at El Alamein. But it was not. When finally the bridge was blown up Rommel was hundreds of miles away in Tripolitania. The difficulties with ELAS should have warned the Foreign Office that ELAS's first objective was less to harass the Germans than to eliminate other guerrilla forces and their leaders. The reports from our liaison officer with the right-wing Greek republican leader Zervas were suppressed in Middle East headquarters because they did not square with the British policy of restoring King George II, who had been rescued from Crete in 1941.* Larry Kirwan and I were genially reviled on the

---

* The King was unpopular because he had supported the Metaxas dictatorship during which political opponents from right as well as left were exiled to the islands.

JIS as unimaginative defeatists by our Air Ministry and Foreign Office colleagues, who thought that the liberation of Greece would smooth away any little political difficulties that had arisen between ELAS and the other guerrilla bands, and that a mere 5000 troops would be needed to establish a new government in Athens. (The figure came from Churchill.[16] When at Christmas 1944 ELAS marched on Athens to seize power 80,000 troops were needed to install Archbishop Damaskinos as Regent and damp down the civil war.) Cairo Intelligence was much to blame.

The person who was most affected by the euphoria of the Italian surrender was not Howard Millis but the Prime Minister. In early September Churchill on his own initiative ordered General Wilson of Middle East Command to seize the Dodecanese islands: a prelude to a 'cascade of ripe plums' that would fall into our laps in the Balkans.[17] Brooke opposed such an operation and warned Churchill that without air cover the operation was not on, unless Rhodes could be taken and the Turks provided air bases – which they refused to do. But on this occasion he gave in to the Prime Minister's wishes and British troops occupied the islands of Cos and Leros. As always the Germans moved fast. They lost ships and aircraft, but they overpowered the Italian garrison on Rhodes. 'The whole thing is sheer madness,' wrote Brooke when Churchill ordered Rhodes to be captured, and he begged Marshall to believe that the adventure was not his brainchild; Marshall sent him a sympathetic message saying he knew who was behind it.[18] Within a month Cos had been lost. By now Churchill was in a fury. Rhodes must be taken. Massive reinforcements must be sent from Italy. No, Leros would not be evacuated: if it was, how could Eden, now in Ankara, persuade the Turks to come in on our side? Telegrams were sent to Roosevelt imploring him to intervene. Roosevelt sent a cold refusal.

The JIS watched in horror. On 27 October we pointed out that the Allies' deception plan, which had succeeded in making the Germans think that the Balkans, and not Sicily, was their objective, had induced them to reinforce the islands.[18] We advised the Joint Planners on the scale of the attack the Germans could mount against Leros, and they accordingly advised that our force should be withdrawn from the islands.[19] We lost six destroyers, two submarines and other vessels; four cruisers and four destroyers were damaged, and many obsolete aircraft were shot down.

Brooke knew he had been wrong to give in to Churchill – though it is hard to see how he could have curbed the Prime Minister's desire, which he shared, to exploit the fall of Italy. His chagrin began to prey on his mind. Perhaps it was his fault not to have convinced the Americans to exploit the Mediterranean. If only he had done so, perhaps Crete and Rhodes would have been taken, the Dardanelles forced and the gateway to the Danube opened. Why were the Americans so inflexible and short-sighted? The remorseless pressure Churchill brought to bear on him day in, day out, and the menacing atmosphere he created began to tell on Brooke; he wrote in his diary that he thought he was not far off a nervous breakdown.[20]

During November there was a brisk exchange of telegrams between Washington and London, and some adroit drafting concerning the overriding importance of Overlord and the necessity to maintain pressure upon the Germans in Italy. The Americans continued to doubt the British commitment to Overlord, and the British continued to chip away at plans to transfer forces away from the Italian front.

Churchill now turned his mind to the Bay of Bengal. He was infuriated that the operation to retake the Andaman islands, approved at the Quebec conference, had been called off. Nature had conspired against us. Floods in Assam had put paid to the plan. When the Indian government asked for half a million tons of grain to feed the starving, Churchill refused, declaring that there had been 'gross mismanagement of Indian affairs'. There had in fact been no mismanagement, and famine struck Bengal: hundreds of thousands died. (Brooke saw to it that next year, when Wavell asked for three quarters of a million tons of grain, the shipping was made available even though military commitments had to be postponed.)

Churchill did not ask for the cancelled operation to be reinstated. Instead he returned to one of his favourite proposals: Sumatra. Time and again the JIS had to rehearse the reasons why his pet scheme to land a force on the tip of Sumatra made no sense. The vital objectives for General Slim and his army were Rangoon, Malaysia and Singapore. We argued that Sumatra was on the perimeter of Japanese possessions; to land there would not draw off troops from Burma, and casualties would be heavier than in island-hopping from Australia to the Celebes and thence on to Borneo.

The opposition to his plans put Churchill in a filthy temper, and he arrived in Cairo for a conference with Roosevelt and the Chinese nationalist leader Chiang Kai-shek grousing and grumbling at our failures. He declared that the build-up of air forces in Italy had hamstrung the Army; that it was madness to remove divisions from Italy to Overlord despite the fact he had agreed to do so; that we had failed to take Rome; that we had failed to hold all the German divisions on our front (some had gone to Russia); and worst of all that we had failed to bring the available landing craft to bear in any theatre and had lost the Aegean. Then he returned to his favourite topic: the length of the Army's tail. Of two million Allied soldiers only 170,000 were in the front line. Finally he was pushed to one side by Roosevelt, who on his own gave Chiang Kai-shek a firm date for an operation by British troops in the Bay of Bengal.

Churchill's anger evaporated in Tehran, where he and Roosevelt met Stalin on 28 November. He was engaged on a great historic occasion that appealed to his imagination. It was the first time the three leaders had met to discuss the strategy to bring Hitler down and to dispel the suspicions and misunderstandings that had arisen between them. Churchill and Brooke had met Stalin in Moscow in August 1942, and it was then that Churchill, at a private meeting with Stalin, had promised to invade France in 1943. Now he was to meet him again with the President of the United States. I remember reading in the War Cabinet Office the minutes of the military meetings between the three heads of state. I read them with a sinking heart. The Prime Minister opened the proceedings. He was garrulous. He ranged from Europe to Turkey to the Mediterranean, a characteristic *tour d'horizon* but with no clear conclusion. Stalin then asked questions, every one to the point. The Mediterranean was important, but one could not invade Germany from it. How many divisions were to be used in Overlord, and how many would come from the Mediterranean? Within a few minutes he possessed

the salient order of battle information. Who was to command Overlord? The President replied that that had not yet been decided.
Stalin said the whole operation would come to nought unless one
man was in authority. The President said there was, of course, a
general in charge of the planning. But, Stalin replied, the supreme
commander when appointed might change those plans. Churchill
bridled when Stalin suggested that all landing craft should leave
the Mediterranean for Overlord. Did the Prime Minister really
believe in Overlord? was Stalin's next question. Churchill side-
stepped: it was our stern duty, he said, to hurl across the Channel
every sinew of our strength.

Delighted by Stalin's unequivocal support for Overlord and the
south of France landings, Roosevelt suggested that the Italian front
might be shut down when the six divisions left to reinforce Overlord. By no means, said Stalin – Hitler would then be able to
transfer divisions to the Russian front. Should the Allies then drive
to Vienna? Certainly not, said Stalin – Overlord was all-important.
In that case, said Roosevelt, the assault on the south of France
could take place in April. Stalin said nothing, though he must have
known that the proposal was ludicrous: annihilation awaited any
force that landed on the Riviera before Overlord absorbed the German reserves. When Brooke questioned the necessity for the south
of France expedition, Stalin snubbed him, saying he could not force
his opinions on the meeting: the heads of state would decide. Finally
Stalin said he wanted an assurance that Overlord would be launched
in May.

Stalin dominated the conference. He came knowing what he
wanted, and he got it. What he wanted was no interference in
south-east Europe or at his back door. Turkey? Yes, indeed Turkey
should be brought into the war – dragged in by the scruff of the
neck if necessary. She was too friendly with too many people. But
it was not worth sending a single soldier to force Turkey's hand.
In true Soviet style Stalin gave nothing in return. Brooke had noted
how Beaverbrook, when he rushed off to Moscow in 1941 as Minister of Aircraft Production and promised to send tanks and aircraft
without bargaining for some recompense, had been rewarded with
nothing but sneers for not organising our convoys efficiently.[21]
Brooke was not taken in by Stalin's geniality. When he met him

for the first time in Moscow in August 1942 he thought he had 'an unpleasantly cold, crafty, cruel face, and whenever I look at him I can imagine him sending off people to their doom without turning a hair'.[22] The plans, possibilities, high sentiments that Churchill deployed meant nothing to him. But unlike Churchill, Stalin was ready to face facts, however unpleasant, and at Tehran Brooke judged that he had a military brain of the very highest calibre.

The Yalta conference in February 1945 was another matter. After the war many criticised Churchill for its outcome, but there he had to play from a weak hand. Roosevelt was dying and in a frame of mind in which he seemed willing to divide the world between the two superpowers. At all events he had not fought the war to save the British Empire, which he wished to see dissolved and the colonies given their liberty. No doubt he and Churchill deluded themselves that deals could be struck with Uncle Joe, though Churchill knew Stalin to be a blood-boltered Macbeth. It was, however, the course of the war rather than delusion that delivered Eastern Europe into Communist hands. What the Red Army occupied, the USSR would dominate. As Stalin said, it could not be otherwise. We were back in the sixteenth century. *Cuius regio, eius religio.*

Meanwhile, both American and British staff officers were trying month after month to increase the number of landing craft and hence the strength of the assault forces for the Normandy beaches. Why not, asked the British, divert to England the landing craft and forces earmarked for the south of France landings? The British hated this operation. They said it would relieve pressure neither on the Normandy nor on the Russian front; and it did in fact remove 40 per cent of the American troops, in particular from General Crittenberger's excellent corps, just as Alexander was hoping to sweep into the Po valley after the capture of Rome. Even after Overlord was launched the British were still trying to get the expedition cancelled. They never seemed to realise that the Americans wanted to land the Free French army as well as their own troops, and to open the ports of Toulon and Marseilles and supply General Devers's Sixth Army Group on the eastern part of the front in France. All the more necessary as it proved, since it was long before the Channel and North Sea ports could be opened.

General Marshall appreciated the irony of the British proposal that the south of France landing be cancelled. He found himself arguing so strongly against it that he wrote to Eisenhower that the American and British positions had now been reversed: 'We have become the Mediterraneanites and they heavily pro-Overlord.' In fact the theatre that suffered was not Overlord but the Indian Ocean, where the British Chiefs of Staff cancelled three amphibious operations in order to provide landing craft for the south of France landings.

But had not a second front been opened against Hitler long before Overlord? This was what the Air Ministry representatives in the JIC/JIS argued. What truth was there in this?

CHAPTER FIVE

❖

The Air Offensive

One of the most contentious issues the Joint Intelligence Staff discussed was the effect of the bombing offensive on Germany. In 1940 Churchill had only two ways of hitting back at Germany: Bomber Command and mustering resistance and sabotage in Europe through SOE ('Set Europe ablaze' was his command). Bomber Command flew lightly armed aircraft designed to bomb by night, but in the early years of the war they did not carry a heavy bomb load and had no navigational aids such as the Knickebein beam, the German device that directed their bombers to the target. How many of our bombers hit their targets? Ultra did not speak much about bomb damage: there was no need to use radio when there were telephone lines and despatch riders. But photographic reconnaissance spoke only too clearly. It showed that in 1940 only one of our aircraft in five was reaching the target. The Prime Minister was onto this failure at once, and in 1941 the War Cabinet secretariat called for a report. It concluded that only a third of our crews dropped their bombs within five miles of the target area. So by 1943 an awkward question was put to Bomber Command: How much damage had actually been inflicted by dropping over 42,000 tons of bombs, at the cost of 718 aircraft?

As the months passed the Ministry of Economic Warfare (MEW) became less and less optimistic. Air Marshal Harris declared that there must have been vast loss of production after such heavy raids: if the photographs showed that a factory had lost its roof, it must be taken as destroyed. But Martin Watson on the JIS maintained that the evidence did not confirm that there had been a serious decline in Germany's industrial output. Not only had the night-bombers found difficulty in pinpointing specific objectives, but as the German night-fighters grew in number and effectiveness the bomber aircraft had to fly on darker nights and at even higher altitudes. It was becoming clear that we could 'not even guarantee to hit towns, let alone individual factories'.[1]

So Harris changed his strategy. He would now concentrate on carrying out one of the tasks allotted to him – the destruction of the morale of the German people. He would flatten German cities by area bombing. This must surely reduce industrial production and drive the inhabitants to despair: they would rise in fury and end the war. In the autumn of 1942 at a Chiefs of Staff meeting Air Chief Marshal Portal had argued that Britain had not the resources both to bomb Germany into submission *and* to invade Europe. Why compromise? The bomber offensive was more certain than an invasion, and more economic. His argument did not get far. It was unthinkable that the Americans would agree to such a strategy; and Pound and Brooke shot him down.

But Bomber Command's hopes leapt up. In July 1943 the bombers used a new device when attacking Hamburg: they dropped metallic strips to confuse the German radar. The result was spectacular. Almost the whole city was destroyed. 'Germany must collapse before this programme which is more than half complete already,' Harris declared in November: had it not been evident after the Hamburg raid that 'the discipline of the people now shows signs of considerable weakening'?[2] Harris now planned to strike at the heart of Germany: 'We can wreck Berlin from end to end,' he said, 'if the US air force will come in on it. It will cost between 400 and 500 aircraft. It will cost Germany the war.'[3] But the raids on Berlin in August and September did not inflict the damage Hamburg had suffered. Photo reconnaissance showed that only twenty-seven of the 1729 sorties dropped their bombs within three miles of the aiming point.[4]

On the bombing of Berlin Harris did not get the support of his colleagues, notably Air Commodore Bufton, in the Air Ministry. The Air Ministry said that to bomb the capital in preference to targets that would reduce German fighter strength was to echo the mistake Hitler made during the Battle of Britain, when he switched the assault from the RAF airfields to London. Harris, however, continued to attack Berlin on 27, 28 and 30 January 1944, again on 15 February and for the last time on 24 March. The casualties inflicted by the German night-fighters were so heavy that Bomber Command had to admit defeat; in a raid on Nuremberg eighty of the 800 bombers failed to return. Finally Portal, overruling Harris's protests, ordered him to bomb Schweinfurt, the centre of the German ball-bearing industry, and later to destroy the V-1 pilotless aircraft sites that had been discovered in north France.

Was German morale at breaking point? Time and again the JIS ruminated, chewing over the evidence. In the days after the Italian surrender in early September the JIS was under the spell of Howard Millis's euphoria, and our masters endorsed a JIS paper which suggested that we should have a plan in readiness to land in France were German resistance suddenly to collapse. Who could have predicted in August 1918, argued Millis, that Germany would sue for an armistice in November? The military situation was not necessarily the best guide: political and economic intelligence, more fragmentary and harder to analyse, must be taken into account: 'If it were not that the political situation is very different from that of 1918, we should unhesitatingly predict that Germany would sue for an armistice before the end of the year.'[5] But by December 1943 the JIS was no longer bewitched by Millis. The War Office worms turned. Instead of us being accused of gross pessimism and distortion of the evidence of the enemy's military strength, Larry Kirwan and I, egged on by Charles Fletcher-Cooke and the Admiralty, raked over the evidence of the effects of the bomber offensive. We were convinced the Air Ministry was being too optimistic, and were adamant that the German army would not withdraw from France before Overlord, nor would civilian morale in Germany disintegrate. There were no signs that the bomber offensive had fomented opposition to the point that would lead to a collapse. The JIC backed our conclusion.

There is, however, a curious passage in F.H. Hinsley's monumental history of British wartime intelligence. He suggests that German morale was on the point of breaking in February 1944. Curious because it summarises a number of reports from MI6 sources to the effect that, while there had been signs of panic in Berlin after the January raids, panic was succeeded by what source after source referred to as 'apathy', rather than simmering unrest. That was a word which raised tempers in Bomber Command. And yet it was an accurate description of the mood of a population that saw no way out of the war. The JIS was not to be browbeaten. We pointed out that several sources not only used the word but considered that German morale picked up again in the spring of 1944. Yet Hinsley declares that 'it does not seem unreasonable to infer that the bombing had brought Germany to a crisis of morale which she had barely survived, and she might well have succumbed to it if Bomber Command had not then been forced to disperse its efforts'; and he cites two decrypts from the Japanese Embassy in Berlin to the effect that there would have been cause for alarm had not the air-raid precautions been so efficient and the SS detachments in the cities dealt so effectively with social unrest after heavy raids.[6] Exactly. We had always stressed the power of the Nazi Party using the SS and Gestapo to suppress defeatism. Anyone who was heard muttering that the war was lost was likely to be strung up on a lamp-post left standing in the ruined and smouldering city.

Was it right to divert Bomber Command? Albert Speer, who was in charge of German war production, declared after the war that disaster had stared him in the face: if the Allies had persisted in their attacks on the ball-bearing industry, tank, aircraft and motor transport production would have seized up.[7] Martin Watson, in a series of papers the JIS drafted in May–June 1944, estimated that the attacks in April had caused ball-bearing production to drop below 50 per cent of the mid-1943 level. Alas, by June it had climbed back to over 80 per cent. This provoked a furious riposte from Harris, who wanted to continue area bombing. MEW, he said, had asserted that this industry was vital; if a reduction of 50 per cent had not proved fatal, then MEW should 'be called upon to account for their own overweening enthusiasm'. He was met by the usual cool, maddening bureaucratic response. MEW said they had never claimed more than that to attack the ball-bearing industry was the best way 'directly to impair the enemy's ability to fight'. Whether or not the results of the attacks were fatal must 'of course depend on the military situation whilst the speed with which it would be felt at the front must depend on the rate of wastage'.[8] In other words, if there was a lull in the fighting, no replacements would be called for and new factories might be built underground.

And yet Harris had a point. Our sources of information about

German production were slender: foreign businessmen, snippets from newspapers and the occasional revelation from Ultra. In 1944 two young American economists, C.P. Kindleberger and Walt Rostow, the latter of whom was to become an implacable hawk on Vietnam under Presidents Kennedy and Johnson, appeared in London. They identified 285 aiming points crucial to German industry, and also came up with techniques for estimating how long repairs would take after a raid and what would be the effect on war potential if the target were partly or wholly destroyed. No one could ever be certain which target – oil, ball-bearings, communications – would have the greatest effect upon the military situation.

The military situation. That was, of course, the real reason why the bomber forces, British and American, were diverted from ball-bearing factories, oil refineries or the aircraft industry. It was not the vacillation of the Allied command in shifting their priorities, but the strength of the German fighter squadrons and the technical response their scientists and engineers made to the Allied offensive. It had been the same in the Battle of the Atlantic. Possibly the worst blot on Portal's record as a strategist was his reluctance to transfer aircraft from Bomber to Coastal Command at the height of the U-boat sinkings in 1942–43. Why, he asked, change them from an offensive to 'an uneconomic defensive role'.[9] Throughout the war Harris mesmerised the sagacious Portal, whatever the military situation.

That situation changed with the arrival in England of the US Eighth Air Force in 1943. Unlike Bomber Command the Americans flew heavily-armed Flying Fortresses designed to bomb by day. They concentrated on a variety of industrial targets. Sometimes it was synthetic oil plants and refineries, sometimes ball-bearing factories, sometimes plant that was producing German air force fighters. From April 1943 they began to penetrate deeper and deeper into Germany. Their raids were to halve German fighter production, but as they flew outside the range of their own fighters who could no longer protect them, their casualties became so appalling that in October their offensive was called off. Both the British and the American air forces needed long-range fighter-bombers.

In 1944 they got them, and once the Eighth Air Force was protected by American Mustangs they began again to fly ever deeper into Germany. From early March the Americans stopped attacking aircraft factories, such as the Messerschmidt works at Regensburg, and concentrated on forcing the German fighters to do battle. Ultra showed how heavy were the German fighter losses. Within a month they had been driven from all their air bases within radio range of the United Kingdom.[10] Allied claims that 20 per cent of German fighter production had been destroyed were accurate: the German air force ran out of fighter pilots, and 40 per cent of their fighter aircraft were non-operational. Ultra decrypts told us the Germans were reinforcing their air force in France from Italy, but we deduced that their squadrons in France were far below their nominal strength.

Although Bomber Command and the Eighth Air Force each continued to follow different policies as the Overlord build-up continued, they were united on one matter. They resisted any order to bomb targets other than those they themselves had chosen to bomb. But there were always unforeseen emergencies threatening Overlord. The Navy might claim there was a new threat from the U-boats in Brest: could the submarine pens please be bombed? And then a new and more sensational threat emerged. Intelligence revealed the existence of the German secret weapons: the V-1 and the V-2.

In March 1943 Generals von Thoma and Crüwell, who had been captured in North Africa, were chatting in a prisoner of war camp near London, not knowing that their talk was being recorded. Von Thoma said: 'I saw it once with Feldmarschall Brauchitsch . . . They've got these huge things, they've always said they would go fifteen kilometres into the stratosphere – you only aim at an area . . . The Major there said "Wait until next year and the fun will start."' Von Thoma added that since he had heard no large explosions, he supposed the fun had not started: perhaps their production had been delayed.[11]

Reading this conversation an MI14 officer, Matthew Pryor, thought that it fitted in with other reports he had read. Pryor was a schoolfriend of Earle who had trained him to take over his job of interpreting air photographs before Earle went on his way to sit in the office of the CIGS. Late in 1942 a Danish engineer had warned MI6 that the Germans were constructing a rocket; there had been a number of references to a secret station at Peenemunde in the Baltic, and Pryor had been intrigued by air photographs of the countryside in the Pas de Calais which revealed numbers of sites with something on them that looked like a ski-jump. He alerted the Director of Military Intelligence (DMI), who informed the Vice-Chief of Staff, and they told the Prime Minister of the possible danger of rocket attack. There was a scientific section under the Air Ministry headed by a scintillating young man, R.V. Jones, who had made his name by discovering how to bend the Knickebein beam, thus diverting German bombers from their target so that their bombs landed in open fields. He next worked on jamming the radar carried by German night-fighters. But the Chiefs of Staff forgot about this section's existence, and suggested to Churchill that he appoint a special committee under his son-in-law Duncan Sandys to investigate the matter. Jones had also been on the trail of rocket intelligence, and he sent Sandys photographic evidence of the rockets' existence. Sandys, behaving like a politician and not a scientist, used the evidence in one of his reports without acknowledgement.

That, to a young scientist who was already in Churchill's good books, was an insult, and Jones declared war on Sandys. He complained to his old mentor, the Prof, and Cherwell told Churchill that he ought to hear Jones's views, even though Cherwell himself discounted all this talk of rockets. The Prime Minister accordingly held a full meeting of the War Cabinet Defence Committee on 29 June 1943. Sandys gave his account of the evidence. Cherwell then said that the estimate of 4000 casualties per rocket was grotesque; the object photographed at Peenemunde and painted white was a dummy; and why should the Germans try to convince us that they had a rocket? – clearly because they were trying to disguise a much more likely weapon: a pilotless aircraft. Churchill then called on Jones to speak. Whenever he made a telling point, Churchill turned to Cherwell and said, 'Hear that. That's a weighty point. Remember, it was you who first introduced him to me.'[12] It was decided to bomb Peenemunde.

Much to Cherwell's credit he bore no ill-will to his old pupil, perhaps because his own guesses were not all off-target. The white-painted rockets may well have been dummies, and Pryor was to produce convincing evidence that the 'ski sites', as they were called, in the Pas de Calais were indeed for launching pilotless aircraft. To add to the confusion Sir Stafford Cripps, who was a lawyer as well as Minister for Aircraft Production, was brought in to consider the evidence. Pryor was astonished to hear that Cripps and his team of analysts and scientists scouted the idea that the sites in northern France were for launching pilotless aircraft – Cripps imagined that such weapons could be despatched from any airfield. At this point the JIC felt they had been elbowed out of this area of intelligence, and in November they set up a special committee, on which Pryor sat, to assess both the German offensive capability and our own defensive measures.

Through the summer and autumn of 1943 Cherwell fought a rearguard action, still maintaining that the rocket was a hoax until the evidence overwhelmed him. On 4 December the JIC told the Chiefs of Staff that the ski sites were indeed intended to launch a pilotless aircraft. A few days later a decrypt gave incontrovertible evidence that the Germans were also building a rocket. Sandys, Cripps and the JIC bowed out, and in the early days of January 1944 the assessment of the weight of attack of both weapons became Jones's responsibility alone.[13] He continued to deduce how the rockets and pilotless aircraft worked – a triumph of scientific intelligence. In May 1944 a rocket came down by the river Bug in Poland – one of many misfires. The Polish underground captured it, prepared a landing ground for a Dakota piloted by a New Zealand airman, and loaded it for despatch to England where it was examined. This confirmed what our air attaché in Stockholm told us when another misfire had landed in Sweden. By the time the attacks from the V-1 and V-2 began, in June and September 1944 respectively, the Chiefs of Staff knew the weight of explosive their warheads carried, and thus the likely scale of the damage. As a result, the bomber forces were diverted to bomb the ski sites.

They were to be diverted again when the planning and intelligence staffs began to ask how the overwhelming Allied air superiority could best be used to support Overlord. The JIS got sucked into a notorious controversy from which we did not emerge with credit. It showed how limited was the power of operational intelligence to influence the Air Force commanders of the day.

By 1944 the numbers of these commanders were legion. At Supreme Headquarters there was Tedder, Eisenhower's deputy commander. There was the Commander of the Allied Expeditionary Air Forces, Trafford Leigh-Mallory, a veteran of the Battle of Britain, and his American deputy General Vandenberg. There was 'Mary' Coningham, Montgomery's air chief. Then came the American chiefs. General Tooey Spaatz was the most powerful. He commanded all the American forces in Europe. Under him were the gigantic heavy-bomber forces, the Eighth Air Force under Doolittle, the Fifteenth in the Mediterranean under Ira Eaker, and the medium bombers of the Ninth under Brereton. Then there was Bert Harris of British Bomber Command. Neither Spaatz nor Harris was likely to allow himself to fall under Leigh-Mallory's command. Ready to spring out of their kennels in defence of the policies of their chiefs were expert guard dogs. Advising Leigh-Mallory at SHAEF were Air Commodore Kingston McCloughry and Professor Solly Zuckerman. Opposed to them was Air Commodore Bufton, head of the Air Ministry's Directorate of Bombing Operations. We in the JIS used to regard him as a counterweight to the extravagant claims Harris made for his area bombing strategy, but in an inter-Allied dogfight he came out barking on Harris's side. Behind Spaatz, Harris and Bufton stood posses of committees and units such as the Combined Strategic Targets Committee and the Committee of Four (a subcommittee of the Joint Technical War Committee). Then there was the American Enemy Objectives Unit of the US Economic Warfare Department. Its chief was a Briton who had become an American citizen, Colonel Richard O'Doyly Hughes; and with him were his young analysts Kindleberger and Rostow.

One of the essential conditions for mounting Overlord was that the Allied build-up of forces in the bridgehead in Normandy must be faster than the Germans could muster their forces in counterattack. How could we impede this build-up? Leigh-Mallory's scientific expert, Solly Zuckerman, thought he had the answer.

Zuckerman was a master operator, and after the war was to make his career as the top British scientific adviser, to whom all doors in the Pentagon as well as Whitehall were open. Young, attractive, bounding with vitality, he had won a reputation outside the laboratory for his study of the sexual habits of apes. Inside the lab he was also a meticulous anatomist, able to trade insults with physical anthropologists about the origins of *homo sapiens*. If crossed he displayed a nice talent for ridicule. He seemed to know everyone, including Cherwell, as they were both Students (i.e. Fellows) of Christ Church, Oxford. He was a fascinator. Like other scientists he used his skill with figures and training in logical inference to impress airmen (who, unlike cavalrymen, were numerate). Zuckerman's first success as a wartime boffin had been made collaborating with J.D. Bernal on a study of the effects of the bombing of Hull and Birmingham in 1941. They showed that the German bombing of our cities had not been as effective as might have been expected, and that the casualties inflicted were considerably lower than feared.[14]

Zuckerman then moved to Allied HQ Algiers, and was on first-name terms with Tooey Spaatz and the American air chiefs. He knew Tedder well, and sold him the idea that the best way to impede the German build-up was to bomb the railway system in France and even back into Germany. To cut the German army's communications would be the best way to prevent them from moving their armoured divisions quickly to crush the Allied forces on the Normandy beaches. Troops, oil, ball-bearings, the components that enable fighter aircraft to be assembled, have to be moved. Attack railways and you impede the movement of all of them.[15] This was the proposal put to the air warlords.

In his autobiography Zuckerman gives an unforgettable description of the warfare within the war that his Transportation plan let loose. The bomber barons were accustomed to work from a loose directive from the Combined Chiefs of Staff that gave them considerable latitude in picking their targets as they saw fit. They were now faced with a proposal that they should all concentrate on one objective. Neither Spaatz nor Harris intended to change his own plan to win the war. MEW and the American and British units who identified sensitive targets in the German economy were also dismayed. On 17 March 1944 the JIS wrote a paper expressing the doubts of Bufton at the Air Ministry, of the new DMI at the War Office, and of the target experts in MEW. We argued that the German army could manage with as few as eighty trains a day, and would be able to substitute road for rail transport. After all, only a fifth of the French railway system was used for military traffic. Zuckerman, who was being advised by my old patron Carl Sherrington and his partner E.W. Brant, responded with a flurry of figures based on experience of the landings in Sicily and Italy.

So on 25 March Portal, with Eisenhower at his side, called a large meeting of all concerned. Spaatz could not understand why his old friend Zuck was on the wrong side; and since he suspected (unjustly) that Harris would weasel his way out of this commitment and resume bombing German cities, with the possibility – horrible to contemplate – that German resistance might collapse and Harris alone would be crowned with laurels, he said we must go on attacking oil production and blasting German fighter aircraft out of the skies. That was the best way to reduce the German build-up against our landings on D-Day. The American target experts backed him. But on this occasion the MEW representative observed that attacks on oil would do nothing to impede the German counterattacks on D-Day. Portal declared that he had not heard a realistic alternative to the Transportation plan, and a few days later the Combined Chiefs of Staff in Washington directed that all air forces should come under Eisenhower.

Yet not until 17 April was Eisenhower able to issue a directive to give the plan top priority. Nor was this surprising, for another critic of the Transportation plan entered the fray. As long ago as October 1943, after Harris had appealed to him, the Prime Minister had dismissed the idea that bombing communications would be effective. Churchill was a wayward supporter of the policy of bombing German cities, but on this occasion he set out to defeat Leigh-Mallory. 'To obtain his way,' wrote Peter Earle as military assistant to Brooke in his diary, 'no trick will be beyond him.'[16] On 5 April Churchill called a meeting, as usual late at night. Unaware that Zuckerman was present, he began by saying the Transportation plan was the 'brainchild of a biologist who happened to be passing through the Mediterranean', and finished by asking Tedder whether he was really in favour of the plan. Tedder said he was. 'You don't know a better plan?' 'There is no better plan.' 'I'll show you a better plan,' said Churchill. Zuckerman noticed Tedder's knuckles whiten as he grasped the edge of the table.[17] Churchill then produced a paper drafted by the JIS declaring that French civilians would suffer terrible casualties if the railways were bombed. It was a bad paper. The Foreign Office and Bufton had plucked the estimate of casualties we quoted out of the air. Portal said that Professor Zuckerman believed the casualty figures were incorrect: Bomber Command had also multiplied the number of sorties required by a factor of three. He predicted that the French, like the British in 1941, would trek when the bombing began. How, asked Churchill, by now in a fury, had the Chiefs of Staff been given wrong figures? At the next meeting Zuckerman produced new figures. If all seventy-four transport targets were bombed, perhaps 12,000 civilians might be killed and 60,000 injured – as against the 40,000 and 120,000 that the Air Ministry had foretold. In the event intelligence sources showed that the casualties were lower than even Zuckerman's estimates. The French who lived near the rail centres did what the British had done: left their homes seeking safety elsewhere.

The Chiefs of Staff were now behind the Transportation plan, yet the Prime Minister continued to oppose it. Of the seventy-four targets, only twelve were to be attacked by Bomber Command, but Churchill insisted that the War Cabinet give permission for them to be bombed. Fighting all the way, he appealed to Roosevelt to intervene. The President declined to do anything that 'might militate against the success of Overlord'.[18] It was not until the first week in May that the War Cabinet grudgingly gave its permission, on the understanding that everything would be done to keep civilian casualties below 10,000. On 10 May Ultra revealed that so many locomotives had been destroyed that the repair shops were overwhelmed.

Even the most successful of operators, however, can nod. Montgomery demanded that the Seine bridges should be destroyed. Zuckerman disagreed. He argued that bridges were easy to repair and that the operation would cost too many casualties among air crews. It would take 260 sorties of B-26s to bomb the bridges and 1200 tons to take out one bridge. Yet Zuckerman must have known that the interdiction of a battlefield by destroying bridges had been established in Italy. Before he and Tedder had left the Mediterranean for Overlord, it had been calculated that the weight of bombs required to take out a bridge was only 375 tons.[19] After Leigh-Mallory was shown the results of attacks on bridges in Italy, he gave the go-ahead.

The American P-47 fighter bombers delivered most of the attacks. On 7 May four of the Seine bridges were destroyed, and by D-Day all twenty-four bridges between Rouen and the sea were out of action; twelve others over major waterways in France and Germany were blocked. Before D-Day Harris did all that he was asked to do.[20] So did Spaatz.[21] Yet this produced further disagreement. Leigh-Mallory became an enthusiast for bridge-bombing, and was rebuked by Tedder for changing his priorities. The truth was that Tedder had changed his. He was now arguing that the greatest threat to the landings was from the German air force, whose airfields ought to be bombed continuously. Leigh-Mallory replied that he thought the threat to the assault force from German armoured divisions was more dangerous.

Was the Transportation plan a success? It certainly was before D-Day. Tedder and Zuckerman intended communications to be the main target until the war ended, but it was not to be. Lieutenant-Colonel Maxwell of Eighth Air Force told the top army commanders at SHAEF, 'Don't count on us to be with you after D-Day', and one of Harris's staff officers warned them that Bomber Command might well have more urgent tasks than direct support for the armies in Normandy. Harris soon reverted to area bombing and on 29 June, to Leigh-Mallory's rage, when the armies were still locked into the bridgehead, the Eighth Air Force bombed aircraft factories and oil plants in southern Germany. After September 1944 Spaatz gave priority to attacks on oil production.[22]

It would be easy to put the confusion of Allied policy down to the personalities of the commanders. Easy to picture them as spoiled movie stars, living luxuriously, refusing to serve under this chief or obey that instruction. Leigh-Mallory was a buttoned-up Briton, with whom the jovial poker-playing American chiefs could never get on terms. He had no friends, not even Tedder. Tedder rarely spoke to Harris, and Brereton would not work with Coningham, who was also disliked by Spaatz and Montgomery. No one in the air forces had Eisenhower's gift of making the alliance a reality. The air chiefs knew the capabilities of the aircraft they commanded: heavy bombers had not been designed to support ground forces. The truth was that the Higher Command failed to command. The Combined Chiefs of Staff never cancelled the original bombing directive issued in 1943. As a result a baron could argue that he was merely carrying out the policy laid down at the highest level. But was it really the highest? Portal has been criticised for not bringing Harris to heel, but in Churchill Harris had a powerful protector. So did Spaatz, in General Arnold on the Combined Chiefs of Staff in Washington.

Each protagonist could appeal to intelligence, a signal from Ultra or other sources to support his case. For instance, Zuckerman could show that between D-Day and 7 July 1944 one SS Panzer division was delayed for a week entraining and two other Panzer divisions had to detrain as far east as Nancy and Bar le Duc.[23] In August a young officer, Derek Ezra (later to become chairman of the National Coal Board), found German documents showing that even before the Seine bridges were destroyed rail traffic in northern France had fallen by 20 per cent.[24] A German Air Ministry report of 13 June said that vital military traffic could still be moved, but all main railway lines were blocked, coastal defences were cut off from their supply bases, and large-scale strategic movement of troops by rail was impossible.

Intelligence, however, also gave Zuckerman's opponents comfort. Examining the evidence, the JIS reported that the offensive against oil production curtailed the training programme of combat divisions and cut supplies to the German navy. When the JIC met the Chiefs of Staff in July 1944 Geoffrey Vickers told them that 'The enemy is being forced to eat into his oil stocks and dumps.' Bomb oil production, and Germany would be unable to fight on three fronts because 'current supplies will fall short by some 35 per cent of the minimum needed to avoid hampering military operations'.[25]

After the war the oil lobby appealed to Albert Speer, Hitler's miracle-worker who kept the German production lines going. Speer said the attacks on oil production gave him his worst headache. But then, did not Speer on another occasion criticise the Allies for not pressing home their attack on ball-bearing factories? And did he not say on another that 'transportation was the greatest bottleneck in our war economy'? And did not General Galland, the German fighter ace, emphasise the crushing effect of the American air offensive in drawing his fighter force into battle? Did he not say that he was losing fifty fighters each time the Eighth Air Force attacked in 1944?[26] The Air Ministry maintained that if oil production had been attacked sooner, 'there can be little doubt that the collapse of Germany would have come sooner'.[27] But bad weather always gave the Germans the chance to repair and disperse production. The JIS pointed out on 1 December 1944 that although ten out of the eleven synthetic oil plants in the Ruhr had been put out of production, the eleven plants in the east and central Germany had been repaired and staged a remarkable recovery; yet the JIS kept on emphasising that in their view the oil offensive should be continued.

In fact there was no more chance of all the bomber forces concentrating on oil production than there had been of it concentrating on the railway system. Harris again ignored the order to bomb oil plants. Even when he was reprimanded in a new directive he refused to obey it. Portal noted sardonically that 'the magnetism of the remaining German cities rather than considerations of weather or tactics' had caused Harris 'to deflect our bombers from their primary objectives'.[28] From November 1944 until January 1945 Portal implored Harris to change his ways, but Harris played his trump card. He would resign. Portal caved in. He would not dismiss Harris, so he said, for fear that the morale of the air crews would suffer.[29] It was a feeble excuse. Neither Brooke nor Montgomery would have tolerated such insubordination in an army commander.

How effective was the heavy-bomber offensive against Germany? In particular, was Harris's policy of area bombing in Germany 'as futile as it was bestial', as it has been described?[30] In fact the bombing of Germany was not futile. Speer admitted that however ingenious and resourceful the Germans were in dispersing industry or burying factories underground, the Allied air offensive created a third front as far as resources were concerned. The German air force became a defensive weapon. They lost air superiority on the Russian front, as fighter planes had to be deployed in defence of their cities; and every anti-aircraft gun in Germany meant one less available for anti-tank warfare in the field. Portal denied that the object of Bomber Command was to kill civilians: it was, he said, to make buildings and installations uninhabitable, and the survivors despair. Only a few protested at the bombings – such as Bishop Bell of Chichester, whose speeches in the House of Lords Churchill's private secretary described as 'notorious'.[31] The rest of us considered that the Germans were reaping the consequences of their attacks on Guernica, Rotterdam and Coventry and their Baedeker raids on historic cities. The callousness war engenders was to have one disastrous consequence: the bombing of Dresden in February 1945.

On 25 January the JIC wrote a paper advocating a gigantic raid on Berlin, in the hope that it would have the same conclusive effect that the destruction of Hiroshima was to have seven months later. The British newspapers were full of stories about the flood of Germans fleeing the Russian advance into Silesia, and Churchill telephoned Sir Archibald Sinclair at the Air Ministry to ask what Bomber Command was doing to add to the confusion. Portal was lukewarm: better, he felt, to stick to bombing oil installations. Sinclair told Churchill that although the time had not yet come for such devastating attacks, they were 'under examination'. This brought a tart response from Churchill: 'I did not ask you about plans for harrying the retreat from Breslau. I asked whether Berlin, and no doubt other large cities in East Germany, should not be considered as especially attractive targets. I am glad that this is "under examination". Pray report to me tomorrow what is going to be done.' Churchill, and Portal with him, then left for the Yalta conference.

The Deputy Chief of Staff at the Air Ministry, alarmed by the blustering tone of Churchill's minute, made a formal report to

Bomber Command to exploit the chaos caused by the flood of refugees by attacking Berlin, Dresden, Chemnitz and Leipzig, adding the weasel words: 'subject to the overriding claims of oil and other approved target systems'.[32] The inclusion of Dresden on the list of targets surprised the Intelligence staff at Bomber Command, and Harris's Chief of Staff, Air Vice-Marshal Robert Saundby, queried the order with the Air Ministry. There was a delay of several days before he was told that Dresden was to be included among the cities to be attacked. Saundby said later that he 'understood' that the attack was part of a programme in which the Prime Minister was personally interested, and that the reply had been delayed because it had to be cleared at Yalta. He 'understood' that the Russians had asked for Dresden to be attacked.[33]

Such a massive operation could succeed only if Spaatz and the American air forces co-operated. Portal told his Vice-Chief on 6 February to ask Spaatz to approve. If he did so, the Combined Bomber Offensive committee should embody the plan in a new directive. The new directive was never issued. The Combined Chiefs never discussed the matter.[34] The plan had a secondary purpose: to help the Russian offensive. And at Yalta General Antonov asked the Allied strategic bomber force to paralyse Berlin and Leipzig. He never mentioned Dresden. This was hardly strange. Ultra informed us that the Russian thrust was directed at Leipzig, not Dresden.[35]

The belief that Antonov had mentioned Dresden arose from events in the previous year. In August 1944 Portal had suggested a massive raid on Berlin, and the American generals Eaker and Quesada remembered the Russian General Novikov asking that Dresden be bombed. But at that time the situation was entirely different: the Red Army had not reached the German frontier, and Dresden had some strategic importance. Churchill's biographer Martin Gilbert states that at Yalta Antonov specifically mentioned Berlin, Leipzig and Dresden; and that the air raids on Dresden were a direct result of the agreement at Yalta.[36] But the official record of Yalta contains no reference to Dresden. There were bomb-line discussions with Antonov, but the only mention of Dresden was made by the American General Kuter, who referred to industrial targets 'in the neighbourhood of Dresden'.[37]

As usual the Russians told the Allies nothing about their intentions, but they used to give us a bomb line. On 6 February they asked us to bomb Leipzig, from which we deduced that Marshal Koniev's armies were to sweep north of Dresden as part of the plan to encircle Berlin. As a result of the Ardennes post-mortem Jim Rose, Bletchley's RAF liaison officer, had been transferred to the Air Ministry to be in charge of operational intelligence. When he discovered that Dresden was the target, he telephoned General Spaatz, who told him that the reason he had been given for bombing Dresden round the clock was that Rundstedt's Panzer divisions were to pass through the city en route for the defence of the Hungarian oilfields. Rose told him that Ultra showed that these divisions were routed west of Prague, and nowhere near Dresden. Spaatz authorised Rose to tell Bomber Command that he would abandon the plan if the British agreed.[38] When Rose rang Saundby at Bomber Command he was told curtly that the operation would go ahead.

Who gave the fatal order? Impossible to say. It may be that no specific order from on high was ever given. Churchill wanted German cities pulverised: but Dresden? When asked at Yalta, he may have simply agreed that Dresden was *one* of the cities that might be attacked. Or Portal may have dealt with the matter. Some have inferred that Churchill wanted to demonstrate to Stalin what the Allies were doing to help him; but this is only an inference. When the Air Ministry confirmed that the inclusion of Dresden was not an error, Saundby 'understood' that Dresden must be bombed, and that it was the Prime Minister's decision. One is reminded of Henry II asking, in a moment of rage, who would revenge him for the injuries he had suffered at the hands of 'this turbulent priest'; he did not specifically order Thomas à Becket to be killed. When Churchill fired off minutes deflecting the Army from its specific objectives, Brooke could reply that what he wanted was not feasible. But for Bomber Command anything, weather permitting, was feasible; and like Henry II's knights, Harris was only too willing to satisfy a thirst for revenge.*

Churchill's conscience troubled him about Dresden. Within a

---

* The deaths of 180 people in London in the winter of 1944–5 from V-2 rockets was not likely to have influenced Churchill – not because of indifference, but from a just sense of priorities.

month he had misgivings about the operation, and he wrote in a minute to the Chiefs of Staff: 'The moment has come when the question of bombing German cities simply for the sake of increasing the terror, though under other pretexts, should be revised . . . The destruction of Dresden remains a serious query against the conduct of Allied bombing.' Portal got Churchill to withdraw this 'rough' minute and to delete the word 'terror' and the reference to Dresden. When Harris heard of Churchill's concern, he said he could not see what the fuss was about. People seemed to have Dresden shepherdesses on their mind. Two and a half weeks later Churchill was puzzled to hear that Potsdam had been bombed.[39] The Mephistopheles of Bomber Command was inexorable, and had Faust in his power; and one of the most beautiful cities in northern Europe lay in ruins.

However much intelligence influenced, or failed to influence, the air war before and after D-Day, the crucial test for intelligence was whether the second and third conditions for launching Overlord had been achieved. How many first-class mobile divisions had the Germans in the west, how many reinforcements could they spare from other fronts, and how fast could they come?

From September 1943 until D-Day we watched the comings and goings of the German divisions. This was by now feasible since Bletchley had broken the German army cyphers one by one, and MI14 could therefore watch what was happening on the Russian front. We relied on the order of battle section in MI14, but by now there were other rivals in the field, double-checking their work: Lieutenant-Colonel John Austin, the order of battle chief in Eisenhower's headquarters, and Brigadier Bill Williams in 21 Army Group. What we saw was a shuttle service of divisions leaving the west for Russia and returning to refit and rest in the west. How right Brooke had been about the advantage the Germans gained by having interior lines of communication. Hitler could move divisions from one front to another in order to plug a hole and avert a crisis. In mid-March the Russians surrounded a Panzer army near Lvov in Galicia. On 27 March we learnt that an SS Panzer division was leaving southern France, the spearhead of an armoured SS corps. Within ten days it was fighting to relieve the encircled army, and with this reinforcement the Panzer army escaped the noose. Two hundred thousand troops got away, though they lost all their heavy weapons and equipment.

So the question began to be put to us week after week: what had happened to the original conditions for Overlord – that there should be no more than twelve German mobile divisions in France and the Low Countries with which to counterattack and no more than fifteen likely to be brought from other fronts? The Japanese Ambassador in Berlin reported that Hitler had told him on 22 January that there were sixty-one divisions in the west – thirty of them mobile reserve divisions, though not all of them were first class. Further decrypts confirmed these figures. General Hollis, the head of the War Cabinet secretariat, told the JIC in early March that the Chiefs of Staff would soon have to review prospects to see whether or not Overlord was on. What was their latest count?

The JIC gave their best appreciation of the war. They were confident that Hitler could not transfer to the west more than eight top-quality divisions within two months of the landings. It was true that there were now sixteen and not twelve first-class mobile divisions, but on the other hand Eisenhower had widened the area of assault and would land more troops in the first forty-eight hours than had been decided in the original plan; and he did not seem to be perturbed. Hollis accepted this answer, and our eyes were glued to the exact whereabouts of every German division. On 20 March the JIS said there were fifty-five divisions in the west. By mid-May the number had risen to sixty. Every day decrypts revealed the comings and goings, the state of refitting, the destination of this or that division. When D-Day dawned the estimate of sixty divisions in the west proved to be almost exactly accurate (there were in fact fifty-eight). But there was a failure. We did not pinpoint the exact spot where 21 Panzer Division or 352 Infantry Division were: and this was to sway the course of the battle in the first forty-eight hours.

We also had to judge whether Hitler had guessed where the Allies would land. Eisenhower and Montgomery knew it was impossible to disguise the fact that France would be invaded across the English Channel. The Germans must realise that we would have to capture a major port soon after the assault; and that pointed to Le Havre or Cherbourg. The bombing of the Seine bridges again suggested Normandy. But might it not be possible to delude Hitler into believing that, having drawn his forces to resist our landings in Normandy, a second but far bigger assault force would be thrown across the Straits of Dover to cut off his armies further south? An elaborate deception plan was therefore concocted. The scheme was for a phantom army group under General Patton to materialise in Kent. Another phantom army was to form in Scotland. Signals buzzed between the two imaginary formations. Our best double agent, who had already been awarded the Iron Cross, reported that without doubt these forces would launch the main attack in the Pas de Calais: any other landing would be a diversion. To preserve security all diplomatic privileges for foreign embassies were stopped. Would Hitler take the bait?

It looked at first as if he would not. In late May the JIS reported that the German High Command was certain that the assault would be launched in the Le Havre–Cherbourg area. Decrypts showed the enemy reinforcing the Cotentin peninsula and moving the 21st Panzer Division closer to Caen. A week later we came to an even more pessimistic conclusion. The Germans seemed to have judged that Normandy was 'a likely, perhaps even the main point of assault'.[40] But on 1 June our spirits rose. Hitler had talked once again to the Japanese ambassador, and had told him that the Allies would make feints at Norway, Denmark, the Bay of Biscay and the south of France. They would then first land in Normandy or Brittany. That, however, would be only an initial landing. The main attack would be launched across the Straits of Dover. This showed that Patton's phantom army group in Kent had acquired a corporeal existence. Still, it did not alter the fact that the enemy would be ready for us in Normandy. But where in Normandy? On 27 May another decrypt from the German air force showed that they thought the Dieppe–Le Havre area the most likely spot. In fact the German High Command never did guess the exact Overlord beaches, nor did they guess the date of the landings.

They did not decide how to meet the assault either. Should they stake all on defeating us on the beaches? Or should they lure the

Allies inland and then annihilate them in a counter-offensive? Rundstedt, the Commander in Chief of the West, favoured the latter; Rommel, commanding Army Group B, the former. We learnt that German divisions were being moved closer to the coast, and Brigadier Williams predicted that Rundstedt would hold the bulk of the armoured divisions under his command, releasing them only when he saw fit. Not until after the war did we learn of the tension between the two great German commanders, nor how effective our deception plan had been. We convinced Hitler that he must hold the armoured divisions in the Pas de Calais to repulse Patton. On 26 June the JIS said that even then the Germans still seemed to expect a landing between the Pas de Calais and the Seine. So successful was the deception that the intelligence chiefs begged the Prime Minister not to listen to the wailings of the Foreign Office but to prolong the suspension of all diplomatic privileges until 21 June so that no embassy should blow the gaffe.

How long would the war last if Overlord was successful? I still saw much of Peter Earle, with whom I had shared a room in those early days in MI14. He was now military assistant to Sir Alan Brooke, and among his duties was to listen in to the CIGS's telephone conversations, so that at any critical moment he could seize a relevant file and lay it before his master as he spoke. (He used to give lifelike imitations of the exchanges between the Prime Minister and the CIGS.) Nevertheless, he was fretting: here he was, a regular soldier, who had still not seen action, and his contemporaries were commanding units in France that were to make or mar their careers in the Army. In his diary he wrote of an evening we spent together in February 1944 during which he lamented that the war would be over by October, and I comforted him by saying that it would last until mid-1945.[41] He was indeed to see action in the last weeks of the war. To my shame, I was not.

So the keystone of Allied grand strategy fell into place. Despite Alan Brooke's fears that the German army possessed a 'mass of manoeuvre', despite Churchill's memories of the Somme and Passchendaele, there was no carnage on the beaches. Lacking the special invasion tanks General Hobart had devised, the Americans took heavy losses on Omaha beach; but they made it. To this day, however, some judges believe we should have left Italy to stew in its own juice, and launched Overlord in 1943.

The most vigorous British advocate of this strategy has been John Grigg.[42] He did not even allow that Tunis should have been taken: the Axis forces there could have been starved out, and several Anglo-American divisions should have been sent back to England to invade France in 1943. So far from suffering a defeat in Sicily and Italy, Hitler bought time – over a year – before he was threatened in the only theatre from which Germany itself could be invaded, namely the Channel coast. It was untrue that the Allies did not have sufficient landing craft in 1943: nine divisions were put ashore in Sicily, two more than in Overlord. Rundstedt admitted to Hitler in October 1943 that the Atlantic Wall in France was ramshackle. The Allies had air superiority, and plenty of troops. Had the firm decision to invade in August been made, Admiral King would not have been able to switch landing craft from Atlantic operations to the Pacific. Even some of the technological triumphs in Overlord, for example the artificial harbours, were mooted in 1942 and could have been developed in time. The fiasco of the Dieppe raid of August 1942 simply showed how not to plan a cross-Channel operation. The new technique of bombing, by marking the target with flares from Mosquito bombers before the heavy bombers went in, was perfected by Wing-Commander Leonard Cheshire in March 1944, but it could have been introduced earlier if mass-production of fast light aircraft had been put in hand in 1942. Roosevelt was in part to blame. He came to the Casablanca conference in the spring of 1942 unprepared, with his military Chief of Staff pro Overlord and his naval Chief of Staff set on the Pacific. All he contributed was his casual off-the-cuff edict of unconditional surrender (which was flouted both by the Italians and the Japanese). As a result, so Grigg argued, the British had their way. Churchill and Brooke dragged their feet at every turn and would not commit themselves to Overlord.

The delay, he went on to say, was disastrous. If the war had ended a year earlier, a million or more Jews would not have perished; Eastern Europe might not have been occupied by the Soviet

Union; the Polish underground would have survived instead of being betrayed by the Russians; de Gaulle could have been a co-operative, instead of an embittered, ally; and if the Anglo-Americans had already formed their second front, the Tehran conference would have been transformed. As it was, victory came by the narrowest of margins. Apart from the atom bomb, Germany was ahead of us in the scientific war: in V-1 and V-2 weapons, new U-boats and jet fighters.

The ghost of General Marshall rises before us. Was his clear, simple plan correct, and could the American divisions with their élan and self-confidence have fought their way ashore alongside the British, held onto a bridgehead and then in the autumn of 1943 streamed across France? No one can say. But it should be allowed that Alan Brooke's strategy had some success. He believed that the Italian campaign (which was needed to provide the shipping) and Overlord were interdependent, not alternatives. Between June 1942 and May 1943 Hitler sent fifty-four battalions to North Africa and the Axis lost 227,000 men, 1200 tanks and 20,000 vehicles there. Whereas in July 1943 the Germans had six divisions in Italy and twelve in south-east Europe, in November they had committed twenty-five in Italy and the Allies only eleven. They suffered four to every three Allied casualties. In 1944 not a single German division left Italy for the west, and only one went to the Russian front.

Some critics argue that the Germans had only 820,000 men in the Mediterranean as opposed to the Allies' 1.6 million. But the disparity in numbers is irrelevant. Whereas the Germans had been forced to withdraw troops from France and the Russian front, there was nowhere else for the Allied troops to fight Hitler. Nowhere else? But there was Normandy. Yet when one observes the fate of the two amphibious landings in Italy, at Salerno and at Anzio – the latter an American operation – it is difficult to believe that an operation against the coast of Normandy could have succeeded without the lessons from Italy having been learnt, without the technological innovations devised during 1943 such as Pluto, the undersea pipeline, without an air-plan for interdiction (i.e. the bombing of bridges and the rail system between the Rhine and the Seine), with the German air force still formidable and able to attack the beaches, without troops experienced in amphibious warfare and the follow-up divisions from America with a year's less training. The build-up against Overlord would have been far heavier but for the Italian campaign. And is Grigg right in assuming that the advance across France in late autumn 1943 would have been as swift as it was in the summer of 1944? Many more Americans and British soldiers would have lain dead in France and Germany.

And what if Overlord in 1943 had been defeated? If the Allies had been thrown back into the sea, the effect on morale would have been devastating and the remounting of the operation immeasurably difficult, because surprise and deception would have gone. It might not have been possible to relaunch the operation until 1945, and by then the Soviet Union would have claimed to have defeated Germany single-handed. The argument that the Allies could have hastened the end of the war by invading France in 1943 looks thin.

❖

CHAPTER SIX

Supreme Headquarters

Once Overlord was launched, the Joint Intelligence Staff could only sit back and watch. It was for the intelligence staffs in the field to analyse and act upon the mass of decrypts that revealed how the German army reacted to the Allied assault. But in the summer we were suddenly called to interpret an event that we had believed was improbable: a plot to kill Hitler.

In 1940 Churchill had insisted on a policy of 'absolute silence' towards any German approach for peace, partly in order to quell any dissenters in the Conservative Party who hankered after a negotiated peace with Hitler; and partly because even high-minded Germans who detested Hitler, such as the Christian mayor of Leipzig Dr Goerdeler, envisaged Germany keeping Austria, the Sudetenland, Alsace-Lorraine and her pre-1914 frontiers. We had also heard of Helmuth von Moltke's Kreisau circle, dedicated Christians who were ashamed of Nazi brutalities. But whereas we stated in January 1944 that no faction likely to overthrow the Nazis existed, in March we said there was some slight evidence of organised opposition. But what did it amount to? The old SPD leaders were in prison, and we doubted whether a few disaffected generals would take 'isolated action'.

At the end of June, however, a key figure in the German resistance, Adam von Trott, met an MI6 officer in Stockholm. Trott, a diplomat who had been a student at Oxford and who knew a number of the younger dons there, was intelligent, idealistic and charming; a touchy patriot, he would flare up in conversation if anyone doubted that there was another Germany, a good Germany, distinct from the Nazis, which wanted only to be treated as an equal in the concert of Europe. Trott asked if the British would modify the terms of unconditional surrender: he was given the brush-off.

The Foreign Office commented: 'These people . . . won't act without our backing which if given might gravely embarrass us later.'* So the British dismissed the approaches by the Lutheran minister Dietrich Bonhoeffer to Bishop Bell (whose criticism of British bombing policy earned him the title in the Foreign Office of 'the pestilent priest') and also by the Abwehr through Swedish contacts. The Americans were less rigid, and Allen Dulles, head of the Office of Strategic Services (OSS) station in Switzerland, kept in touch with the German opposition. To no avail. The July plot failed.

British Intelligence has sometimes been blamed for its indifference to Stauffenberg and his fellow plotters. But there is no evidence that they faltered or changed their plans because the British were sceptical towards their aims. Nor is it credible that a sizeable swatch of German generals and influential civilians were only waiting for a sign from the Allies of generous treatment after the war to trigger them to overthrow Hitler. The Nazi apparatus of social control – the SS, the Gestapo, the Gauleiters in the provinces – were too strong right until the end of the war for any plot against Hitler to gain significant support. In late April 1945 suspects of the July plot were being executed even though their executioners knew the end of the Reich was imminent.

Why was the Foreign Office so sceptical? To the Foreign Office embarrassment is almost worse than diplomatic defeat, because embarrassment is a continuing state of discomfort, like a running sore. They had no wish to be confronted by a group of Prussian Junkers who, they considered, would be scarcely less nationalist than the Nazis when putting forward conditions for peace. How could we convince Roosevelt to go back on his demand for 'unconditional surrender'? – though in effect he had done so in Italy. How could we convince Stalin that we were not plotting a deal with the German military elite? After all, Stalin himself, we suspected in mid-1943, had sent emissaries to listen to Hitler's proposals for a

---

* Trott, most unjustly, was regarded as an equivocal figure. After the British had failed to respond to General Beck's overtures to call Hitler's bluff at the time of Munich, Trott visited Britain in the summer of 1939. It was said that he advocated coming to an agreement with Hitler over Danzig: once that was out of the way, the conspirators would get rid of him. He seemed to have moved, therefore, into the camp of the appeasers. He was in fact always an opponent of all the Nazis stood for.[1]

separate Soviet–Nazi peace. For the British Labour Party, and for many Conservatives, the Prussian military caste was held to be almost as responsible as the Nazis for the war. Had not General Hans von Seeckt, who masterminded the rebirth of the Reichswehr after the First World War, secretly broken the Versailles Treaty? Less than fifteen years before he had rearmed and retrained a German army larger than the Treaty permitted. Many of the German generals who had won battles in the first three years of the war closed their ears to the stories of the atrocities the SS committed within the territory the army had conquered. Even after Hitler's crazy declaration of war against America and the turn of the tide in Russia they could not bring themselves to act.

But one young officer even before Stalingrad had already prepared to do so. Colonel Claus von Stauffenberg asked General Zeitzler, the chief of staff of the German War Office (OKH) in July 1942 if he could visit Manstein. He told Manstein that the war was lost and urged him for over an hour to take command of the army. Manstein was friendly, but sat mum. In desperation Stauffenberg made his final plea in one word: 'Tauroggen' – the place where in 1808 General von Yorck on his own authority abandoned Prussia's alliance with Napoleon and changed sides. These officers lived by military history.

Manstein remained unmoved. 'Prussian field marshals do not mutiny,' he said. How could a commander expect his soldiers to lay down their lives for victory and then, by his own hands, precipitate defeat? He sent a message to Zeitzler that Stauffenberg had been too long on the staff and should be sent to the front (Stauffenberg was sent to North Africa in February 1943, where he was so badly wounded in Tunisia that he returned to staff duties.)

Alexander Stahlberg, Manstein's adjutant, who heard and recorded the conversation, kept on bringing to Manstein's attention fresh Nazi bestialities. So too did Generals Fellgiebel and Hans Oster, who were to perish after the failure of the plot. Of the 3–9 million Russian prisoners of war taken by February 1942, a quarter of a million were shot and only a million or so survived. Any Jews found among the civilian population were killed at once. Even when Hitler sacked Manstein from commanding Army Group South in Russia, Manstein kept on hoping that stalemate on the

Russian front would compel Hitler to call for an armistice.[2]

The aristocratic officer caste were caught in a bind. They despised Hitler and the lower-middle-class riff-raff and thugs among the Nazi and SS leadership. They knew Hitler was losing the war by his strategic blunders. But many considered they were bound by their officers' oath of allegiance. In Italy the monarchy offered an alternative centre of loyalty to Mussolini. In Germany there was none. We in the JIS believed that the army alone could overthrow the regime; but after the failure of the Stauffenberg plot the German army and its General Staff would fall under the command and surveillance of the Nazi Party. Only military defeat, not a political coup, would bring the war to an end. The old tight-knit General Staff, who knew and trusted each other, was now diluted, and numbers of generals were Nazi supporters. The vast majority had not scrupled to break their oath to the Weimar Republic, and after 20 July they hastened to congratulate Hitler on his escape (though had they not done so they would probably have been arrested).[3]

In retrospect, however, the Allied reaction to the failure of the plotters, if comprehensible, is chilling. Let dog eat dog – 'Let the generals kill the corporal or vice-versa, preferably both,' said the *New York Herald Tribune*.[4] Roosevelt was determined not to find himself in President Wilson's shoes, defending Fourteen Points that had been agreed with the German resistance. In Moscow there was some confusion. At first the plotters were hailed as anti-Nazi allies. Then the Party line was laid down: they were a capitalist clique whose sole aim was to preserve their own property and the military order. In Britain the word was put out that the plotters were nationalists trying to salvage as much as possible of Germany's ill-gotten gains. An appalling misjudgement followed when the BBC broadcast the names of those who might be supposed to be in the plot, leading the Gestapo to arrest several who had not been suspected. They were executed.

At the time the JIS knew all too little about the plotters. Some were utopians, or mystics like Helmuth von Moltke; some were old-style authoritarians and committed Christians like Goerdeler; others intelligent officers and officials like Stauffenberg, Schulenburg, and Trott. They regarded Britain as the moral leader of

Europe – had she not acknowledged the injustice of the Versailles Treaty? They wanted a peace that acknowledged that injustice. But they had not the faintest idea how loathed Germany was. They had two ambitions, as the agonising last letters they wrote before their execution showed: to be true to their conscience and to uphold their honour. They knew they would be vilified as traitors, but by honour they meant preserving Germany, the country of Kant and Goethe, as a great power.

The plotters were heroic. They recognised how slim were their chances of success. Only those who have lived under a totalitarian regime with secret police and a servile judiciary can understand how difficult it was to plot and how ferocious the system of repression. Difficult to visualise also how dense was the security screen wrapped around the Führer: squads of SS bodyguards never allowed the army to drive or even cook a meal for him on the rare occasions when he visited an army group headquarters.* We in JIS were heartless but right to discount any possibility of further resistance. The Foreign Office attitude, endorsed by the historian John Wheeler-Bennett, was expressed by Oliver Harvey: 'Our enemies are both the Nazis and the generals. We should make peace with neither . . . it was to our interest that the coup failed.'[5] On the other hand, what is one to say of the Foreign Office, who *after* the war suppressed documents, manipulated evidence and refused to acknowledge or even give minimal recognition to the widows and children of the executed plotters? They even tampered with evidence that might have helped Ernst von Weizsäcker when the Americans put him on trial.[6] That is a squalid little chapter.

---

* And yet equally difficult to visualise was the ability of Berliners to evade the repression, as described in the memoirs of 'Missy' Vassiltchikov and Christabel Bielenberg. Even more strange is the story of Aimee and Jaguar, as told by Erica Fischer. In 1944 a middle-aged housewife and Nazi sympathiser became infatuated by a young lesbian Jewess, and involuntarily protected a circle of lesbians, some of them Jews, who had become 'U-boats', i.e. torn the yellow star of David from their clothing and gone underground. They bathed in the lakes and went to parties. Only one of them was discovered and died in Auschwitz. In Berlin, as in London, life in wartime was full of improbabilities and excitement.

Once the Allied armies began to break out of Normandy and stream across northern France, the old euphoria in the JIS returned. We were asked to predict how long the Germans would continue to resist. On 14 July the JIC forecast that the war would end in December. On 5 September we declared that, since the German front in the west (unlike that in Russia) was held by 'nothing but disorganised remnants', German resistance would disintegrate, though we could not predict how long it would take. Our optimism was modest compared with that of SHAEF, 21 Army Group and MI14 intelligence staffs.

One man dissented: the Prime Minister. On 8 September 1944 Churchill wrote a memorandum in which he foresaw that Patton would be halted at the Metz–Nancy line. Montgomery, he judged, could hardly advance until he had got the Channel ports working and the Scheldt cleared. He criticised the JIC report for not showing how many and where the German divisions were and how many and where they were expected to be at the end of September. Would the Germans be able to find troops by withdrawal from Italy or from the twenty-five to thirty-five divisions in the Baltic states? 'It is at least as likely that Hitler will be fighting on 1st January as that he will collapse before then. If he does the reasons will be political rather than purely military.' Brooke's biographer David Fraser compared Brooke on this matter to Churchill: 'There is no doubt which way the balance tips; Churchill wins at all points.'[7] Churchill predicted that Hitler would find troops from somewhere and stand on the Siegfried Line, on which in 1939 the British sang that they would hang out their washing.[8] They found, in the words of the song, the Siegfried Line still there.

Churchill had read the decrypts, especially that of 3 September in which Hitler gave orders to deny the Scheldt estuary in Belgium to the Allies. So had Admiral Ramsay, the naval commander of Overlord. The Chiefs of Staff and my colonel, Larry Kirwan, were at the Quebec conference, and they too saw the significance of the Scheldt. Neither Eisenhower nor Montgomery did – uncharacteristically, years later Montgomery acknowledged his mistake.[9] Montgomery had the excuse that at the time he was embroiled with Eisenhower on strategy and with the Canadian Commander General Crerar. He had torn a strip off Crerar for attending a memorial service for the Canadian soldiers who died at Dieppe in 1942 instead of attending his conference of army commanders, and had had to apologise.[10] Now he ordered Crerar to eliminate the German garrisons in Boulogne, Calais and on the Scheldt, but he did not give him the administrative back-up to do so. No ship unloaded at Antwerp until eighty-five days after its capture.[11]

Montgomery was in the grip of an obsession. Too slow in pursuit of Rommel after El Alamein, too plodding in Normandy, he now intended to show his critics in the press how fast he could move. He believed he could drive to Berlin if only Eisenhower would halt the other two army groups and put two American armies under his command. Later he came up with a more modest proposal to seize a bridgehead over the Rhine and outflank the Ruhr. Between 6 and 9 September the decrypts showed German forces building up in the Arnhem area, with references to 9 and 10 Panzer Divisions which were to rest and refit under a Panzer corps. These divisions did not show up again in Ultra. The British Second Army intelligence concluded: 'There can either be rest and refit, or defence of the west wall and Holland. There cannot be both.'[12] But SHAEF was more alive to danger, and Bedell-Smith, Eisenhower's Chief of Staff, visited 21 Army Group to warn Montgomery. The warning fell on deaf ears; the German tanks were to turn the scales at the battle of Arnhem.

In August General Strong, head of intelligence at SHAEF, said he wanted a closer relationship with the JIC in London, and I flew to Paris to see him. I discovered that he was thinking of setting up a Joint Intelligence Staff of his own in G2, the intelligence section: would I join him? By this time the centre of interest in intelligence had shifted. The JIS and their cousins the Planners had turned their attention to another war. For months the JIS had been advising on the scale of Japanese resistance to numbers of operations in Burma, Malaya and beyond. There was one secret that the planners and intelligence staffs did not know: the existence of the atom bomb. So by the autumn of 1944 we had charted the progress of the island-hopping strategy which in 1948 would bring about the final defeat of the Japanese army on the mainland. It seemed to me that there was little more the JIS could do in London, and with the blessing of the DMI and Larry Kirwan I set out for Versailles.

Some years later Andrew Noble, then a Counsellor in Buenos Aires, wrote to me summing up our days in the JIS: 'It was hellish hard work, and one was often so tired that one could hardly think straight; but there was zest to it. We were at the centre of things and could often see the fruits of our work. What is more, we were a happy band. We had some glorious arguments, but there was a blessed absence of rancour; once the battle was over we could adjourn to the Mess for a drink and unite in damning the Planners.'[13]

One's complexion after working underground for months resembled a potato, but compared with most others our lot was a happy one. Perhaps the most nerve-racking tension was security. When one became overtired, it was hard to remember whether one had seen some succulent item in Ultra, a Cabinet Office document, *The Times* or the *Daily Mirror*. Journalists often made sensible military predictions that were not all that far off what was in fact being planned. Noble was right. The work was exhilarating: very different from my work at SHAEF.

The routine at SHAEF was like my days at the War Cabinet Offices. Every morning I walked, not across the Horse Guards to the War Office, but from the Hôtel Trianon, the main headquarters across the park of the Palace of Versailles, to the Petite Ecurie and past the touching statue of the gardener who crouches sickle in hand. There I called on John Austin, running his order of battle section, and picked up the latest Ultra teleprints. Every night I returned to my billet and read French poetry in my comfortable but icy bedroom. The wife of the family on whom I was billeted was as charming as her Vichyssois husband was not. Did I not know, he said – I assuredly did know, but would not admit it – that Admiral Darlan, Pétain's commander of the Vichy French armed forces, had been assassinated on the orders of the British in 1942? '*Et je vous assure, monsieur, que quand nous monterons au ciel, nous verrons l'amiral Darlan et Jeanne d'Arc se serrant la main*' ('And I can promise you, Monsieur, that when we ascend to heaven we shall see Admiral Darlan and Joan of Arc shaking hands').

In MI14, 1941

Joint Intelligence Staff, 1943: Francis Ogilvy, Henry Haslam, Ken Sloan, NA,
Charles Fletcher-Cooke.

Arthur Marshall.

Major-General Kenneth Strong at SHAEF.

A Chiefs of Staff meeting in April 1945: Major-General Hollis, Admiral
Sir Andrew Cunningham, Field Marshal Sir Alan Brooke.

Lieutenant-Colonel Peter Earle.

Brooding over Germany at the Blase house.

Ilse Martos-Imhorst and Cecil King.

Farewell party at the Blase house: Leo Long, Peter Domieson, NA, Austen Albu,
Jack Rathbone, Dusty Rhodes, Robert Harcourt, Alan Flanders.

Christopher Steel, Anne White and Austen Albu.

Kurt Schumacher,
addressing an SPD rally,
October 1946.

Konrad Adenauer,
photographed in
1952.

Schumacher (right) studies the election results as they come through on
9 November 1946.

The work at Supreme Headquarters was never exacting. It was a factory designed to cement the Anglo-American alliance. The bonding took this form: a British major would answer to an American colonel who in turn answered to a British brigadier who was deputy to an American major-general. As soon as I arrived Strong summoned me to his office at the Hôtel Trianon. I found him sharing a room with an American brigadier-general, and he delivered a homily on the supreme importance of Anglo-American relations: backbiting and sneers about our ally were not tolerated in the headquarters. 'Here you see I sit with General Betts – what passes over my desk, passes over his.'

The harmony between the allies at SHAEF was exemplified by General Eisenhower. By his personal modesty, his charm, his genius for informality and his determination to make the Anglo-American alliance a reality, Eisenhower evoked intense loyalty and affection from his staff. My friend Arthur Marshall in the counter-intelligence section once found himself alone with Eisenhower in an air-raid shelter at the Bushy Park headquarters. The flying-bomb offensive on London had just begun. As one passed overhead and exploded in the distance Eisenhower said, 'You know, every time I pray "Oh Lord, keep that engine going" I feel kinda mean.'[14] Harmony reigned between the British and American officers in his headquarters. It became the mark of a good British SHAEF officer to express dismay at the behaviour of Montgomery. Had he not challenged Eisenhower's broad-front advance across France? Had he not then intrigued to be reinstated as Commander in Chief of the land forces and usurp Eisenhower's position? Did he not treat Eisenhower with contempt, refusing to visit him at his head-quarters? Why could he not understand that American forces now far outnumbered the British? The American generals were insisting that they should run the war – having not been all that impressed by the way Montgomery ran it in Normandy. Such certainly were the views of Kenneth Strong, who since Algiers days had been Eisenhower's intelligence chief.

I noticed that my old chief had changed. By now Strong had the sleek, well-fed look of a senior staff officer who had adopted the lifestyle of the American top brass in Algiers. Like Solly Zuckerman he responded to the generosity and informality of Americans, and had learnt a lot about the in-fighting between one headquarters and another. Under him were a British brigadier for operational intelligence and an American colonel for counter-intelligence, i.e. security. He had picked as his aide-de-camp a Welsh Guards officer, Kenneth Keith, who already had that nose for a deal and for inside information that was to make him a leading merchant banker at Hill-Samuel after the war. Another financial wizard helped John Austin, his American counterpart: a sharp, quick-witted Wall Street analyst, John Petito.

Supreme Headquarters was gigantic. The forward echelon to which I belonged was equivalent in numbers to a division; how large the rear echelon was I never discovered. Strong's staff alone numbered over a thousand men and women. It was not as if the vast staff helped Eisenhower to take strategic decisions: they had already been taken at meetings between Eisenhower, his army group commanders and General Patton. At such meetings Bedell-Smith and senior staff officers such as Bull, Whiteley and Strong might contribute their views as well. As a result the plans SHAEF produced were rarely clear or convincing, since they were a series of compromises; and the staff spent more of their time producing papers to justify these decisions to the Combined Chiefs of Staff than in producing the data on which plans could be made. A SHAEF general would announce a plan was on; a day or so later an army group chief of staff would announce it was off. Not that matters at Mountbatten's headquarters of South-East Asia Command in Kandy were any better. 'All balls and rackets' was the view taken of it by General Slim's staff officers. Perhaps it is inevitable that Supreme Headquarters, whether in Versailles, Cairo or Kandy, being at the interface of politics and strategy, earn a bad reputation. The Oberkommando der Wehrmacht was no exception to this rule.

Intelligence at SHAEF was governed by what one might call the Happy Hypothesis. This was that the German army had now been so shattered in Normandy and battered in Russia that it was only a matter of two or three months before the war would end. When I arrived at SHAEF I formed the impression that the intelligence appreciations were tuned to justify Eisenhower's policy to attack all along the line. This policy required intelligence to report the German army as being incapable of mounting an offensive. Strong was later to say that intelligence officers were regarded as defeatist if they did not believe that the end of the war was in sight.[15] All the warlords, despite their rivalries, agreed that this was so. But it was not so. The most spectacular blunder of the interpreters of intelligence was our failure to forecast the German offensive in the Ardennes on 16 December 1944. How did this happen?

It was not the fault of the staff at Bletchley Park. Seen with the benefit of hindsight, the story Ultra told was this: in August Hitler told the Japanese Ambassador that he was mobilising all resources and would deliver a counterstroke in November or December. Ultra did not spell out the miracles Speer was achieving in increasing production, nor that boys, and from October girls, were serving as *Flakhelfer* (anti-aircraft auxiliaries), enabling anti-aircraft soldiers to be redeployed as part of a final comb-out of headquarters troops, nor that aged men became Volksgrenadieren, and farm workers were being assigned to the Volkssturm (the German equivalent of the Home Guard).[16] But Ultra did reveal the effect of the mobilisation. At the end of September an armoured corps consisting of three Panzer divisions was put under 6 Panzer Army, commanded by the Nazi General Sepp Dietrich. They were ordered to move east to Westphalia to rest, refit and train, and were to be allocated new tanks and guns. Together with another armoured division, Panzer Lehr, they were designated, so we learnt on 22 October, as the OKW (German High Command) reserve. The Germans had difficulty in extracting several of these and other divisions from the battle, and Rundstedt fought an able withdrawal to the Siegfried Line.

Then on 2 November the German air force began to jabber. Fighter patrols were to protect the unloading of train transports in two areas west of Cologne, one of which was opposite the Ardennes. Two batches of trains, the first of forty-one, the second of twenty-eight, were to be unloaded at Cologne. A further 200 trains, carrying in all a dozen divisions and other units, were to be unloaded in the Eiffel and Saar areas. The rail authorities were to ensure that the trains arrived punctually. The next signal, which should have astonished us, was that Kesselring in Italy was told to transfer a thousand lorries to 6 Panzer Army. On 29 November jet fighters were told to reconnoitre the crossings over the river Meuse daily, and on 5 December a conference of fighter squadron commanders was fixed outside Koblenz.[17] Lastly there was an item whose significance escaped everyone's attention: U-boats in the Atlantic were ordered to make weather reports. These were said to be 'of great importance for the war on land and in the air' – by December twenty reports a day were being made.[18]

Sifted in this way, the evidence looks overwhelming. The very obscurity of all this activity should have suggested that strict security was being maintained by the Germans for some purpose. Rundstedt was maintaining it to deceive his own forces, just as on several occasions our own troops were led to believe they were destined for some theatre only to find themselves detailed for somewhere different. No one, not even at Bletchley, asked themselves why U-boats were asked to report on the weather: the reason was that bad weather was essential for a German offensive, to prevent it from being blunted at the outset by the Allied air forces. No one asked why the fighter aircraft were retained on the western front while the Allied bomber offensive against German cities and industry continued. No one remarked that one division was rapped over the knuckles for being twelve hours behind schedule. No one remembered how in 1943 the Germans improvised a front in Italy.

How, then, was the evidence interpreted? In mid-October Strong received a visit from two officers from Bletchley. One was a former member of his staff at MI14, Captain Alan Pryce-Jones, the other the RAF Liaison Officer Wing-Commander Jim Rose. Debonair as ever, Pryce-Jones sat on the corner of Strong's desk and asked him why he was so confident Germany would collapse. Strong told him that the Germans were losing the equivalent of a division a month in countering Eisenhower's war of attrition. Pryce-Jones said that if Strong believed that, he could believe anything: all the signs were that the Germans were replacing their losses and gathering reserves. It was a measure of Strong's sympathetic treatment of the civilians in uniform who worked for him – and of Pryce-Jones's considerable charm – that he did not turn rough. He accordingly warned Bedell-Smith that what Pryce-Jones had told him might be so. Perhaps this was why on 15 October Strong wrote a report saying that Rundstedt was gathering crack troops to act as a 'fire brigade', and referred on 19 October to Hitler's wish to launch a

November offensive and put in a 'spoiling attack' in the north.[19] In London the DMI, General Sinclair, had a hunch that the Germans would attack the flank of the Allied salient at Aachen. The Air Ministry liked the phrase 'spoiling attack' but when MI14 dissented, changed it to a 'defensive spoiling attack'. My old colleagues in the JIS were unconvinced. They said that a spoiling attack was unlikely: the OKW would use 6 Panzer Army to blunt the forthcoming Allied offensive. Millis and my RAF opposite number Francis Ogilvy, however, insisted on adding a paragraph saying: 'The enemy are planning to spring a surprise which would almost certainly include attacks on Allied airfields.' But when the Chiefs of Staff received the JIC paper they struck the paragraph out.[20]

Then the pendulum swung the other way. Strong's October forebodings evaporated in November. On a visit to London he told Peter Earle that the war would be over within a month or two. On 6 December Air Intelligence backtracked: 'Whatever intentions the German air force may have for further reinforcement of western front, the original plan for "lightning blow" and sudden attack may with some certainty be said to have lapsed . . . The German air force is also already thrown back on the defensive.'[21] SHAEF thought that none of the OKW reserve divisions was near the front: 'The outward surface remains unchanged but there have been considerable stirrings within the sepulchre.'[22] The metaphor is revealing.

Yet at SHAEF there was some mild dissent. According to Strong, John Austin, John Petito, Alan Crick (who had served in North Africa) and I put another argument to him.[23] If all the formations we knew were opposite the Ardennes continued to stay there, and more particularly if yet another division, reported to be on its way, arrived, 'some relieving attack' must be considered likely. Unfortunately the division on its way was mistakenly reported still to be in the Saar. Strong temporised. He circulated at SHAEF and to other headquarters a series of three options open to the German High Command. The last of these was 'some relieving attack' in the Ardennes.[24] Eisenhower told him to warn General Omar Bradley, who commanded the US 12th Army Group, of the last possibility. Strong said he saw Bradley, and on the 14th he sent a signal to the three army groups outlining the three options open to the OKW reserves: they could be sent to Russia; counterattack an Allied penetration of their front; or 'stage a relieving attack through the Ardennes'.

The reaction to this muffled warning was interesting. Montgomery's staff were the most dismissive: 'the enemy is at present fighting a defensive campaign on all fronts: his situation is that he cannot stage major offensive operations'.[25] Bradley was also unimpressed. He told Strong that he had earmarked certain divisions to move to the Ardennes if the enemy attacked there. He never did so, and no record of such a plan exists. His intelligence chief General Sibert was sceptical. Plans were drawn up instead for a new attack on the Roer dams. Bradley was visiting Eisenhower when the first reports of a German attack came through on the night of 16 December, but Sibert told him he saw no reason for him to return from SHAEF.

Yet in fact Sibert had been alerted to the danger. Five days earlier Colonel Dickson, the senior G2 (Intelligence) officer of the First US Army, which was in Bradley's Army Group, had become convinced by prisoner of war interrogations and by information from patrols that what he sometimes called an 'all-out counter-offensive' and at other times an 'all-out counterattack' – two very different things – was imminent. In late November a German order in his sector had fallen into his hands calling for men who spoke English and could simulate an American accent. Meanwhile he had tabulated German concentrations of armour as well as dumps of bridging equipment and ammunition: but when General Hodges, commanding First Army, and his tactical air commander General Quesada asked for them to be bombed, Spaatz replied, 'Target unremunerative.' Then German prisoners of war began blabbing about the recapture of Aachen as a Christmas present for the Führer. So Dickson took the line that the Aachen sector, north of the Ardennes, would be the focal point for the German attack. Yet on the night of 14 December, when a staff conference was held at the headquarters of First Army, Dickson suddenly slapped the map and said, 'It's the Ardennes.'

Nobody paid much attention. Dickson was regarded as an oddball, given to impetuous judgements. In September he had woken General Hodges saying that he had heard on the radio that Rundstedt had ordered the German army to disarm the SS and would now obtain an honourable peace. The report turned out to be American black propaganda. Dickson's own G3 (Operations) at First Army and Sibert at 12th Army Group did not have much faith in him. The day after he slapped the map he left for a leave in Paris. His leave had been long delayed. Still, that was hardly the action of an officer expecting instant action throughout First Army as the result of his warning.[26]

The Germans launched their Ardennes offensive on 16 December; it petered out in mid-January. Since then, many autopsies have been carried out on the corpse. Bedell-Smith at once had to meet criticism from the American press: his investigation cleared everyone personally of blame. The Chiefs of Staff set up an inquiry under the Vice-CIGS, General Nye, who commissioned Peter Calvocoressi and F.L. Lucas at Bletchley to comb Ultra's contribution to the jigsaw puzzle. There was no lack of Ultra: some 11,000 decrypts were sent to intelligence staffs between 1 October and the end of January, of which over half were about the western front. Staffs were more in danger of being swamped than starved. Calvocoressi and Lucas pointed out that intelligence staffs had been too apt to assume that Ultra would tell them everything. We could not always expect, as at Alam Halfa, to learn in full the enemy's plan of attack. They said that Ultra 'gave clear warning that a counter-offensive was coming, and some warning, though at short notice, of when it was coming'. Intelligence had become too wedded to one view of enemy intentions. Calvocoressi and Lucas added that it would be 'interesting to know how much reconnaissance was flown over the Eiffel sector on the US First Army front'. The DMI added that there seemed to have been no vigorous patrolling or determination to capture prisoners. (That was not so.) Nye concluded that too great a reliance had been placed on Ultra, and insufficient use had been made of other ways of obtaining information; but, he added, 'while it was possible from this evidence to draw the correct deduction from it, the odds were very much against our doing so . . .'[27] As everyone from the Chiefs of Staff downwards had discounted a German offensive, it was hardly surprising that Bedell-Smith and Nye granted absolution.

The autopsies by historians have been more damning. Hinsley granted that until 6 December much of the evidence could have been interpreted either way. Acute shortage of petrol and need for economy did not necessarily indicate stockpiling for an offensive. But after that date the 'stirrings in the sepulchre' – the troop movements and the train traffic Crick and I had noted – reported by Ultra were so loud that SHAEF should have recognised that they were listening to an imminent resurrection. Hinsley's colleague at Bletchley, Ralph Bennett, considered that the Ultra evidence was more than enough to prevent the complete surprise the Germans achieved. The overconfidence of August might serve as an excuse for the failure to open the port of Antwerp, but 'it wears thin for Arnhem and is threadbare by mid-December'.[28] Reconsidering the matter fifteen years later, Bennett was even more severe. Strong's account, he judged, was evasive and equivocal. Eisenhower, distracted by the continued British attempts to persuade him to appoint a land forces commander and abandon his strategy of attacking all along the line, was ill-served by his intelligence staff.*

The verdict is just: SHAEF hedged their bets. To give options including the 'worst case' is bad intelligence. Intelligence officers must give their commander a clear lead, right or wrong, about what they think the enemy is likely to do: it is up to him to accept or reject that advice. If one genuinely believes that the commander must guard against an eventuality, then one must issue a clarion call, warning him to change his dispositions. Bradley did not receive such a call. Ultra provided such authentic information, thought Bill Williams, that the recipient could forget the value of other less reliable, but still important, sources. It not only devoured other bacilli, but overpowered the common sense on which all intelligence is based. Williams did not spare himself. The exuberance of that September when the German army was being scattered like chaff was permissible at an Army headquarters. But intelligence

---

* Bennett concluded that JIC was most to blame: 'If anyone was equipped to undertake lengthy research and to see nothing was overlooked' it was surely them. But that was never JIC's job: they attempted only to reconcile and make sense of what their respective ministries produced. The blame in Whitehall must rest with MI14 and Air Intelligence, and in the field with SHAEF and 12th Army Group. Bennett, however, stops short of Solly Zuckerman, who thought that those who neglected Dickson's warning should be 'put up against a wall and shot'.[29] But then, Zuckerman was a man of great self-assurance.

officers at Army Groups should have been passion-free, Aristotelian analysts.[30]

Yet even if the headquarters in the field and intelligence in Whitehall all misread Ultra, there was other evidence which could have alerted us at SHAEF: the evidence Dickson at First Army accumulated from prisoners of war and other sources, which was stifled in Bradley's headquarters. SHAEF did not see it. And on one matter SHAEF and the Army Groups were right. We said that the Germans had not the strength or resources to reach the Meuse, still less to take Antwerp. The American divisions they overwhelmed were either under strength or had hardly seen battle (the American system of replacing casualties was not working well[31]), but the Germans were surprised by the toughness of the American troops who held Bastogne. The Ardennes was an absurd gamble, and at the end of it the Germans had suffered 80,000 casualties. But 8000 Americans were taken prisoner, and 70,000 killed, wounded or missing. Those dead and wounded are the measure of our failure.

In my view Strong was more to blame for an episode that turned the drama into farce. Spearheading the German advance was a unit under Major Skorzeny, who had rescued Mussolini when the deposed dictator was imprisoned in the mountainous Gran Sasso in central Italy. The unit wore American uniforms and rode on captured American vehicles and tanks. It had orders to cause maximum confusion behind the Allied lines and if possible to seize bridgeheads over the Meuse. One report – more likely than not it was part of the unit's propaganda – said that Skorzeny had orders to assassinate Eisenhower. Colonel Gordon Sheen, the officer under Strong responsible for security, burst into a room at SHAEF headquarters in the Hôtel Trianon crying 'Skorzeny is driving on Paris!' On the strength of what was no more than rumour, Strong persuaded Eisenhower to incarcerate himself near his headquarters in Versailles, surrounded by a bodyguard of armoured vehicles. Yet that was the moment when Eisenhower should have been on the move to see Montgomery and Bradley and their army commanders.

One day in March 1945 Strong asked me to accompany him to see the battlefield in the Ardennes. We drove until the roads were so churned up by tanks that his staff car could go no further. I had lost my old admiration for him by then. He was too keen to keep in with everyone, and too apt to flinch if he stuck his neck out. I got a mild rebuke from his brigadier afterwards for upsetting him by saying that we were all being criticised for our failure over the Ardennes. Listening to Strong, one picked up the gossip of the SHAEF generals. I was alarmed to hear him say: 'When the Germans are finished, we shall just push the Russians back to their pre-war frontiers – just push them back.' The notion that the American and British armies, despite their firepower, could take on the enormous weight of the Red Army, an army indifferent to casualties, that had outfought the German forces, seemed to me so absurd that I fell silent. As Goethe said, *'Man merkt die Absicht und man ist verstimmt'* ('One spots the intention, and it turns one off').

Nevertheless, I enjoyed Strong's company. He talked of his days in Berlin as assistant military attaché and of the German officers he had known then, nearly all now generals. One of them, Generaloberst Gerd von Schwerin, had been taken prisoner in Italy in April, and Strong had him brought to Reims, where SHAEF was now established. In January 1939, when Schwerin had been head of the intelligence section in charge of Britain, he had called on Strong in Berlin and told him that Hitler respected nothing but strength. Chamberlain was a symbol of weakness. 'What are Germany's aims?' asked Strong. 'World domination,' Schwerin replied. In June 1939 Schwerin had arrived in London with the same message. Convince Hitler you mean business over Danzig; when Germany sent a cruiser to Danzig, Britain should have sent a battleship; take Churchill into the Cabinet; Hitler despises Chamberlain and Halifax; Send your air squadrons to France and station them there. His opposite number, Colonel Hotblack, the head of the German intelligence section, dismissed him: his visit was 'bloody cheek'. It took the Navy, in the person of Admiral Godfrey, to invite Gladwyn Jebb of the Foreign Office and later the DMI to meet Schwerin. The Foreign Office flannelled: 'It would be difficult to draw the line between a firm attitude and a provocative threat.' Schwerin reported to the German General Staff Godfrey's blunt statement that Britain would fight. The Wilhelmstrasse was no different from the Foreign Office: 'Enemy propaganda', someone wrote in the margin of his report. Schwerin was reprimanded, dismissed from the General Staff, and joined an armoured unit.[32]

Strong asked George Bailey, a young American intelligence officer and brilliant linguist, and myself to accompany Schwerin to the headquarters of the OSS to meet its chief, Bill Donovan, in the hope that he would consent to broadcast to the German forces telling them to surrender as the war was over. At one point he asked where we were going. '*Ach, Paris. Ich habe gute Freunde in Paris – sind aber keine Collaborateure*' ('I have good friends in Paris, but they're not collaborators'). Other German generals when captured would lecture their interrogators: how mistaken the Allies were not to realise that Germany was saving Europe from communism – but soon all would be well, and we would be fighting on the same side against the Russians. Schwerin did not lecture us; but he told us that fighting on the Russian front was of a brutality unimaginable in Italy or France. He refused to broadcast, asking us to imagine what would happen to his wife and children in Germany if he did so.[33]

In the final month of the war in Europe intelligence at SHAEF seemed to me to become more and more fantastical. As a last desperate throw the Nazis were said to be building a National Redoubt in the Alpine depths of Bavaria. Desperadoes in disguise, called werewolves, were said to be planning sabotage and assassinations; a werewolf headquarters was said to have been captured. Strong excused himself for taking these phantoms seriously by saying that after the Ardennes he would not risk another miscalculation of German resistance; and the werewolves were not all wraiths – the mayor of Aachen appointed by the Americans had been assassinated.

The JIC in London were dismissive; much of this rubbish reflected further policy rifts between the British and Americans. On a visit to London Strong told Cavendish-Bentinck that Eisenhower off his own bat had agreed with Stalin that the Allies would not attempt to take Berlin. Churchill and Brooke were furious. Ninth US Army and their divisional commanders begged to advance – nothing, they said, stood in their way. This was puzzling, because in the Harz mountains there was fanatical German resistance, and one of the American bridgeheads over the Elbe estab-lished by the First US Army was driven in.[34] As usual the Russians refused to provide any information about their own forces, and Eisenhower was determined to avoid a clash with this touchy ally. So he ordered Patton to drive towards Prague and Hodges to halt on the border of the future Soviet zone.

Was it a mistake? By this time the Germans were so anxious to fall into the hands of the West rather than the Russians that Brad-ley's forces would not have suffered the casualties in taking Berlin that Eisenhower feared. Still, the Russians suffered over 200,000 killed or wounded in their assault on Berlin, and British troops were meeting resistance in the last week of April as they fought to the Elbe. Was the propaganda victory of being the first to enter Berlin worth the life of a single soldier, especially when the occupa-tion zones had been fixed at Yalta and our forces would have had to abandon whatever land they had seized in the Soviet zone?

Some months before, Peter Earle had begged Brooke to release him: as a regular officer he must see action before the war ended. 'They expect one to have been shot at. Silly fellows,' said his master, and commended him to Montgomery, who made him one of his liaison officers. These officers were Montgomery's only com-panions in his tactical headquarters and were sent out to the front line in Jeeps each day to bring back accurate information about the state of the battle and the immediate plans of divisional com-manders. On 21 April Earle and John Poston, who had joined Monty as his ADC in Cairo, set out to obtain General Barker's plan for crossing the Elbe with 53 Division. On the way back over Luneburg heath they ran into a German roadblock. Earle rammed the machine-gunner and killed him, but the Jeep overturned. In revenge the Germans bayoneted Poston and looted his body. But they spared Earle and left him, wounded in the head, leg and back, with a farmer.

So the end came, and I watched the German plenipotentiaries, General Jodl and Admiral Friedeburg, sign the document of uncon-ditional surrender in the school room at Reims. At last I saw in the flesh one of those German generals whose name I had learnt within a week or so of joining MI14. Jodl was Chief of Staff of the German High Command, the OKW. He turned out to be a small man, expressionless but not without dignity. By prevarication he had gained a respite of forty-eight hours to allow as many German troops as possible to become prisoners of the Allies rather than the Russians. But at 2 a.m. on 7 May 1945 he and Friedeburg signed. He made a little speech: the Germans had suffered much. He hoped the victors would treat his people with generosity. He was met with silence.

CHAPTER SEVEN

❦

Fathoming Hitler

'In intelligence the opportunities for mistakes are almost unlimited,' wrote Walter Laqueur, one of the best analysts of the business.[1] Our knowledge is always insufficient: we are deceived by the enemy's clever ruses, we are biased or surprised by some clever stroke we had not foreseen, or so over-confident that we fail to read the enemy's intentions. Suspicion can be as misleading as complacency: Stalin suspected everyone, and was unable to decide which suspect was most dangerous. The assumptions we make about foreign governments are often misleading. The Establishment in Britain before and during the war never understood that the fascist regimes were mass movements, with genuine widespread support, and not just reactionary dictatorships.

There are more technical reasons for the failure of intelligence. Intelligence officers can be confused by what they call 'noise', a mass of irrelevant signals: the amount of evidence is so great and so contradictory that none of it makes sense. They can fall into the error of mirror-imaging: of thinking that what we know, the enemy knows, and that therefore he is certain to do such and such because that is what we would do, were we him. Or our team makes a penetrating analysis, so convincing to us and to our superiors that, even when new and contradictory evidence emerges, we cannot endure the pain of breaking up the theory and starting afresh. Indeed, when one thinks of how unsuccessful forecasters of the future of the world are, with few restrictions on the use of the information on which they base their predictions, it is hardly odd that intelligence officers in wartime are not more successful.

The most successful were those scientists who were set to crack technological problems; and perhaps if more scientists had been available to interpret the evidence from Ultra and other sources, our predictions would have improved. Scientists can ask for an item of information that is crucial if an answer is to be truthful: if it is not forthcoming, they will point out that the answer must be speculative. Most jobs in intelligence, however, do not demand exceptional talent: diligence or commonsense are more important. It is only the top men and women who need a quality always in rare supply and unpredictable: flair – *Fingerspitzengefühl* – the instinct to spot that something is wrong, or something is suspicious, or something is likely to happen despite the odds.

No single interpretation of a strategic situation is ever likely to be accepted by all the different staffs who ponder over it. There are too many variables. Ralph Bennett questions how successful the JIC and JIS were in reconciling the conflicting views of the service ministries.[2] He points out that the War Office and Air Ministry never settled their differences over bombing policy, nor the Admiralty and Air Ministry over aircraft for Coastal Command. In those days there was no Defence Ministry, but even so, major strategic differences between the three services are not all that rare today. It is a mistake to regard the JIC and JIS as composed of dispassionate scientific experts wafted from outer space to resolve all disputes. Each of us, in true Whitehall style, represented the views of his ministry. I was there to put forward the War Office interpretation of the evidence: if I could not prevail, I had to try to insert as many points as I could from my brief and modify if possible the majority view so that the DMI could sign the final version of the paper without feeling that he was putting his name to a document for which he could be sacked. So there were sometimes weasel-words inserted to satisfy the apprehensions of our bosses in the JIC. Of course at times you were convinced that your colleagues' interpretation of the evidence was right and your own ministry was wrong: then you had to defend the majority view to your chief and persuade him to change his mind. Nevertheless, we did not commit all the sins that intelligence officers are tempted to commit. We did not refuse to give a lead and make predictions. We did not hedge against all possibilities, leaving the Chiefs of Staff uncertain what line the enemy might take. We did not suck up to our chiefs and tell them what they wanted to hear. We stuck our neck out. We were wrong more times than I like to remember, but we gave a verdict.

We were, however, at the mercy of our organisation. Each of us brought to the table what his own ministry deemed relevant, and it was up to us to rummage within the MI departments and the sections of the German branch to unearth material. We had to read and reflect on Ultra. But the assessment of evidence, the piecing together of items, had to be done within the ministries. The JIS was not a research organisation: it was too busy drafting papers. I cannot recall any information that the War Office suppressed; but why did the Air Ministry never reveal the Zuckerman–Bernal research in 1941 on the bombing of Hull and Birmingham? Or did their report lie buried in the files of the Home Office, invisible to Air Intelligence? The JIS can boast that it never endorsed the view that Germany could be bombed into submission, nor that Hitler had a strategic reserve that could be shunted from the Russian front to crush Overlord – one view dear to Portal, the other to Brooke.

Our failings were manifold. We did not spend enough time considering how the enemy might react when things were going badly. All five ministries got caught out at times. For the Admiralty the battle of the Atlantic was a ding-dong affair; first one side gained the technological advantage and then the other; if the war had not ended before the Schnorkel U-boats were built in number, the battle of the Atlantic might have taken a turn for the worse. Air Intelligence would not accept that the new tactics and dispositions put into effect by the Luftwaffe, which had caused Bomber Command and the US Eighth Air Force to recoil as the toll of casualties became prohibitive, had given German industry time to recover. They did not recognise that Speer was being successful in moving industry from the Ruhr to south and central Germany, and was countering the Allied bombing offensive by dispersing production, dismantling factories and putting them underground. At the War Office MI14, and we on the JIS, underestimated the genius for improvisation of the German General Staff. When the game was up in Sicily, they did what the British had done at Dunkirk, commandeering little ships to get their troops across the Straits of Messina. When the Allies landed at Anzio, the Germans formed battalions at the railway station in Rome from troops returning from leave, and flung them into battle. In the Dodecanese they diverted aircraft from all over the Balkans. With inexorable logic my colleagues would prove that every German division was committed in Russia, in the Mediterranean or in defence of the west: yet always some unsuspected reserve emerged to plug a breach in their defences or quell the partisans. The Ministry of Economic Warfare misread Germany's resources, and had to admit that production was higher in 1945 than it had been in 1939. It made an astonishing leap in 1944 because Speer rationalised resources and made industrial organisation more efficient.[3] The very fact that the British were more efficient than the Nazis in organising their manpower meant that Hitler in the last few months of the war was still able to comb out men from business and the armed forces' administration to form new cadres and reinforce his armies. The Foreign Office was right in predicting that Franco would remain neutral, and that the French in Algeria would not long resist. But in 1944 they misread the political situation in Greece and the unpopularity of the King for having backed the Metaxas dictatorship. The warnings of our liaison officers were suppressed or ignored by Middle East Command, with the result that we underestimated the number of British troops needed to stop the communist-led guerrillas ELAS from seizing power.* Some of the errors were due to commanders rather than to Intelligence. The record of operational intelligence between El Alamein and Overlord is not a triumphant story.

Perhaps our greatest, and yet most comprehensible, failure was to get inside Hitler's mind and think like him. The problem was insoluble: how could one persuade the Chiefs of Staff that Hitler would take decisions that were the despair of his finest strategists, like Manstein? Here was a man who seemingly understood the new tactics of armoured warfare, the *Schwerpunkt* and the Blitzkrieg: yet in reality he was enslaved by his memories as a front-line soldier in the First World War, refusing to fight a battle of manoeuvre and insisting that every inch of territory conquered must be held. In the Ardennes we made the mistake of asking ourselves: 'What

---

* So unpopular in America was the British intervention against ELAS that Admiral King ordered American landing craft to be withdrawn and ships bringing supplies to the Piraeus to fly the red ensign rather than appear to be supporting British imperialist war aims. Roosevelt's troubleshooter Harry Hopkins got the order countermanded.[4]

would an experienced commander like Rundstedt do?' It was not Rundstedt we should have thought of, but Hitler. Hitler did what no one expected him to do. And yet, was it not in Hitler's character to recall that it was he who had backed Manstein's plan to break through the Ardennes in 1940? Should we not have guessed that he could hear destiny calling him once again to choose the Ardennes, seize Antwerp and encircle with his three Panzer armies the British as he had done in 1940? None of us could rise to such a flight of imagination.

Or of fantasy. When Schwerin told Strong in 1939 that Hitler's aim was world domination, he was not exaggerating. Hitler wanted *Lebensraum* in Eastern Europe. First Poland, then the Ukraine. When Britain and France tried to stop him, he turned on them first, defeated France, and returned to his original purpose. A Blitzkrieg, he believed, would finish Soviet Russia, and he would make peace with Stalin after he had obtained the Ukraine. Then Britain would be eliminated. After that he would build his navy, perfect the new weapon of rocketry and develop the atom bomb preparatory to the final attack on the United States. That was why he postponed the invasion of Britain in 1941 and why he declared war on America. That was why he would not abandon conquered territory in Russia. That was why he still believed in 1944 that he could defeat Overlord, split the Anglo-American alliance and once more turn his full might against Russia. This time he would force Stalin to agree to an armistice. That was why he rejected all approaches by Mussolini and the Japanese to make his peace with Stalin in 1943.

To fathom the workings of Hitler's mind required intelligence of a very high order. The most distinguished British Germanist of my generation was Peter Stern, whose study of Hitler[5] is rewarding and disturbing. Stern argued that German literature at the turn of the century, and indeed before then, was inspired by an ideology which writers, however apparently opposed, accepted: that man can be redeemed only by the most heroic sacrifice – a sacrifice that he must himself will – and the more costly the sacrifice, the more noble the redemption. The hero must be prepared to forfeit all in order to achieve his goal. He must be ready to lose his life, his sanity, love and salvation, even to be damned in order to achieve his supreme aim in this world. Stern called this belief 'the dear purchase'. One can purchase fame only if one is willing to pay the highest price. It was this idea that inspired Nietzsche, Mann and Jünger.

It also inspired Hitler. He declared that he knew by his own experiences in the front line, by his insight into Jewry, what had to be done. To achieve it, he would exert his Will. He believed that only his Will, his strenuous determination to overcome all obstacles, enabled the German army to survive the Russian winter of 1941–42 with no winter equipment. He believed his Will could prevail at Stalingrad. He demanded that Germans should give everything in the struggle: if Germany perished, then the great tragedy of defeat had been dearly purchased.

Whatever difficulties intelligence staffs had in getting inside the mind of this evil fanatic, there is less excuse for the revisionist historians who like to portray Churchill's decision to resist in 1940 as absurd: absurd in that the decision to fight on was beyond Britain's capabilities and led to the break-up of the British Empire and our inevitable decline in the second half of this century. The Empire was dissolving into self-governing status before 1939. As for decline, what is the present state of Britain today compared with what it would have been had Hitler broken his word and occupied Britain? To the revisionist historians the fate of the Jews – or the gypsies, or the prisoners in the east who were slaughtered – is irrelevant. And what of Hitler's intention when Britain was defeated to deport all males between the ages of seventeen and forty-five to the Continent? Grotesque? But so was the unimaginable evil of the Holocaust.

Plutarch in his *Lives of the Noble Grecians and Romans* used to compare his heroes – 'The Comparison of Fabius with Pericles' or 'The Comparison of Aristides with Marcus Cato' – and shortly after the war Isaiah Berlin made a memorable comparison between Churchill and Roosevelt.[6] Those who were young then are right to see them as heroes. For us, who learnt Macaulay's *Lays of Ancient Rome* as children, it is not fanciful to see Churchill as our Horatius, who 'kept the bridge' in the brave days of old against Lars Porsena and his Tuscan hordes, Churchill, who defied the Nazis in 1940 when they threatened to cross the bridge and who echoed Horatius in thinking:

And how can man die better,
Than facing fearful odds,
For the ashes of his fathers,
And the temples of his Gods?

Nor is it wrong to see Roosevelt, the American Scipio, as the man who gave hope to his countrymen during the Depression and, not only to Americans, but to those in other nations who were not prepared to believe that the only alternative to fascism was communism. Did he not leave his country after his death the most powerful state in the world, and the arbiter of the West?

Historians in the twenty-first century are, however, certain to see these two men in another guise. They may dwell on Roosevelt's failure to revive America's economy in the thirties. All his schemes and gimmicks failed, and they will confirm that it was not until war in Europe began that in America the Depression and mass unemployment became a mist in the past. They may declare that Roosevelt never intended to enter the war, preferring to let America profit by draining Britain's resources. They may say that he went to war only when Japan kicked him into it, and that at its end he was gulled into believing that he and Stalin should dissolve the colonial empires of Britain, France, Portugal and the Netherlands and rule the world as a dyarchy. And will not Churchill's record look even more equivocal? What was his life but a repetition of failure: Gallipoli, Chanak, the reimposition of the Gold Standard, the intransigence over India and the belligerence that made him the *bête noire* of organised labour, a man so mistrusted that he could not awaken his party to the menace of Hitler?

These historians may well latch on to the less attractive side of the personalities of these two leaders. Both relished the delectable comforts that power brings: the life where everything is smoothed and ordered by secretaries, aides, servants; where one steps from an aircraft into a limousine and is cosseted in a mansion that the state or hosts have provided, where dishes are cooked for their special pleasure and whatever drink they demand is instantly to hand; where the diary that rules the waking hours of great executives can be changed to suit a whim. Everyone and everything is at their call.

So much did they relish power that neither gave a thought to the duty they owed to the state when they fell ill. From the early days of 1944 Roosevelt knew he might drop dead any day, yet it did not cross his mind to bow out after his third term as President. During that year he spent perhaps only half a day on the fortunes of the United States. No one will blame Churchill for his resolution in defeating the pneumonia that laid him low in North Africa in 1943. But what is one to say to his obstinate determination, aided by family and civil servants, to conceal the effects of the stroke that brought him down in 1953 and left him a shadow – a mighty shadow, but still a shadow – of his former self? Roosevelt was a great seducer: he charmed practically everyone, and those who moved into the orbit of his giant planet became satellites. There they revolved, but many were burnt out or collided with each other because his administration was haphazard, agencies being set against each other and none knowing where his sphere in orbit precisely was. Churchill was a fascinator: but few have been more inconsiderate to those who served him or more ungrateful to friends who stood by him when he was in exile.

Try as they will to disguise it, a moralist lurks in the soul of every historian of international affairs, and as the years pass and historical perspective lengthens, the fortunes of nations cast shadows or sunlight upon their protagonists. Statesmen are but men; and more than in any other calling, they embody the defects of their merits. The imperious leader who appears to dictate the future is at the mercy of unpredictable events and the impersonal forces of history; at the mercy too of the hesitations and doubts of those he has to trust to carry out his commands. On the other hand, the sagacious, rational conciliators see their humane plans swept aside by crude demagogues, and are unable, precisely because they appeal to reason, to defeat the emotional slogans of opponents who know how to play on the prejudice of their compatriots.

Yet for those who were young when Roosevelt and Churchill ruled, they remain heroic figures, and their defects pale because they were then, and still appear, larger than life, men who enjoyed, as well as responded to, their call to destiny. Those who were alive when Lincoln was President or Palmerston and Gladstone were Prime Minister no doubt felt that lesser men stepped into their shoes. This is exaggerated: there were some formidable politicians at the turn of that century. So there were in the 1980s. But that peculiar blend of gaiety, enjoyment of life, contempt for dull, grey, prudent policy, that spontaneity and imaginative belief in a better or a more glorious world, is something that has disappeared from public life at the end of this century.

CHAPTER EIGHT

❧

Britain's New Colony

One day in the autumn of 1944 when I was visiting some French friends of my parents in Paris, Antoinette de Grandmaison said to me, 'Everyone knows' (it was supposed to be secret) 'that le grand Etat-Major is moving from Versailles to Reims. You must call when you are there on a friend of Saint Exupéry. She's called Simone de Vogüé – I'll write a letter of introduction.' The meeting was a success. Madame de Vogüé lived with her two sons aged twelve and eleven, a daughter aged three, and her handsome elderly father, who had the air of one who still appreciated pretty, smart women. Immediately the Allies landed in Normandy the Germans had taken her husband hostage and imprisoned him in Neuengamme concentration camp.

This was hardly surprising. Her brother-in-law had been sentenced to death, she told me, for his part in the Resistance. My face assumed a melancholy expression. But no; he had been reprieved. 'Naturally,' she explained, 'we appealed to le Maréchal.' Pétain had exercised his right to demand, once a month, clemency for one of the condemned.

My political education improved. I began to tear up the monochrome daguerreotype that the war and isolation in England had printed on my mind, in which all Germans were wicked or deluded and weak, and all Frenchmen heroic, supine or, worse still, collaborators. The politics of an occupied country, I learnt, were more complicated and agonised than the British imagined. My moral, as well as my political, education also advanced. My conception of a Catholic French family had been formed by Mauriac's novels and other severe critics of the *gratin*. Yet here was a woman as witty as she was sensible, never giving way to her anxiety about her husband, agog for gossip, watchful of the *formation morale* of her children yet at the same time relishing the ridiculous in her efforts to bring them up. After she had explained to her boys the mysteries of reproduction one of them asked, '*Mais, Maman, est-ce que c'est liquide ou solide?*' Her voice rose in a shriek of laughter: '*Mais, liquide!*'

Soon after we met Simone de Vogüé asked me whether I was wedded to the life of my mess. If not, would I like to lodge in her house? She would have the benefit of my rations and I would have the benefit of her wine – her father and she were part-owners of Veuve Clicquot. Generous as American rations were, they did not go far in the family, and dinner was sometimes a meal of contrasts. The main course would be a dish of mangel-wurzels while at my elbow Maurice the butler would murmur '*La maison, vingt-et-un.*' As the end of the war approached the boys would mark up the map with pins showing the line which the exuberant French radio had announced Allied troops had reached, and every evening, to maintain a faint connection with reality, I would move the pins back some 50 kilometres to cries of shame.

On 8 May, the day after the unconditional surrender had been signed at Reims, I had a travel order made out and, as one could do in those days of elated chaos, hitched an aircraft to Hamburg and went to Neuengamme to find Bertrand de Vogüé. Alas, when I got there it was swarming with Poles and thousands of other 'displaced persons'. I hitched a plane back to Brussels and sat in the cockpit on a sunny, cloudless evening wondering how I could break the news to Simone that I had failed to find her husband and had only the vaguest news about where he and his fellow prisoners might have been marched. A month later he appeared, emaciated, from somewhere near the Czechoslovak border.

Shortly afterwards Supreme Headquarters moved to Frankfurt. Our offices were in the head office of the great German chemical complex I.G. Farben. Flats had been built for the employees, and Arthur Marshall and I shared one in which we lolled at ease. There was no work whatsoever to do except to write the odd paper summarising the state of German resistance to the occupation, which as there was none was not time-consuming. Many of my colleagues, Arthur included, expected to be demobilised in July, or August at the latest. But I was twenty-nine and older officers had priority, so it would be a year or longer before I could hope to return to

England. One day to my surprise I saw Bill Cavendish-Bentinck, who asked me what I was going to do. 'The Foreign Office needs some satraps in Germany,' he said, 'and you should be one of them.' So even before SHAEF broke up, I moved north to the little Westphalian town of Lübbecke to join the political division of the British Control Commission*; when accommodation had been found in Berlin, part of the division moved there. I was at last in the capital of the Third Reich.

What should be done with Germany? At first there had been much talk of dismemberment and returning to the days before the *Zoll-verein*, or customs union, was formed, the first stage in the unification of Germany in the nineteenth century. Roosevelt and Stalin were still talking dismemberment at Yalta, and Churchill and Eden went along with them, but both knew that Whitehall was sceptical.[1] How was a Germany of little states to be kept from reuniting? The British wanted to abolish or detach Prussia, but as in 1943 they had feared that the Soviet Union might be tempted to make peace unilaterally, they took the view that Germany should be divided into zones but treated as a unity. They also proposed that Berlin should be put deep into the Soviet zone: that would give the USSR a prize to keep in their sights. For many months Roosevelt fought for the Americans to occupy the north-western zone. He too had his fears. Might not political chaos in France cut communications with the American armies? But the British pointed out that their armies would be on the north-west flank when they advanced into Germany, and as a maritime nation their interests lay there. The impasse was solved by giving the Americans Bremen, as a port through which their forces would be supplied.

Meanwhile Roosevelt had become enchanted by his old friend and Secretary of the Treasury Henry Morgenthau's plan for the future of Germany. Morgenthau proposed that Germany should be deprived of its heavy industry in order to demilitarise the country

---

* The Control Commission was to take the place of a German government. It consisted of representatives of the four powers, and its headquarters were in Berlin.

once and for all. The mines should be closed, the steel industry dismantled; part of the heavy industry that remained should be internationalised and part given to the French. Four million Germans would be shifted from industry into agriculture and transported to farm lands east of Berlin. The Allied occupation was to last for twenty years, and no assistance should be given to the German economy. The plan was solemnly initialled by Roosevelt and Churchill at Quebec in September 1944.

At first there was much self-congratulation.[2] Roosevelt insisted that a 1944 SHAEF handbook for military government officers be withdrawn since it envisaged a German central government and the rehabilitation of essential services in Germany. Eventually it was agreed that Germany should not be totally stripped of industrial plant.[3] Then reality broke through. Cordell Hull and Henry Stimson, the Secretary of State and Secretary of War respectively, were appalled. In the winter of 1944–45 it became clear that Stalin was going to shift Poland's frontiers to the west, and the land Morgenthau had earmarked for the four million displaced Germans would be farmed by Poles, not Germans. Stalin also demanded reparations. That meant that British and American tax-payers would have to feed millions of German unemployed. Morgenthau's plan was a gift to Goebbels. If this was what unconditional surrender meant, then better die fighting than endure such a future. The Morgenthau plan died at the Potsdam conference of July–August 1945, but its ghost walked for many months and bedevilled occupation policy. Germany was to be treated as a conquered nation, said the new SHAEF directive, and no fraternisation with Germans was permitted. Military Government officers were told by 21 Army Group to give Germans orders, not requests.[4]

At Potsdam the differences between Britain, America and the Soviet Union were not resolved. In effect the Americans made a deal with the Soviet Union. Germany was to be treated as a unity and would be ruled by the four powers (the French, at British insistence, were to be given their own zone carved out of the British and American zones), and they would set up a body called the Kommendatura in Berlin. Each power would create in its own zone a series of divisions that corresponded to shadow central ministries in Berlin – Trade and Industries, Transport, Finance, Legal, Manpower, Political, Internal Affairs etc. The Kommendatura would hand down directives to these divisions. In the British zone these divisions, scattered among three small Westphalian towns, in turn passed instructions to five regional headquarters. Three of these – Hamburg, Schleswig-Holstein and our sector in Berlin – did not need to be subdivided; but the North Rhine, Westphalia and Hanover provinces each had half a dozen or more detachments corresponding to the cities within them; and beneath them were the urban and rural counties (*Kreise*), in each of which military government operated.

Each occupying power interpreted the Potsdam Agreements in its own way. At one end of the spectrum were the French. They did not consider they were bound by Potsdam. Why should they? They had been excluded from the conference, and they wanted Germany dismembered. For months they vetoed any proposals that would have created in the future a central German government in Berlin.

At the other end of the spectrum were the Russians. They insisted that the directives of the four powers must be implemented in the letter as well as the spirit. The Soviet Union had one advantage that the Western powers lacked. They had a coherent policy. They had suffered loss of territory at Brest-Litovsk in 1917. Very well, they would regain that territory, and more. The West had built a *cordon sanitaire* against communism in 1919. Very well, they would build a *cordon sanitaire* against capitalism in the countries whose territory their armies had occupied. Their industry west of the Don and Moscow had been destroyed and the country devastated. Very well, they would remove German factories and their technicians and rebuild those factories within the Soviet Union. They had suffered appalling losses of men. Very well, German prisoners of war would be held until they had helped to rebuild the Soviet infrastructure.

The Soviet Union intended to reform Germany by rebuilding its institutions from the top down. They brought back from Moscow leading German communists who had fled the country in the 1930s, including Wilhelm Pieck and Walther Ulbricht, to impose their policies. Although by the Potsdam Agreements no German was permitted to criticise Allied policy, the German Communist Party,

Germany after World War II

BERLIN

HQ
FRENCH
BRITISH RUSSIAN
HQ
HQ AMERICAN HQ
HQ HQ
Allied
Command
Spree

Lübbecke • • Mecklenburg

Hamburg

HOLLAND

Bremen
AMERICAN

R U S S I A N

Ems

POLAND

Oder

Elbe

BERLIN
Potsdam

Bielefeld

Hanover

Z O N E

Münster

Detmold

Weser

Brunswick

B R I T I S H   Z O N E

• Wuppertal
Düsseldorf
Cologne

Aachen
Bonn

Rhine

Leipzig •

Elbe

Dresden

BELGIUM

G E R M A N Y

F R E N C H

• Frankfurt

• Nuremberg

CZECHOSLOVAKIA

Z O N E

A M E R I C A N   Z O N E

FRANCE

Rhine

• Stuttgart

• Munich

AUSTRIA

SWITZERLAND

the KPD, devised a means whereby they could get round this. The Party line was simple. Life in the Russian zone alone was tolerable. There, the people had work and owned the means of production. There, reform had given the soil back to the people. They had food, whereas the British zone was threatened with starvation. That was the fault of the British: the shortages would disappear overnight if they removed Nazis from the administration. Industry too would flourish if the cartels were destroyed. The Soviets intended the four powers to set up a central German administration in Berlin, to which they would dictate. Therefore any form of federalism, decentralisation of power or of functions to the provinces (*Länder*) was an abomination and against the Potsdam Agreements. Marx taught that the cause of injustice was a capitalist economy. Change the economy, establish a dictatorship of the people, change the structures from the top down, and a peaceful Germany would be born. If, owing to their anachronistic ideology, the economy of the Western zones fell into disarray, the Germans, driven to revolution by starvation, would take their lead from the East and acquiesce in a regime established in Berlin that would bring communism to the Rhine.

The Russians' long-term plan, however, was frustrated by their own behaviour. Hitler had treated Slavs as *Untermenschen*, subhumans, to be treated as slaves, shot or starved when they were no longer of use. The Russian army took its revenge and sacked Berlin and other German cities with rape and pillage, as Tilly and Wallenstein had done in the seventeenth century. In the Western zone the tales of millions of refugees nullified communist propaganda.

The Soviets continued to treat their allies as they had during the war. They were suspicious, ungenerous, disagreeable, uncooperative and obstructive. The British urged the Americans not to withdraw from those parts of the Russian zone they had both occupied in the last days of the war, so the Allies could bargain over the status of Poland and her frontiers. The Russians countered by refusing to allow the Allies to occupy their sectors in Berlin.* They

---

* The Americans were all set to enter Berlin on Independence Day 1945, when the British were told that Marshal Zhukov considered a bridge on their route of entry was unsafe: they must therefore use the American road. As a SNAFU of major proportions would have resulted, General Lyne refused; and so, a day later, the British made their entry, the bridge having been miraculously strengthened overnight.[5]

had good reason for behaving as they did. This policy had worked to date beyond their expectations. It had succeeded because in their conferences at Tehran and Yalta they held the cards.

The Americans were no longer harnessed to the British. The wartime alliance between the two, which despite differences had been close, now began to dissolve. In the last months of his life Roosevelt was looking for a settlement of the world's problems. Europe took second place. That remarkable man, so generous and imaginative in peace, so naturally liberal and disposed to help the oppressed and the victims of the Depression, was not averse to seeing the eclipse of that imperial power his own countrymen had defeated at Saratoga in 1784. For Roosevelt the British empire was an anachronism. He saw the future of the world as being ruled in harmony by two great non-imperialist powers. In mid-century they would liberate subject peoples from the chains of the European colonial powers, just as the United States had liberated the Spanish colonies in America at the beginning of the century. Once the British empire and the other colonial domains were dissolved, the people would be free to choose their rulers.

Many of Roosevelt's entourage wanted to dissolve the Anglo-American alliance of the war for different reasons. Cordell Hull had a horror of 'spheres of influence' and 'balance of power' – relics of 'an unhappy past'.[6] He wanted Britain to accept free trade, free investment, free access to raw materials, and to abandon the Ottawa Agreements and protectionism. Britain, with its struggling post-war economy, found it hard to accept this. American foreign policy harked back to the peace they had lost – the peace of Versailles. This time they were determined to set up an international world order which would work – and it would work provided the four great powers (China being the fourth) acted in harmony. In effect this meant, for Roosevelt, a condominium of the USA and USSR. What did it matter if Poland's frontiers were rearranged; or if Eastern Europe was within the Russian sphere of influence?

The new American President Harry Truman, thrown into international politics by Roosevelt's death in April 1945, at first followed his predecessor's policies. He sent Harry Hopkins to Moscow to tell Stalin that America, unlike Britain, had no territorial ambitions anywhere (they certainly had in the Pacific). When Joseph Davies, the former US Ambassador in Moscow, turned up in London to admonish the British for following the foreign policy of Hitler and Goebbels towards the Soviet Union, Anthony Eden was astonished and outraged. He said Davies seemed to be as willing as Chamberlain had been to appease the new bully of Europe.

The Americans had three objectives in Germany: to de-Nazify government and business; to decentralise government; and to destroy the cartels in industry and set up a free competitive economy. They wanted to get the hell out of governing Germany as fast as possible. The British were rocked back on their heels when Roosevelt casually announced at Yalta that American troops would leave Germany two years after the end of the war. After only five months the Americans left the administration of the urban and rural districts to the Germans. They did not give a damn which Germans were elected to govern, so long as they were not notorious Nazis. From the start the Americans were the most humane of all the four powers towards Germans. They did not put their resources into programmes for re-educating them, but into agencies, often staffed by Americans of German origin, to bring Nazis and war criminals to trial. They ran their zone on the principles of common sense, and flew by the seat of their pants.

The British, therefore, found themselves isolated and even further out on a limb than they had been at Yalta. When the new Prime Minister Clement Attlee and his Foreign Minister Ernest Bevin came to the table after the triumph of the Labour Party in the General Election of July 1945, they found themselves in a dilemma. They wanted good relations with the Soviet Union, and had been shocked by a paper written by the Chiefs of Staff who argued that if Russia turned hostile Britain would have to incorporate as large a part of Germany as possible within the Western sphere. But they found that Stalin's demands conflicted with British interests. Keynes had written a celebrated polemic against the Treaty of Versailles after the First World War, exposing the folly of exacting vast sums in reparations. If the Ruhr was to be stripped of all its machinery and earning power to pay Russia in reparations, the British public would have to foot the bill. 'Paying reparations to Germany' the Chancellor of the Exchequer, Hugh Dalton, was later to call it.

All Attlee and Bevin could do at Potsdam was to try some horse-trading on the percentage of German industrial output that should go to Soviet Russia in reparations. Stalin had no worries. Of Attlee he said, 'He does not look a greedy man.'[7] He himself was. He was as determined as Clemenceau at Versailles to bleed Germany white and to make the prisoners of war repair the devastation in Russia. Stalin insisted on an astronomical sum in reparations and in forced labour. His demands were understandable enough, and Attlee and Bevin had no choice other than to protest at the scale of reparations. The decision about reparations, and the British expostulation that it would be the British as well as the Germans who would be paying the price, established the matrix for the future of Germany. All talk about a central government – reunification, de-Nazification, frontiers and the rest – was secondary to the decision about reparations. That decision determined that the Western powers would be responsible for the German economy in their zones. Subject to that decision the British aim was to revive democracy in Germany. But in their zone democracy was to be built from the bottom. Political parties and trade unions were to form at the lowest level of city and rural council and in the factory: there was to be no voting for lists of candidates imposed by party bosses.

Bevin hated the Germans and refused to visit Germany, but he did not allow his feelings – which went back to a sense of betrayal by the German trade unions in the First World War – to influence his policy. He appointed J.B. Hynd, a trade union MP who spoke German, to be minister in charge of the Control Commission. Hynd was not in the Cabinet and carried no political clout, though he was given as Permanent Secretary a splendid civil servant, Sir Arthur Street, who died after a few years from overwork. Unlike Churchill, Bevin enjoyed negotiation, and wanted to make four-power government in Germany work. He had no illusions about the Soviet Union, or about communists, whose disruption in the trade union movement he knew only too well, but he was also the man who in 1920 had threatened dock strikes when Lloyd George supported the Poles against the Soviet Union.[8] Official British

policy was to accept the Potsdam Agreements and enforce the directives of the Kommendatura.

The mood of the British in May 1945 was bitter. They felt that no
country had done more than Britain, indeed had done too much at
Munich, in trying to meet Germany halfway towards its legitimate
aspirations. In the twenties both the middle-aged and the young
had been pulled emotionally towards Germany. The war veterans
had formed lively 'No More War' Associations with their former
foes; the unsophisticated young enjoyed Bavarian heartiness and
respected the famous athlete Dr Peltzer; intellectuals lived in Hamburg and Berlin and admired the Bauhaus, the Expressionists, Ufa
movies and Brecht-Weill. And what had been the result? Hitler.
When the British contemplated the ruined German cities they felt
hardly a twinge: they remembered only too well Nazi leaders and
the Luftwaffe gloating over Coventry and a dozen other English
cities. The Americans whose own homeland was unscathed found
the non-fraternisation policy impossible to follow – they were too
generous and outgoing. The British did not find it all that hard.
They entered Germany believing that the Germans had got what
they deserved and that this time, unlike in 1918, they were going
to be made to feel the yoke, to submit, to acknowledge that they
had been militarily defeated. This time the legend, put about by
the Freikorps after 1918, that the German army had not been
defeated but had been betrayed by a stab in the back, must be
buried. Had not the Germans started five wars within the space of
a century? Did not the lesson of history teach us that Prussian
Junkertum was the seat of German militarism? Prussia therefore
should be destroyed.

There was another dimension to British anger: the Holocaust.
The discovery of Belsen on 15 April showed how the Nazis had
exterminated political prisoners and hostages. That was only the
prelude to the discovery of what had occurred in the concentration
camps in east Germany and Poland. It took some time, however,
for the enormity of Germany's crimes against the Jews to sink in.
In intelligence we knew of the gas ovens, but not of the scale, the

thoroughness, the bureaucratic efficiency with which Jews had been hunted down and slaughtered. No one at the end of the war, as I recollect, realised that the figure of Jewish dead ran into millions. Yet the knowledge of Belsen alone did not make it hard for soldiers to accept the policy of non-fraternisation in the early days of the occupation, even though it became impracticable within a few weeks.

It became impracticable because almost at once the British came up against the brute facts of those terrible days. What were they to do in the country they now were ruling? Millions of people were on the move. Millions of displaced persons from all the countries which Germany had enslaved were on their way home or had decided that under no circumstances would they return home. Russian and Polish prisoners of war roamed the countryside: some took to rape and murder in revenge. In mid-August I attended a Military Government summary court and saw a Pole condemned to death for possessing arms and belonging to a raiding party – though the Commander in Chief had power to commute the sentence. Our troops who at first considered the Germans were getting just deserts became ever more sympathetic to them and hostile to the DPs when they had to turn out night after night to stop some affray.[9]

It was not only the displaced persons who were on the move – millions of Germans expelled from Silesia and Czechoslovakia – or indeed by the British who had commandeered their homes – were moving from east to west. Baroness Dönhoff, later to be editor of *Die Zeit*, made the journey from East Prussia to Hamburg on a horse. The two great canals were blocked. Trains crept over improvised bridges: only 650 out of 8000 miles of track were operating. You drove along roads where every few miles you met a sign, '*Umleitung*', and you were diverted down tracks and side-roads. The devastation of the bombed cities beggared description. Three out of four houses were destroyed, seven out of eight damaged and shattered. Scarcely a city of any size and importance had escaped. In Berlin the trees in the Tiergarten were cut down for firewood, and a familiar sight was of some wizened old man hauling a little cart with a few sticks in it, and of chains of men and women passing chunks of rubble from hand to hand in an attempt to clear a site. The spectacle of misery pervaded one's life. Calloused as our sensibility has become since then by the images on television and in the press, year in year out, of millions of human beings in Asia and Africa murdered or dispossessed in our brutal and violent century, the memory of Germany in defeat has never faded from my mind. Particularly since we, the new lords of creation, swept by in our cars bound for some snug mess remote from hunger and cold.

West Germany had been cut off from its natural source of food supply in the Russian zone and the Soviet authorities had no intention of releasing a morsel. When P.J. Grigg, Secretary of State for War, saw the man whom Montgomery appointed to be the Military Governor of the British zone, he told him he must resign himself to the fact that two million people would die of starvation in Europe after the war.[10] General Sir Gerald Templer had no intention of resigning himself to any such calamity. He was a ruthless, incisive, dynamic commander, biting or disarming as occasion demanded. His smile was ferocious: like a wolf. In 1943 he was driving in his jeep up to the front line in Italy where he was commanding a division. An approaching lorry pulled over onto the verge, struck a mine and he was hit in the back by its rear wheel – he thought his back was broken. The lorry belonged to the Guards Brigade, and was bringing back a piano among other comforts for the Guards while they were resting. Templer used to say that it was the piano that hit him, together with a bucket of ice and bottles of champagne, 'all part of the Grenadiers' normal front-line equipment'.[11] By now he was fighting fit. As soon as he took over he sacked the dug-outs and failures who had been shunted into Military Government. He organised at once an operation to feed the Dutch who were on the verge of starvation. Then he got medicine and food to the concentration camps. Helping two and a half million displaced persons was his next concern. By June 1946 1.8 million had been repatriated. He then set up Operation Barleycorn, in which half a million German prisoners of war and women got in the harvest.[12] When that was achieved he got German staff officers in the prisoner of war camps to identify former miners and recruit others to raise coal production – despite protests from the Russians in the Kommendatura that he was keeping the German army in being. Then he moved to provide pit-props and so on.

How was the labour for these schemes to be provided? Templer simply kept the German army in being – though without badges of rank – and called these prisoners of war *Dienstgruppen* (Service detachments). This created some apprehension in Control Commission headquarters, apprehension which was justified when Marshal Zhukov circulated a memorandum accusing the British of breaking the Potsdam Agreements. Montgomery went in to bat at the Kommendatura on a sticky wicket, but he did not take his metaphor from cricket as he had at Alamein, when he told Eighth Army they were going to hit the Germans for six out of Egypt. His jaunty report to London began: 'I drove straight down the fairway on principle that I must seize and hold the initiative.' The US General McNarney, deputising for Eisenhower, was 'inclined to be hostile and when he had finished the ball was in the rough'. The French representative 'put the ball back in the fairway', but Marshal Zhukov 'selected a club with great care and proceeded to try to put the ball into the deepest part of the rough', although 'his club slipped and the shot was a poor one'. We were now, Montgomery concluded, in a good position to win the match. The truth was that the Field Marshal was in a bunker so deep that he had no hope of reaching the green. He had to order General Templer to dissolve the *Dienstgruppen* in an operation appropriately named 'Clobber'.[13]

Templer's energy transformed the British zone. Military Government officers, who had previously spent happy hours commandeering the best houses and stocking up the messes with wine and schnapps, found themselves working late hours reconstituting the German administration and putting Templer's emergency plans into operation. Horses were gathered at three centres and sent by train to the main agricultural areas; 800 railway bridges and 7000 miles of track were repaired by the end of the year. But the food crisis did not disappear, the black market raged, and people left work to deal in it or went to the farms to barter their possessions.

Who were these new rulers in Germany whom Templer galvanised? Some were senior officers, generals and brigadiers, who a few months earlier had been commanding military units. Indeed during 1945 most of the Military Government detachments were manned by army officers, some like myself waiting to be demobilised. (German officials used to lament that no sooner had they learnt to work with a Military Government officer than he departed to resume his civilian life in Britain.) Then there were the civilians, many wearing ill-fitting uniforms and somewhat despised by the regular officers. Some were civil servants. Ministries had been asked to release experienced administrators, but few were willing to let their best men and women go when Britain was converting from a war to a peacetime economy. Others came from the Colonial Service. Some were young idealists who hoped for a lifetime career in the Control Commission – described by Con O'Neill of the Foreign Office as 'low-level zealots'. Quite a few, singularly lacking in zeal, were there for the pickings. This was hardly surprising, since to the fury of Ivone Kirkpatrick, the senior officer at the Foreign Office responsible for Germany, the Treasury insisted on one-year contracts and inadequate salaries.[14]

These were to be my colleagues when I moved from SHAEF to join the Political Division. I had already met my new chief. Christopher Steel had been the British Political Officer at SHAEF. He looked like a soldier. Bluff, red-faced, no intellectual but canny and forthright, he had been educated at Wellington College, that nursery of generals, and had been chosen for his ability to get on with them. Although I could never believe it, he was said to have been the prototype for the sophisticated hero of Terence Rattigan's *French Without Tears*, and he certainly put first things first. Delighted to hear that I had the entrée at Veuve Clicquot, he set off with me for Reims and loaded up the Foreign Office truck there. As we came over the rise before dropping down to Bingen Steel gazed across the Rhine at the Johannisberger vineyard. 'What a bloody marvellous sight,' he said. He saw to it that he and his staff lived in comfort in Lübbecke and later in Berlin where we set up our mess at the Herbertstrasse in the Grunewald.

I found myself working with Goronwy Rees, an amusing, intelligent companion who had served on Montgomery's staff. I had first met him in Oxford when Maurice Bowra walked me over to All Souls' to rout him out of bed one Sunday morning. His father was a Calvinist Methodist minister and he a brilliant grammar school boy from Wales with curly dark hair and a mobile face at once seductive and quizzical. At Oxford he had carried all before him, and in London he had moved from the arms of Elizabeth Bowen into those of Rosamond Lehmann. By now, however, he was married and waiting to be demobilised.[15]

Routine business never passed across Goronwy's desk, although occasionally it might be disfigured by a small sheet of paper. But he knew pre-war Germany well from his Marxisant days in the thirties; and sometimes a news item caught his attention. For instance, when he read that Otto Springorum was to be appointed to the newly constituted steel board of Krupps, Goronwy remembered him as one of the industrialists who had financed Hitler, and got Steel to take action to cancel the appointment. He was one of the few officers who talked to me about the political significance of the atom bomb which had been dropped on 6 August. His technological knowledge was not quite the equal of his political sagacity, as I remember him assuring me that the bomb was about the size of a golf ball. He had a journalist's nose for events that might give him some clues about the state of Germany. We were meant to report on events in the country, and Goronwy suggested we test the quadripartite alliance in Berlin by driving to the Nickolaussee, deep in the Soviet sector; we were duly arrested, but released after half an hour with warnings about the danger of being taken for spies. On another occasion we went to the Soviet sector to attend a demonstration by former concentration camp victims, who processed in their striped prison uniforms round an arena before the speeches began. In the despatch Goronwy drafted he described this as an impressive spectacle of working-class grief, though I myself thought the occasion was no more spontaneous than a Nazi rally.

Goronwy was at his best in describing the Victory Parade on 7 September. Marshal Zhukov had insisted that the Russians should have pride of place, and in order to forestall any attempt to upstage him, he paraded his troops at 4 a.m. and called them to attention at seven for the march-past to begin at eleven. The Russians, Goronwy wrote, 'threw in their heaviest armour, including Marshal Zhukov, his burly chest blazing with decorations from his belt to his epaulettes, and one wonders what impression it made on the eight visiting American Congressmen who in snap-brim hats, chewing gum, and smoking cigars, looked as invincibly civilian as the Marshal looked warlike'.[16]

When Goronwy departed in September I was left on my own to analyse what was happening in German politics and to prepare a regular summary of political developments in Berlin and the zone for Strang to sign. I had one invaluable source of information. One of the divisions in the Control Commission was entitled Intelligence, and in each Military Government area there was an Intelligence unit which was not under local Military Government control. For instance the unit at Cologne was run by Lieutenant-Colonel Ronald Grierson, a German by birth who was later to become a director of Warburg's and chairman of the South Bank Board. At Hamburg there was Major Randell, who had identified Himmler when interrogating hordes of German prisoners; and there was Lance Pope, who became one of the best-known officers in the business. These units became my eyes and ears. They told me what Military Government was doing in the British zone, and sometimes asked me to intervene when they saw a scandal developing.

The Political Division resembled a diplomatic mission abroad. There was a Chancery that concerned itself with the four powers' activities in governing Germany through the Control Commission. There was a consular branch, and a skeleton staff remained in Westphalia to deal with, say, Swiss nationals who were engaged in salvaging what was left of their factory or business, or indeed with British firms and individuals with interests in the zone. The Foreign Office does not regard itself as an executive branch of government. Its members report and advise on events, and negotiate with foreign governments. The ambassador meets the head of the government and his ministers and his staff, the many departments of state and influential citizens. In Germany there was no government and no ministers, and soon telegrams began arriving from London: What were the Germans doing? What were they saying? Was an underground resistance forming, and what were these anti-fascist groups that had emerged offering to help the Military Government detachments? Could we explain why prominent Nazis were being employed by the Military Government in such and such a town? Why had no members of the SPD (Social Democratic Party) been appointed to any post in another? Why was the directive on reparations being ignored in such and such an industry? Why was Military Government so slow to license political parties or newspapers? Kit Steel told me that Sir William Strang, the Political Adviser to the Commander in Chief, was somewhat troubled by these telegrams. He had already toured the British zone in July with

Goronwy Rees, and now he wanted to make another reconnaissance. Would I please accompany him and keep a diary which he could forward as an annexe to the despatch he would send to Berlin?

The Political Adviser held the rank of ambassador and was on the same level as General Robertson, Montgomery's deputy. Robertson was in effect the head of the Control Commission in Berlin, to whom even Templer was responsible. Sir William Strang was an obvious choice for the post. He knew the Soviet Foreign Minister Molotov and Deputy Commissar for Foreign Affairs Vyshinsky from the time when he was sent on a luckless mission to Moscow to attempt to persuade Stalin to declare war on Germany if Hitler attacked Poland.* Strang bore no resemblance either to Cavendish-Bentinck or to Steel. He had gone to a grammar school and then to University College London where he enjoyed the grind of Old and Middle English, Anglo-Saxon and Gothic. In the trenches during the First World War he had seen bravery and cowardice. He looked like a confidential clerk, but if he considered his opponent on the other side of the table obstructive he became a terrier and tore his arguments to shreds. On his first tour of the zone he had met the patrician Rudolf Petersen, whom the Military Government had appointed Bürgermeister of Hamburg. Petersen had talked of Germany's 'folly' in going to war, and said that she must now be given some hope for the future. Strang snapped that Anglo-German friendship was not the first item on the agenda: the first item was the eradication of Nazism and militarism. The needs of other countries came before those of Germany, who must endure 'a long apprenticeship'.[17]

The first stop on my tour was at Münster, the seat of the provincial government of Westphalia. Brigadier Chadwick told us he held a conference with the German heads of departments once a fortnight

---

* As the Poles would not allow the Red Army to move across Poland if Germany attacked them, and as the Western powers would not agree to declare war if Germany threatened the independence of the Baltic states, the mission failed, and Molotov and Ribbentrop concluded the Nazi-Soviet Pact. Strang was chairman of the Governing Body of University College London when I became Provost there in 1966.

and insisted that each spoke his mind, to the surprise of the Oberpräsident Herr Amelunxen, who had expected to speak for all of
them.* We heard how 20 per cent of the police had to be armed
to cope with the murders and pillage committed by the displaced
persons. De-Nazification was in full swing, and the chief economic
officer said that his departments had been so thoroughly purged
that British officers had to keep essential services going. Industry
was switching to night shifts to spread the peak load on electricity.
From there we went to Dortmund to see a camp of 4500 displaced
persons, largely Poles, and run efficiently by Polish officers. 'Welcome to our guests,' shouted Stasha, head of the youngest form in
the school they had started in the camp. Eighty per cent intended
to return to Poland. At the extreme end of the camp we came to
a block occupied by Hungarians, Yugoslavs, Finns and Romanians.
I wrote in my account: 'Of all the sights which we beheld on our
tour this was the most pitiful. Cut off from the social life of the
rest of the camp, ignorant of when they might be moved, and of
the conditions in their countries, they stood out as an isolated
collection of individuals, united only by misfortune.'[19] When we
left a Romanian boy seized my hand and kissed it wet with his tears.

At Aachen we heard how Dutch and Belgians came across the
border to steal food and how an American lorry stacked with Persian
carpets had been turned back at the frontier. Only 7 per cent of
industry had been reactivated, but the schools were in full swing.
Lieutenant-Colonel Black, the deputy commander of the detachment, considered there was enough housing if only the authorities
would force the well-to-do to surrender empty rooms to the home-
less. At Jülich it had fallen to him to organise the collection of
garbage, since the fascination of this task seemed lost on the Germans. I wrote: 'We were impressed by the joy and pride this
Detachment took in their work.'[20] Each detachment in turn spoke

---

* A hierarchical bureaucracy in which a minister receives advice solely through the
top civil servant was not specifically German. When Roy Jenkins became Home
Secretary in 1965, each item that crossed his desk consisted of a short summary of
the issue and a recommendation from the Permanent Secretary, a procedure which
had already destroyed the reputation of the last two Home Secretaries. Jenkins insisted
on seeing the file to learn whether there were any dissenting opinions or other options
and what were the background documents.[18]

of the numbers of Nazis that had been dismissed, but several commanders asked whether we were not creating a body of able and clever malcontents so long as we deprived them of their pensions. Surely, too, some of the denunciations of Nazis were attempts to pay off old scores. We were also told that discipline needed to be restored in the coalmines, where miners were denouncing their foremen as Nazis, otherwise the supply of coal would fail.

We went on to visit Düsseldorf, Bonn, Cologne and Wuppertal. At our last port of call, the small town of Weidenbruck near Bielefeld, we were given a cup of tea in the detachment mess in a charming house that had belonged to a fervent Nazi, Herr Knobel. It was built, as an inscription on the chimneypiece proclaimed, in the year that Hitler had freed Germany. What, asked Strang, head on one side, looking like an old secretary bird, had happened to Herr Knobel? Oh, he was living in his factory that made furniture, and was doing a roaring trade. Yet here in this backwater there was, I reported, at any rate one happy group: 'They were a body of handsome Hungarian Jewesses who, despite a regrettable propensity to burn their furniture as fuel, were in constant demand by the troops for dances. Americans had arrived to fête them, and on one occasion they had disappeared for an unofficial holiday in Munich. From these experiences they returned invigorated.'[21]

And politics? To most Military Government officers German politicians – indeed all politicians – were an irrelevant nuisance given to criticising the occupying powers and nursing absurd pretensions. They could have no power: the British were running the zone. The only Germans who mattered were the bureaucrats who carried out British orders. They saw politicians as a premonition of their own demise. One might have concluded that it was British policy to impede rather than nurture political parties. Parties had to apply for a license to form and were warned that the process might take a long time. It did. The Internal Affairs Division scrutinised each application in six copies as if it were a time bomb. If an irregularity was detected, back it went for amendment.*

---

* Bernard Burrows at the Foreign Office commented on this bureaucratic nightmare. If the Internal Affairs and the Political Division had to be consulted on each application by each party in each *Kreis*, 'was there not some danger of the whole thing getting jammed?' – particularly since the Political Division was so understaffed. We should

The tour with Strang opened my eyes to the assumptions on which Military Government officers worked. Grotesque as it may sound today, they assumed that the occupation of Germany would last for twenty years. The plan was to allow political activities to develop at a leisurely pace. First there would be elections in the *Gemeinde* (parishes); then in the *Kreise* (counties and boroughs). After an interval, elections in the *Länder* (provinces) would follow. National parties campaigning in a nationwide election were but a shadow on the horizon. Until then the Germans were to learn how to conduct democratic government at each level. The British were somewhat priggish in the way they set about this task. The model was unquestionably colonial: British methods of voting and organising local government were to be introduced. Professor W.A. Robson of the London School of Economics had popularised the notion that German *Bürgertum* was too authoritarian. He advocated introducing the British system, in which the mayor and council were elected and were advised by the town clerk, a non-political administrator responsible for carrying out the council's policy.[22] The British insistence on introducing this arrangement bewildered the German officials. Hardly surprising. The German system was common to many European countries and not unknown in the United States. Nor was this all. In true colonial style the British set up nominated councils as the first faltering step on the path to democracy, and a redoubtable former colonial servant, Harold Ingrams, saw to it that the policy was implemented. Ingrams was apt to treat Germans as if they were a specially intelligent tribe of Bedouins. Discussion in the shady tent was permitted until the Resident Officer struck the ground with his stick and gave his decision. This attitude exasperated the Germans. Schumacher, the most likely leader of the Social Democrat Party, thought the proposals disastrous. '*Wir sind kein Negervolk*' ('We are not blacks'), he once said to me.[23]

None of the detachments Strang visited had a good word to say for the nominated councils. Each contained a quota of businessmen, women, trade unionists, lawyers, religious leaders and, as an

decentralise. On another matter Military Government was no less bureaucratic. Germans whose houses had been requisitioned could receive compensation, but the forms were so complicated that no one could fathom how to fill them in.

afterthought, a representative of three or four of the political parties applying to form. What were these councils to do, and how could they take decisions, when all power was in the hands of local government officials supervised by Military Government? The Colonel at Bielefeld said he enjoyed the cut and thrust of local politics, but we discovered that when the nominated council was about to pass a vote of no confidence in the mayor he ordered it to be dissolved. What was true of nominated councils was surely also true of trade unions. Colonel Strangeways, the head of intelligence at 1 Corps headquarters, was puzzled by what a trade union was to do if it was prohibited from calling a strike or from collective bargaining? In fact the nominated council in Hanover became by 1947 a responsible and confident body, and the local government reforms in the opinion of some British historians 'have always been considered the most successful aspect of British occupation policy'.[24] The British system survived for many years in some German cities. But most Germans were unimpressed, and the conception of a de-politicised civil service ran up against the objection that to call oneself 'non-party' at this time was a euphemism for ex-Nazi.[25] The old civil service, argued the SPD, had been far too non-political, willing to serve any master.

One German historian has dismissed the British administrative reforms as an example of 'amateur reforming zeal . . . the product of far-reaching ignorance or misunderstanding of German history and of Germany's administrative traditions'.[26] That is too severe a judgement. The British could chalk up two successes. The transformation of the German police and the restoration of an independent judiciary was one. The second was the creation of a responsible trade union movement. The British stopped Hans Böckler, the father of the modern German trade union movement, from forming one gigantic trade union representing every type of worker (he envisaged it as a political force). They told him on no account to follow British practice and allow a multitude of craft unions to form. Instead the Germans formed a number of large trade unions and won rights to representation on the boards of companies.

Over lunch or dinner in the messes of the Military Government detachments who entertained Strang and myself, one topic never failed to emerge: could we 're-educate' the Germans? In the opinion of Donald Watt this was the positive core and inspiration of the Control Commission. The notion that Germans had to be re-educated was dear to the hearts of Military Government, who believed the British should knock the elementary rules of democracy into their heads; the British resembled, as I once said in a note to Steel, a housemaster coaching his Colts in the nets.[27] If you mentioned that some of the men who were now forming political parties had suffered for their loyalty to democracy at the hands of the Nazis you were met by the reply, 'Well, they failed to stop them, didn't they?' Strang had been listening to such talk in the Foreign Office for some years. The older generation there had been as unsympathetic to the Weimar Republic as they had been to Hitler. 'No normal Germany has existed for fifty years or more' was the current view, and it was not confined to the Foreign Office: Fabian Society intellectuals and trade unionists also found German politics unsympathetic.[28] John Troutbeck, the adviser to the Cabinet on Germany, wanted to 'stamp on the tradition on which the German nation had been built'.[29] He had no patience with Dick Crossman at SHAEF who argued that there were plenty of noble Germans who had resisted Hitler and who, put into posts of responsibility, could re-educate their countrymen better than the British. Kit Steel had even less patience. Crossman, he felt, should be turned off Foreign Office turf and told to lay off promoting 'dubiously repentant Huns'.[30] As late as 1952 Chaput de Saintonge, the head of the German Education Department at the Foreign Office, minuted: 'It is unlikely democracy will develop in Germany in the near future' – a sentence Ivone Kirkpatrick insisted should be redrafted, for if it were true the occupation of Germany would be prolonged indefinitely, and de Saintonge's department expanded instead of being wound up.[31] Nevertheless, the Foreign Office always argued that the object of British policy was to restore Germany, de-Nazified and demilitarised, to the European family.

This negative Foreign Office line was institutionalised in the Control Commission's Information Services and Public Relations Division. Michael Balfour was an influential figure there. He was a persistent debunker of the 20 July plotters: they may have plotted, but how many of them believed in democracy? The guilt of the German people must be brought home to them – though Balfour drew gossamer distinctions between collective guilt and collective responsibility. 'Any attempt to re-educate the German people,' he wrote in October 1946, 'is bound to fail because the German people are in no mood to be re-educated.'[32] In the end he took the line that re-education meant publicising the British way of doing things, rather than using our resources to discuss ideals and the meaning of life.

Ideals and the meaning of life, however, inspired many who had joined the Control Commission. The handbook that was issued to them teemed with delineations of the German character and the need to change it. How, for instance, could one inculcate a sense of personal responsibility in people used to obeying orders without reflection? I heard some astonishing suggestions emanating from those whom Con O'Neill had called 'low-level zealots', people who were convinced they had discovered the antidote to Nazism. There was the lady who begged me to use my influence to have all performances of Wagner banned because his music inculcated the *Führerprinzip*. Another officer stood the Nazi racist Alfred Rosenberg on his head. Pondering whether the Germans could be civilised, he concluded that it was just possible, provided that their 'biological foundations' were changed by intermarriage and 'extensive mixing of blood with other nationals'.[33] Another proposal was to put all ex-Nazis and their families on an island called Adelheide in the North Sea. But, asked Robert Birley, would not the children, going to school on the mainland, infect others with their ideas? The proposal was dropped.[34]

The re-educators were by no means all cranks. They could congratulate themselves on the de-Nazification of school textbooks, even if the de-Nazification of 16,000 teachers left the schools understaffed. But, as in the civil service, the Germans found the imposition of British practices baffling. If the British wished to make Germans less authoritarian, why did they advocate a system in which the headmaster was all-powerful, and responsible only to a local education authority? In Schleswig-Holstein an SPD administration was to try to transform the German secondary school system, based on the *Gymnasium* and *Abitur*, into a comprehensive system. When Germans assumed responsibility for education that initiative collapsed. Nor was it favoured by the British, with the Butler Act of 1944, which had effectively divided secondary education into grammar and secondary modern schools, fresh in their minds.

British attempts to reform the universities met with spectacular failure. When I was in Germany, it was an achievement to keep the universities open; the students warmed their hands at the bunsen burners in order to write in notebooks discarded by British schools. In 1948 'Sandy' Lindsay, the former Master of Balliol and now Vice-Chancellor of the first new British post-war university at Keele, appalled at the way German universities had become so divorced from society, used his influence to set up a committee to make proposals. The Report on University Reform 1948 won enthusiastic plaudits from the German press, which compared its ninety-five propositions to those of Luther. The massed Rektors and professors refused to implement them. Anything that weakened professorial oligarchy was anathema. Until 1955 there were only twelve universities in Germany, and the qualification (*Abitur*) could be obtained only if one went to a *Gymnasium* (i.e. grammar school), and was so exacting that less than 150,000 students graduated: anything that adulterated the standard was unacceptable. (Years later I was to hear identical arguments in Britain.) Geoffrey Bird recalled how the Rektor of Göttingen was 'highly suspicious of the appointment of young progressive lecturers'.[35] The universities remained unchanged for another decade, manned by professors whose outlook, as my colleague, Cecil King, said in a letter to me 'would have brought them honour and preferment in the days of Bismarck'.[36]

The most famous of all the British educators in Germany was Robert Birley. Birley left the headmastership of Charterhouse to become educational adviser to General Robertson. He won many hearts in Germany because he said he was in the business of education, not re-education. He wanted to awaken Germans to the part of their cultural tradition that Troutbeck ignored: the tradition of Kant and Goethe. Birley's ideal was certainly realised in the most successful British innovations: the exchange of visits between British and German teachers, the provision of British libraries and youth and adult education centres (*Die Brücke* – 'the bridges' – as these enterprises were called). Most imaginative of all was the Wilton Park Centre run by Heinz Koeppler, to which dozens of selected German prisoners of war who were to rebuild their country came. They later regarded themselves as a special fraternity, so enlightened and unlike propaganda the course turned out to be. From these beginnings came the annual Königswinter conferences run by the redoubtable Frau Lilo Milchsach, where British and German men and women in public life met to talk together.

Nevertheless, Birley was to lose the battle inside the Control Commission. The new head of information services, General Balfour, complained that his ideas were weakening 'the British projection'. Re-education for Balfour meant 'promoting British policy and projecting British civilisation'. Birley protested: was he to 'find false beards for my Education Control officers'?[37] General Robertson ruled against him. Robertson saw that, lacking a Parliament or a lively press, Military Government was without a forum in which to defend itself against the suspicions, complaints and innuendoes about British policy. Birley accordingly resigned to become headmaster of Eton where, after Claude Elliott's retirement, a considerable task of re-education awaited him.

I returned from my tour with Strang in a sombre state of mind. The hostility of Military Government to any kind of German political initiative disturbed me. Sooner or later, and unlike these Military Government officers I thought sooner, the Germans were going to rule themselves again. Military Government had one objective in mind that overrode all others: stability. The forces of instability – displaced persons, German refugees expelled from East Prussia, Poland and Czechoslovakia, hunger, homelessness and hopelessness – were strong enough. Why add to them by restructuring German institutions? Some Germans imagined that the Labour Government in London would insist on nationalising German industry, but Military Government's first concern was to get German industry back to work to provide minimal needs of the zone and to pay reparations. Whereas Soviet military government was inspired by politics, the British were technocrats. They preferred the status quo. From the start they regarded the SPD with suspicion, because the left endangered the status quo: 'It therefore had to be discouraged and it was.'[38] Works councils were forbidden. Nazis might be turned out of their flats by the British, but not by zealous Germans. Some city administrators tried to compel known Nazis to clear rubble: Military Government forbade it. When a committee of concentration camp victims was formed to supervise releases from the camps it was at once banned. Even a commemorative service for the victims of Nazism was forbidden: why, that would be equivalent to staging a demonstration – and were not demonstrations by their nature disturbances?[39] There was therefore no sense of a new beginning. When Military Government called on the ordinary German citizen to help them distinguish between repulsive, fervent Nazis and merely nominal members of the party, the ordinary German citizen replied '*Ohne mich*' – count me out.

Sublimely self-confident as Military Government officers were in governing Germany, two minor incidents reminded them that there were supra-national forces – morality and the rule of law – that could call them to account. That great prince of the Church, Cardinal Archbishop von Galen of Münster, who was renowned for his outspoken criticism of the Nazis, was not likely to be intimidated by the British. In August he stated that the policy of non-fraternisation was 'a denial of justice and love if it is declared that every German person participated in the guilt of each criminal act'.[40] Galen determined to call on General Templer to protest that the British were starving his flock. On the appointed day a few of us waited outside Templer's headquarters to receive him. We watched his car draw up, and a towering figure in all the panoply of his office stepped out. The Brigadier in charge of religious affairs, who was a Roman Catholic, dropped to his knee to kiss the episcopal ring. 'I say, whose side is that fellow on?' General Bishop anxiously asked me. The two commanders, spiritual and temporal, took to each other at once, and when later Templer gathered all the bishops in the zone together for coffee, cigarettes and unbridled criticism, Galen said, 'I shall tell the Holy Father that we are dealing with Christian gentlemen.'*[41]

Another renowned British commander also met with a check.

---

* Strang recognised Galen's strength of character, but referred to him as 'a German nationalist out and out'.

General Horrocks, Commander of 30 Corps, issued an order in the autumn of 1945 that any German boys who mocked or insulted British soldiers should be summarily caned on the spot. Mr Wilberforce of the Legal Division in Berlin (a Fellow of All Souls' who became the senior Lord of Appeal in the House of Lords) sent Horrocks an instruction to cancel the order at once: if the British purported to be reintroducing the rule of law to Germany, they must abide by it themselves. Gradually it seeped into the minds of Military Government officers that there were limits to their power.

The art of interpretation in history – its hermeneutics – lies in recognising signs that resemble those weather-beaten wooden finger-posts half hidden by brambles in the English countryside. The British attempt to change the structure of German local government was such a finger-post.

The British are proud of their system of governance. In theory the elected politicians, whether in Parliament or in local councils, are separate from the civil service or local government officials who are permanent and under an obligation to carry out the policy of the people's elected representatives. Several academic studies – and the outstanding television comedy series *Yes, Minister* – have shown how in fact the permanent officials, using time-honoured bureaucratic devices, thwart politicians who try to change things. In Britain there is no formal separation of powers between executive and legislature as there is in the United States Constitution. But the power of politicians is checked by a multitude of pressure groups and lobbies and dozens of semi-official bodies representing professions such as the Inns of Court and the Law Society for lawyers, or the General Medical Council and British Medical Association for doctors. They police the practitioners, but are the first to campaign in their defence. Even individuals can form ginger-groups to defeat schemes to cut rail services or to construct motorways or bypasses. New associations of consumers and environmentalists sprout and block what their elected representatives and their officials have proposed. When told that the man in Whitehall knows best, the British show how much they distrust bureaucracy. The

Whig historians were not wrong to find the roots of this tradition of consent and dissent embedded in the seventeenth century.

How different is the tradition of governance in Germany and France. In France Napoleon transformed the *intendant* of the *ancien régime* into the *préfet de département* of modern times. Germany too owes its governance partly to Napoleon. After winning the battles of Jena and Auerstedt he imposed upon Prussia such harsh terms that the country was destitute, the population reduced by his annexations from 10½ to 4½ million, paying a huge indemnity, and its economy ruined by his blockade of trade with Britain. Reform was inevitable. Scharnhorst transformed the army from Frederick the Great's regiments of blind obedience into a thinking, technocratic fighting force; and Stein, Hardenberg, Schön and others set to work on the economy and administration. Historians say that the reforms failed. Certainly they failed to produce what Hardenberg called the 'democratic principle in a monarchical government'. Prussia remained an absolute monarchy, though the King now ruled through ministers of state; and they ruled through an autocracy of bureaucrats. But the reformers succeeded in creating a free enterprise economy with only one tariff at the frontiers; in creating meritocratic schools and universities and a respect for technical education; and establishing the best system of justice and the least corrupt bureaucracy in Europe – and one which could exact obedience to all its edicts.

The year 1945 has been called in Germany *Stunde Null*, zero-hour, a black hole into which the past disappeared. This never happens in history. The past, in one form or another, continues to exist and to exert its influence, however catastrophic the present may be. Germans were determined this time to build a Western democratic state, and substantial powers were devolved to the *Länder*: no longer could a Goebbels broadcast on a national radio. But the old system, in which the elected politician is the head executive in local as well as in national politics, survived; and the authoritarian tradition of governance helped Germany's politicians perform the Economic Miracle. Hitler had destroyed the elites; as in Frederick William III's time, a new meritocracy formed.

When Britain joined the European Economic Community in 1973, it found a governmental machine at Brussels manufactured on the Napoleonic and Prussian model, and a legal system based on Roman law that appealed to principle, as distinct from the Anglo-American system that is based on precedent. Britain's Parliament sat for many weeks longer than Continental legislatures, and amended legislation that civil servants had drafted. The British were unused to a form of government in which a bureaucracy directed by a powerful President put forward directives to a Council of Ministers who, though they could challenge one or another of them, were expected to give their agreement to the rest. How little did I realise in 1945 that the trifling dispute about the imposition upon German government of the British system of an elected mayor and permanent town clerk was a finger-post pointing to a discord between Britain and the European Union in the future.

Certainly in October 1945 when I was accompanying Strang on his tour I had another matter much more in my mind. When we dined at the headquarters of the North Rhine province in Düsseldorf the topic of conversation that dominated the evening was the sacking of the Oberbürgermeister of Cologne: Konrad Adenauer.

CHAPTER NINE

Germany's Political Parties Form

Three days before I left on the tour with Strang, the telephone rang in my office. One of my sources in the zone was speaking. 'Have you heard Military Government has sacked Adenauer as Oberbürgermeister of Cologne?' 'Good God!' I said. 'Why didn't they consult us? What's the story?'

The story has often been told – not least by Adenauer himself.[1] The facts were these. Towards the end of September 1945 General Templer had visited Cologne. He was disgusted that the elementary services of gas, electricity and sewerage had still not been restored; the Rhine was blocked; and far less seemed to have been done than elsewhere in clearing streets and providing emergency housing. He met the Oberbürgermeister, then in his seventy-first year, and was not impressed. Adenauer seemed to think it was up to the British to repair the city's services. Templer told the Military Governor of the North Rhine Province, Brigadier Barraclough, a former parachute officer, that a younger and more energetic man was needed as mayor. The decision to sack Adenauer was taken by Barraclough, but Templer propelled him.[2]

Barraclough went at once to Adenauer and talked to him for two hours. Adenauer pulled out a portfolio of drawings showing him what Cologne would look like in twenty years' time. He had already refused to cut down the trees in the green belt to the west of the city to provide pit-props and fuel for the population, and said he was doing all that could be done. Back at his headquarters Barraclough dictated a letter of dismissal, which was translated into German and typed.

Adenauer had been disturbed by Barraclough's visit, and resorted to the only weapon in his hands: politics. He at once gave an interview to British journalists in which he criticised the British authorities for refusing to give coal to the people of Cologne, and went on to praise de Gaulle and to speculate about the future of the Saar. This was a deliberate act of provocation. No German was permitted only five months after the end of the war in Europe to make public political pronouncements. Barraclough was furious. He summoned Adenauer to his office and read the terms of his dismissal to him, making him stand throughout the interview. But he did more than dismiss him. Since Adenauer's brother-in-law, Dr Willi Suth, would take over as temporary mayor, Barraclough forbade Adenauer to remain in Cologne or to engage in any political activity outside it.

Barraclough was right to dismiss Adenauer. He had already dismissed Dr Fuchs, the Oberpräsident of North Rhine, on grounds of age and excessive partiality to old-guard officials, and had put in his place Dr Robert Lehr, a caricature of the German official: gleaming bald head, grey moustache, blue eyes and an authoritarian manner. A caricature of German efficiency too: when Barraclough ordered him to evacuate 600,000 people from the Rhineland because there were no houses for them, Lehr pleaded to put forward counter-proposals. Given three days he did so, and in two months his plan to produce accommodation for them got under way: it finally produced shelter for a million.[3] On the other hand, if Barraclough was right in dismissing an inefficient mayor, he was wrong to let himself be provoked. It never crossed his mind that there could be any repercussions about the manner and terms of Adenauer's dismissal. But there were.

The officer who telephoned me from the British Zone was Captain Michael Thomas, a remarkable young man. He was the son of Felix Hollaender, a prolific novelist who had been director of the Max Reinhardt Theatre in Berlin. Prevented from taking his degree at Tübingen because he was a Jew, Thomas left Germany in disgust and became one of the few Germans to graduate from the Pioneer Corps and be commissioned in the British Army (he was called 'the Prussian baron' by his platoon because he made them shower and clean their teeth each day). In Normandy he had been liaison officer with the Polish Armoured Division, and on arrival in Germany he began networking with those Germans who seemed to be emerging as potential leaders, such as Petersen in

Hamburg and the old Social Democrat minister Karl Severing. His reports impressed Templer, who asked his commanding officer, 'He is a Prussian, can you trust him?' and then appointed Thomas his roving liaison officer.[4]*

He had been on his way to see Adenauer when he heard of the dismissal, and hurried to Adenauer's home, where he found him in a state of shock. Parachute generals, said Adenauer, were stupid fellows, in whatever army they served. The instruction to sack him must have come from the Foreign Office. He had never met de Gaulle, he said (he did not disclose that he had seen an emissary of the General), and was indignant at the way he had been dismissed. It was not true that he hated England, but, alas, Englishmen were gentlemen no longer. Speaking in his habitual Rhineland accent he said, '*Sehnse, ich bin'ne alte Mann, ich habe jar keine politische Ehrjeiz mehr*' ('Look, I'm an old man, I've got no further political ambition'). This was too much for Thomas, who said, 'Herr Dr Adenauer, I am not buying that one.'[5] He told Adenauer he would find out the true cause of his dismissal, and asked him to believe he would tell him the truth.

Michael Thomas was not only clever; he was intelligent. His bright eyes darted to and fro as he spoke. Politically he was a strong conservative, and he made penetrating judgements of those he met. Of all my sources in the British Zone, he was the best, and despite his anomalous position he won the confidence of the Germans, though he was regarded with suspicion by Military Government officers. I liked him and knew I could trust him.

It was at a reception Military Government gave for Strang that I had arranged to meet Thomas. He told me he had asked Barraclough whether the Foreign Office had intervened in Adenauer's dismissal. Barraclough had shown him Adenauer's file, and nothing

---

* Thomas had direct access to Templer, which did not please his punctilious and unimaginative Chief of Staff Brigadier Britten. In 1946 Templer issued an order prohibiting Germans from wearing military uniform even if stripped of badges of rank. Thomas protested, and told him that for thousands of men their uniforms were the only clothes they possessed. Templer was irritated, and Thomas lost his access to him. He then found himself at the mercy of the staff. When a new commanding officer, Lieutenant-Colonel Pearson, referred to him as a 'Jew-boy' he quit the army when he was entitled to be demobilised, and, after further service in the Control Commission as a civilian, later made a fortune in business in Germany.

in it suggested that they had. The only document from London was a letter from a First World War general who warned that Adenauer had been much too pro-French during the occupation of the Rhineland. Adenauer was disappointed to be told that the Labour government had nothing to do with his dismissal, and he continued to maintain for the rest of his days that politics was behind it. Perhaps this was natural. None of us likes to admit that we have been a failure in any job. Michael Thomas also told me that Barraclough had twice been rebuked by the Commander of I Corps, and that after Templer's visit he had received another stinging message from the Corps Commander, who told him that Cologne 'had the worst record of debris clearance in the British Zone'. In other words, Barraclough had received a rocket, and that, Thomas believed, made him so vindictive when he sacked Adenauer. So it may have been; but when Thomas told me how Adenauer had been made to stand while Barraclough read to him the terms of his dismissal, I became convinced that Barraclough had wanted to make an example of Adenauer.

At first sight this might seem strange. Adenauer appeared to be exactly the kind of German the British needed: a man with an impeccable anti-Nazi record, who had suffered imprisonment by the Gestapo; a staunch Catholic in a city and region predominantly Catholic; and a conservative. He hated Prussia and *Junkertum*, and prided himself on being a citizen, not an aristocrat. But to Barraclough he was a political intriguer, and indeed Adenauer spent many hours not in restoring Cologne but in building a new party – the Christian Democratic Union (CDU). The fact that he had been floating the idea of a strong Rhine-Ruhr Province joined in economic union to the West appeared to be a monstrous interference in affairs which were solely the concern of the occupying powers. Barraclough wanted a sober, unambitious German *Beamter*, *tuchtig und fleiszig* (an efficient and hard-working official). Military Government officers had been told to check at once any sign of German arrogance; and what else, Barraclough may have wondered, was Adenauer displaying than that? Many Germans still had no conception of the world's verdict on their conduct in occupied Europe. (In 1946 a British Member of Parliament speaking to German university students was asked why Britain had not launched an offensive against Russia to release German prisoners of war and, if we did not intend to do so, why not? The question was greeted with deafening applause.) Barraclough may have thought that he had rumbled exactly the kind of German who despite his anti-Nazi record should be kept out of a position of power.

I considered the terms of Adenauer's dismissal disastrous. His wife was ill, and he was allowed to see her only twice a week: to comply with his ban he had to drive round the city. Here was a man who already looked as if he would be the leader of the most powerful party in the Catholic Rhineland, and possibly in the zone. No German would believe he had been dismissed for inefficiency, and he would gain credit for having stood up to the British. I told Michael Thomas that I would intercede, and had no difficulty in persuading Kit Steel to get General Robertson to countermand Barraclough's order. To save the face of Military Government, a few weeks were allowed to elapse before I called on Brigadier Barraclough to tell him that if Adenauer became a political martyr he would become all the more powerful as a symbol of British injustice.

Barraclough was by no means as difficult to deal with as some other senior British officers. He neither blustered nor excused himself, but he pleaded that he could not reinstate Adenauer as Mayor of Cologne. This I accepted; having once made a judgement about Adenauer's competence, Military Government could not now reverse it. But I told Barraclough that he would have to rescind the order of house arrest, and that I would call on Adenauer and admit to him frankly that an error had been made.

Thus it was that shortly afterwards I found myself being greeted by Dr Adenauer in his sitting room and watching that flat, impassive, curiously Tartar face with those minute, watchful eyes that one had seen in portraits by Cranach and Dürer – a face which reminded one how much Germany belonged to eastern as well as western Europe. Adenauer received me without recrimination, but with what is usually referred to in diplomatic circles as reserve. He said first that we could not talk politics because he was forbidden to do so, but then added that we had only to drive a few miles south into the French Zone and he would be free to talk. Enjoying his irony, I laughed and he began to thaw. Prudence alone dictated that I should treat him as a statesman of the future. But there was another reason why I should take his part. To me Dr Adenauer exemplified the virtues of that 'other' Germany which so many Englishmen had admired for over a century. I wanted to listen to him, and I hoped he would listen to me.

In that I had no difficulty. Adenauer listened to what I had to say with dignity. We talked about the difficulties Military Government faced: I tried neither to claim nor to concede too much; and Adenauer for his part never attempted to deny the curse that the Nazis had laid on his country. I told him that the ban on his political activity would be lifted immediately, and when I remarked that his dismissal as Oberbürgermeister would be much to his advantage in his search for political support, he permitted himself a faint smile. We also talked of his role in the Rhineland after the First World War, and I told him that some concern was felt that he had in those days been thought to be anti-British. He denied this, but admitted that he found difficulty in seeing Britain as a European state.

At one point Adenauer asked me what I would do when I was demobilised. I told him that I was an historian and hoped to return to Cambridge University to teach and write history. 'Then,' he said, 'you will be able to tell me what was the greatest mistake that the English ever made in their relations with Germany.' Thinking that discretion was the better part of valour, I asked Dr Adenauer if *he* would tell *me*. 'It was at the Congress of Vienna,' he replied, 'when you so foolishly put Prussia on the Rhine as a safeguard against France and another Napoleon.'

A few weeks later Ronnie Grierson invited Adenauer to meet Kit Steel and myself over lunch at his house in the Leyboldstrasse in Cologne. On that occasion Adenauer unfolded his political philosophy. He spoke of his concern that *westliches Christentum und abendländische Kultur* (Western Christianity and culture) should be preserved. These were phrases which the British at that time did not much like to hear. They were too like the arguments used during the war by those who wanted America and Britain to sign a separate peace with Germany. But nothing changes so quickly as alliances after a war. The more decisively one country is defeated, the more clearly the balance of power is upset. The

British had to take account of the fact that many of its European allies, from Greece to France, were threatened by communist takeovers.

My tour with Strang convinced me that whether or not Germans could be re-educated, there was an overwhelming case for educating Military Government. In late September I had already begun to draft a memorandum of political guidance that could be distributed to all detachments. Meanwhile I set off on a series of tours in the British Zone. Yes, it was true, I would explain to a Kreis commander, that the theoretical foundations of the Social Democrat Party were Marxist; but that did not mean that it was a crypto-communist organisation. On the contrary: the SPD was our best bulwark against communist expansion. Or I would suggest that a nominated council should bear some relation in its composition to the likely politics of the population. When I told the Military Governor of Hamburg, Brigadier Armytage, a grizzled old warrior of the First World War who looked like a malevolent tortoise, that his nominated council was almost entirely middle class and that his fine patrician Bürgermeister would never be returned in an election, he received this advice with undisguised distaste. Michael Thomas warned Templer that Petersen was under threat, and Templer told Armytage that Petersen should stay. But when elections came almost the whole of his nominated council was swept away and Hamburg returned an SPD mayor.

Meanwhile Templer, with characteristic élan, had determined to hold a conference at Detmold in November. He would address the Oberpräsidenten and Oberbürgermeisteren and other top German officials, and some of the politicians who had emerged. He intended to ask Karl Severing, who had been Minister of the Interior in the late 1920s, to act as chairman of the German delegates. I told Steel that this was unwise. Here was a man who was symbolic of the surrender of Weimar democracy to Hitler: did we want him to become the leader of a revived SPD? I was not alone in being alarmed by the name of Severing: Ernest Bevin himself was displeased to hear it. Templer was disconcerted to be told by Steel that as he had resurrected Severing, it was up to him to reinter him.[6]

It had never crossed anyone's mind to consult the Political Division when Adenauer was dismissed or Severing courted. Military Government thought of the Political Division as being merely concerned with diplomatic relations with the missions of the other three powers. When I returned to Berlin I found that my draft memorandum of political guidance to Military Government officers had sunk into the Serbonian bog of the bureaucracy. Surely the Four Power Directive of 10 September would be good enough? Perhaps, thought Strang, I should re-read the Potsdam decisions on which all political activity was based.[7] Should the guidance be a secret paper? If it were to leak to the Russians, would they not gain a propaganda coup by distorting its meaning?[8] Surely no example should be given of unsatisfactory appointments in the zone? Should not the letter of guidance include advice about de-Nazification and democratisation? It was then decided that a passage advocating political neutrality, welcoming a 'sound and vigorous Social Democratic Party' and being 'not averse to the aims of the Christian Democrat Party' (though warning that some reactionaries might masquerade as such) should be deleted. Eventually a document signed by Steel went to the six Regional Commissioners with the warning that 'though you may and should discuss it with your officers, its contents should on no account be . . . bandied about in casual conversation'.[9] After four months' gestation, a mouse was born.

I had slightly better luck with the speech I was to make to the German politicians. I told Steel how damaging the Military Government restrictions were, and how far behind the Americans and Russians we were in announcing elections and a degree of self-government. It was ridiculous to expect national parties to emerge in each Kreis: they ought to be encouraged to organise nationally – at least at the level of our own zone. The Foreign Office had displayed a worldly scepticism about some of the more idealistic aims of the Control Commission. It took the line that German politicians should be allowed to criticise Military Government and flaunt their own ideas about the future; how else was freedom of speech to be inculcated?[10] Steel was splendid. He convinced General Robertson that the British must change their time-table for elections, and told me to invite delegations from the parties to a conference to explain the changes. As a matter of courtesy I passed a draft of this speech to the Internal Affairs Division. The reply I received was characteristic of the tone of Military Government: 'I think this very good on the whole,' wrote the staff officer in his reply. 'My only general comment is that it is too friendly.' Why should I thank Germans for attending? I should make it clear I had ordered them to do so. (When I saw the emaciated faces of those who had come hundreds of kilometres across broken bridges and cratered roads, I was glad that I did thank them.) The officer then went on to suggest fourteen redrafts to make the text of my speech considerably less friendly.[11]

I ignored his advice and told the German politicians that they were to be permitted to form national political parties. Meetings between themselves, which had hitherto been held clandestinely because they could have been judged illegal, were now to be welcomed. Political newspapers would be licensed; speeches by political leaders would be permitted over the Nordwestdeutscher Rundfunk in Hamburg; and local elections would take place in the British Zone in the spring next year.

The response was touching: 'This news is better for us than white bread,' said one old social democrat. Here were men with sallow faces and with the strained expression that hunger gives, men who were prepared to devote themselves to the unrewarding task of being a politician. I recognised during the time I spent in Germany a spirit of dedication to parliamentary democracy which sprang from the knowledge of what dictatorship had been, and still was in the Soviet Zone of Germany. I have never failed to be struck by this spirit whenever I have returned to the Federal Republic.

Who were these politicians, and what did they stand for? I spent most of my time until the end of the year compiling evidence for a despatch which Strang endorsed and sent to the Foreign Office.[12]

I began by describing politics in the Soviet Zone, where as early as June 1945 the Russians had permitted political parties to form, and had recognised them. They were expected to work as a 'united front'. The Social Democrat Party was under constant pressure to toe the KPD (Communist Party) line, and its newspapers were censored. CDU meetings in the Soviet Zone were broken up as 'fascist rallies'. The Soviet conception of politics was put to me in primitive German by a Russian officer I met at a reception: '*CDU ist guter Partei: aber kleiner Partei.*' If the Christian Democrat Union was a bourgeois party, and the bourgeoisie were by definition only a small percentage of the population, how could the CDU be anything other than small?

The KPD was run by émigrés from Moscow. The chairman, Wilhelm Pieck, white-haired, square-shouldered, was a jovial front man. The real power was in the hands of the hard-line Secretary of the Party, Walther Ulbricht, Marshal Zhukov's political adviser, a masterly and unscrupulous tactician. Ulbricht made his name in the Spanish Civil War liquidating anti-Stalinist revolutionary combatants (i.e. Anarchists), and was adept at infiltrating left-wing organisations for the Party. A Spanish war comrade in exile in Mexico described his face, with its Lenin-beard, as 'stiff with a malice that was conscious of its own ugliness . . . His eyes, the right sharply observant, and the left half-closed [gave him] the look of a lapsed priest who visits shady houses.'[13] In the Soviet Zone the other parties had been informed that opposition to land reform (i.e. the expropriation of large estates) would be regarded as opposition to the Soviet Military Government; and the social democrats were not best pleased when they saw the expropriated land parcelled out to the 'politically reliable'. Only 'anti-fascist' youth could enter Berlin University; all youth organisations other than that run by Heinz Kessler, an active communist, were banned. Most sinister of all, the Nazi *Blockleiter*, or street warden, had been transmogrified into the communist *Hausobmann*.

In my despatch I acknowledged that the KPD alone among the parties preached fidelity to the Potsdam Agreements and the Oder-Neisse frontier with Poland; but they 'cannot resist the temptation to capture and twist every democratic institution to their own end'.[14] Even in the earliest days of the occupation in the west this was so. The invading Allied armies were sometimes met by anti-fascist committees. Some of their members were genuine idealists who had lain low and who offered to de-Nazify their cities and reorganise their administration. But just as the Provisional IRA were quick to take over the civil rights movement in Ulster in the

176

1960s, the communists moved in on the 'Antifa' committees. The KPD presented their applications to form local parties quicker and more efficiently than other groups. In the Ruhr under Max Reimann, and in Hamburg under Dettmann, they took the Party line from their comrades in Berlin. When Reimann held a rally, the mass clapping and chanting reminded observers of the Nazis.[15]

I next described the Social Democrat Party (SPD), which I judged to be potentially the most powerful party in Germany, although in December 1945 it was split. In Berlin there were veterans like Gustav Dahrendorf who remembered the disastrous hostility between the two working class parties, and hankered after a united workers' party. Schmedemann recalled how in 1933 he had proposed to organise underground opposition to Hitler, and had been told by the older SPD leaders that to do so would be a crime against both the state and the workers. (It was the memory of such incidents that had induced me to bury Severing.) The leader of the SPD in Berlin, Otto Grotewohl, had twice been summoned by the Russians and accused of anti-Soviet activities. His committee had decided to fight the elections as a separate party, not on a single list; and most of the abler administrators in the Soviet Zone were SPD supporters. But naturally he stood for co-operation with the KPD.

In the British Zone, however, he had a formidable rival: 'One-armed, spare, intense, with cunning eyes, Dr Kurt Schumacher has taken the lead in organising the party not only in the British but also in the American Zone.' Schumacher stood for implacable opposition to the communists, and was therefore bound to challenge Grotewohl. He claimed to have the support of the Kreis leaders, in his own words, 'from Munich to the sea'. He did not see eye to eye with Karl Meitmann in Hamburg nor Wilhelm Hoegner in Bavaria: but Hoegner, having been appointed Oberpräsident of the province, was out of the running. Schumacher's call for land reform and nationalisation of major industries was orthodox. But what was alarming was the unbridled nationalism of his speeches. I first met him when I was ordered to remonstrate at his public statement that the SPD refused to recognise the Oder-Neisse frontier. He received my rebuke, I reported, 'in stubborn and defiant silence'.[16] In return he complained that Military Government favoured the CDU in their appointments. He could not understand why the Labour government in London did not impose a socialist policy in the British Zone. Why had the British stopped the trade union movement from allying itself with the SPD? He complained that in Hanover only six of the ten administrative departments were headed by SPD supporters. Why did the British treat all parties equally? To do so was to discriminate against those who were democrats before the British arrived. Why had Military Government forbidden delegates from Berlin to attend when he held a conference at Wennigser on 5–7 October? Why was Bratke, an excellent chief of police in Hanover, so reluctant to de-Nazify his force thoroughly? Must administrative convenience always come first?[17] Schumacher argued that the SPD was the only genuinely anti-Nazi party (apart from the hateful KPD) because it was the only party dedicated to the destruction of militarism, capitalism in the form of cartels and the other sociological causes of Nazism. Put authority in its hands and it would make the revolution in Germany that a Labour government must surely desire.

Schumacher's aggressiveness was counter-balanced by a familiar failing among the rank and file of the party. Excessive idealism, I said, still lay heavily upon it: 'The speeches by delegates at recent party conferences were as stratospheric as the combined ages of the speakers were astronomical. The elderly leaders will not concern themselves with details of organisation of the local branches and practical politics at which the communists excel.'[18] Conciliatory as Grotewohl was when they met, Schumacher insisted that the SPD in the British Zone would not subordinate itself to the Control Committee in Berlin. I thought then that Grotewohl, who seemed to be standing up to Soviet pressures to amalgamate the SPD with the KPD, was, compared to Schumacher, 'the abler and better man'. I was soon to change my opinion.

The Christian Democratic Union was the most fascinating of the new parties to watch. With remarkable speed its adherents established a network throughout western Germany. The Cardinals, Frings and Galen in the British Zone, and the sinister Faulhaber in Bavaria, were naturally prominent supporters and the faithful, as in Italy, were enjoined to vote CDU. The Church declared that Germans could not be held responsible for Nazism: it was a disease that had infected the population.[19]

The CDU at once came under suspicion of being a bolthole for old nationalists and ex-Nazis. The Americans had sacked Dr Schaeffer, the Oberpräsident of Bavaria, for excessive partiality to former Nazis. Adenauer practised what Schumacher preached. His CDU administration in Cologne excluded all other parties from holding major posts (with the exception of one Social Democrat, responsible for the city's gardens and cemeteries). The strength of the party rested on its predominance in the administration of the Rhineland-Westphalia: fourteen out of eighteen head officials in Münster district were CDU. Adenauer had some rivals for the leadership. In Schleswig-Holstein there was Schlange-Schoenigen, in the Rhineland Holzapfel and in Berlin Andreas Hermes, an anti-Nazi 'with close-cropped hair and a dry unsmiling countenance who had been kept in chains since the July plot, daily expecting execution'. He also had 'the distinction of being described by the *Daily Worker* correspondent in Berlin as one of the most dangerous men in Germany today'.[20] The CDU in Berlin stood well to the left of the party in the British Zone and included two trade unionists, Jakob Kaiser and Ernst Lemmer. The editor of the CDU newspaper, Emil Dovivat, took every opportunity to emphasise the differences between the Soviet Union and the Western powers, and he was attacked unsparingly by the communists who dug up his not entirely spotless past.

There were some other political fledglings. The old Catholic Zentrumpartei revived in Westphalia as a breakaway from the CDU, though Cardinal Frings made it clear that the line of the Catholic Church was to follow the CDU. There was the Lower Saxony Party, that pronounced its loyalty to the House of Hanover and wanted the province to become part of the British Empire. Some parties were strangled at birth, such as the Deutsche Aufbau Party, whose moving spirit was a Reinhold Wulle, a notorious anti-Semite who was banned from political activity in 1946. Major-General Remer's party did not hide its admiration for Hitler, and it too was suppressed. Rather late in the day the Free Democrat Party emerged, supporting free enterprise in industry and a federal constitution for Germany. In 1945 it was more nationalist than liberal, and it won support from those who disliked the Catholic influence in the CDU and the CDU's admirable insistence on the rights of workers and the duties their employers owed to them.

With true Foreign Office courtesy the Secretary of State replied to my memorandum that this comprehensive report had been appreciated and read with great interest. Bevin was no reader, and of course he didn't read it himself. But others did. 'This is certainly an excellent report on the German political parties, much the best we have had yet,' wrote Con O'Neill at the Foreign Office, and other congratulatory minutes followed. 'We cannot,' O'Neill wrote, 'have things both ways. We cannot ourselves retain supreme authority in Germany and wholesale Military Government, and at the same time help German political parties to develop a sense of responsibility.' Why, he went on, did we insist that Germans could not criticise the actions of Military Government and Allied policy? In his covering note to my memorandum Strang pointed out the dilemma facing the British. If they handed over a bankrupt, starving zone to the German politicians, they would be discredited at once and people would sigh for the return of the Nazis. If, on the other hand, we retained full control for years, political parties would become a farce.

German historians of the Occupation often quote my memorandum, but I blush when I read it today. Schumacher's name was misspelt throughout, and my prediction that the SPD was probably the party with the largest support was wrong. Michael Thomas used to tell me that I was backing the wrong horse, and foretold that the CDU would win when elections were held in the West; and within a few months I agreed. The heartland of the SPD lay buried in the Soviet Zone, and the working class in the Ruhr were not solid socialist voters. I used to tell Thomas that my worries lay elsewhere. The CDU did not need encouragement: three of the four Oberpräsidenten in the British Zone belonged to the party. As a British officer I was, however, bound to be more concerned in those early days about the development of the SPD. For it was vital to us that the left in Germany did not fall into communist hands. The KPD did everything they could to discredit Military Government by spreading rumours about the closure of factories which according to them 'could not happen in the Russian Zone';

and in December 1945 they began their campaign to fuse the Communist and Social Democrat parties.

Meanwhile I watched with interest Adenauer's masterly campaign to become the leader of the CDU, first in the British Zone and then in the West. I had met him for a second time when I addressed the German politicians (he received an *order* from Barraclough to attend). His ambition had been hobbled by the ban on his political activity. Hermes and Jakob Kaiser had been permitted by the Russians to go to the West, where they called a meeting at Bad Godesberg to form a national party. Adenauer attended but did not speak. Some months later Hermes was expelled by the Russians from the Soviet Zone for refusing to endorse the policy of land reform. A few days after he arrived in the British Zone the zonal party of the CDU met at Herford to elect a chairman. As a householder in Cologne Hermes was eligible, and he duly turned up at the meeting only to be told by Adenauer, who had taken the chair, that because the British had given permission only to certain named persons to take part, Hermes could not attend. Hermes at once left Herford, and Adenauer was elected chairman of the zonal party. Later he wrote to Hermes to say how astonished he was that Hermes had abandoned his candidature for the leadership.

Adenauer was to display similar guile in 1949 when on 21 August a meeting was held to decide who should lead the CDU/CSU in the three Western zones. He held the meeting in his own home and as host was careful to take the chair. As no one was prepared to move he be voted out of it he was elected chairman of the party in the West. What an old fox he was!

There was another reason why my prime concern was the rebirth of the SPD. Schumacher was wired to the SPD exiles in London led by Erich Ollenhauer; and they in turn were tuned in to the Labour Party. Some of the most articulate Labour Members of Parliament belonged to the left wing of the party and regarded Military Government with suspicion. They were men and women of the thirties who looked with undisguised hostility at the world of 1939 – a world whose leaders were Hitler, Mussolini and a variety of petty kings and dictators in the Balkans, a world (as they saw it) in which the inefficiency of capitalism had produced mass unemployment, a world that had become engulfed in war because the ruling class of every country, including our own, would rather appease Hitler than run the risk of a socialist government. Moreover, the left believed that foreign policy during the war was largely the creation of Churchill and Eden, and that the War Cabinet had played little part – a belief that Churchill himself did nothing to discourage. This was not in fact so: Bevin and Attlee had been involved in Cabinet discussions on foreign affairs. But to the left all was clear: there must be a decisive break with the foreign policy of the wartime coalition. The Foreign Office must be purged, for surely it was self-evident that the Etonians and Oxbridge birds of prey in that reactionary nest must be expelled and in their place cooing socialist doves should nestle. Only then could a true socialist foreign policy be followed. Had not Bevin himself said 'left understands left, but the right does not'?* That was why the Soviet Union should not be over-criticised. The left believed that in 1945 Europe was on the verge of a people's revolution. The reactionary regimes of Eastern Europe had been overthrown by the Red Army. Why then did a Labour government prevent the communist-led resistance in Greece from taking over, and authorise a plebiscite to be held in September 1946 to enable King George II to return? Why did it concern itself with the reactionary London Poles, for whose right to be included in a Polish government Churchill had fought? Why did it slaver over capitalist America and reject Britain's natural ally, Soviet Russia? And at home, why did the government listen to the voice of sound finance in 1947 and rein in the housing programme? Was the Labour movement once again being betrayed by a Labour government?

It was not only the left who wanted to play down differences with the Soviet Union. That had been the policy during and after the war of *The Times* under its editor Barrington-Ward; and its leader writer the historian E.H. Carr, whose *The Twenty Years Crisis*

---

* Bevin made this remark before the war; he was referring to the Popular Front in France, but the comment was seized on by the left and applied to relations with the USSR.

was a scarcely veiled apology for the appeasement of Hitler, and whose *Conditions of Peace* (1942) took the same line towards the Soviet Union.[21]

Meeting Kingsley Martin, the editor of the *New Statesman*, on my return from Germany at the end of 1946, I discovered that he believed that but for the presence of Anglo-American armies all Europe would have been governed by socialist regimes installed by popular acclamation. Left-wing Labour MPs like Dick Crossman and Barbara Castle, as well as fellow-travellers like Konni Zilliacus, peddled this scenario. Some surprising people took the same line. In 1945 Major Denis Healey urged at the Labour Party conference that Labour should dissociate itself from Tory foreign policy and 'assist the socialist revolution wherever it appears'. Labour, he said, should not be 'too pious and self-righteous when occasionally facts are brought to one's notice that our comrades on the Continent are being extremist'. These comrades were right to use their police to punish the 'depraved, dissolute and decadent upper classes'.

In fact, the vision of Labour's left and the fellow-travellers bore no relation to the simple desires of human beings all over Europe. All they wanted was food and shelter and freedom from the secret police and the authorities. It did not take long for Denis Healey to see what was what. In 1947, when Crossman and others published a pamphlet entitled 'Keep Left', Healey replied with 'Cards on the Table', a tough defence of Bevin's foreign policy. He slated the Soviet Union for its propaganda offensive that depicted Britain as a 'decadent reactionary power'.

I was among those young army officers who in 1945 voted Labour. It was not that I did not admire Churchill – for me he was the saviour of our country, magnanimous in victory, a statesman who judged events in relation to the great sweep of history, an incomparable leader who insisted that the military commanders and his ministers should not dally but get business done. Nor was it his eccentricity as a strategist that persuaded me to vote against him. I doubted whether he understood what the country needed after the war. I also thought him so tired that oratory had taken the place of intuition.

That did not mean that I questioned Churchill's new-found disillusionment with the Soviet Union. My years on the Joint

Intelligence Staff had shown me how the Soviets had treated Poland. I had seen how the communist guerrillas in Greece used the arms the British sent them not so much to harass the German army, as to overpower other guerrilla units and eventually to march on Athens and attack British forces. British policy in Germany was right to fear the emergence through a communist coup of a German-Soviet alliance. It was also right to fear that America could quit Europe two years after the Yalta Agreements. Whatever happened among the four powers in the Control Commission, America must not be goaded into isolation. Ernest Bevin pursued this policy with courage, and I admired his resolution. No one can accuse him of fomenting the Cold War. He tried for months to come to an understanding with the Soviet Union about Germany, and was always trying, on tiny as well as big issues, to make the four-power government work.[22] But John Hynd, the Minister of the Control Office for Germany and Austria, was being criticised from all parts of the Labour Party for not having visited Germany; and Geoffrey de Freitas was among those in the centre of the party who urged Bevin to send out a Labour political adviser to the British Zone. The sniping from the left, and in particular the criticism that Military Government was not as ardent as it should have been in de-Nazification, led Bevin to tell Hynd to go to Germany and see what was happening.

I accompanied Hynd on his tour. Bevin had chosen him as a man who would not be taken in by the log-rollers. He was a simple, decent trade unionist who at first gave the impression that the revival of democracy in Germany depended on elections being conducted on the same lines as in the National Union of Railwaymen. The top Military Government officials hardly bothered to conceal their contempt for him. This vexed me because, although Hynd was unimpressive, he was honest and unprejudiced. During the journey I talked to him about the political vacuum in the British Zone and tried to explain the difficulties facing Military Government. The Control Commission in Berlin had hardly had time to dredge a channel through French obstruction, which was preventing clear policy decisions from flowing to Military Government in the British Zone. I told him that whereas the Soviet Union had legalised political parties as early as June 1945, it had taken Military

Government until September to allow them to form in the British Zone, and the regulations were in my opinion unnecessarily cumbersome. In the Russian Zone political parties in the administration were given executive power to carry out de-Nazification and to organise the collection of fuel, welfare and allocation of housing. In our zone these matters were left to allegedly non-political German officials supervised by Military Government, and the political parties were regarded as superfluous nuisances. During his visit Hynd met some SPD leaders who told him how dismayed they were that the Labour Government was neglecting its comrades in Germany. Labour distrusted the CDU. Had not its predecessor, the Zentrumpartei, voted for the Enabling Act which brought Hitler to power?

To take the wind out of the left's sails, Bevin decided to send a sound Labour Party supporter to supervise political development in the British Zone and ensure that the German political parties should bear some of the responsibilities in taking decisions. His emissary was Austen Albu, who came of a well-known Jewish family and who later sat for many years as Labour Member for Edmonton. He was a voluble right-winger and had some experience – rare among Labour politicians – of management in industry. What was more, he knew something of German politics before 1933, and had been friends of the SPD refugees who in exile in London had formed the *Gruppe Neubeginnen*. A new unit, the German Political Branch, was to be formed. Albu would be its head in Berlin, I his deputy in the zone, and he was to be on a level with Steel. (In mid-1946 he became senior to Steel when he was promoted to the ornate rank of President of the Governmental Sub-Commission.) It says much for Albu's good sense and Kit Steel's urbanity – for Steel could be touchy, and regarded Albu's appointment as something of a slur upon his integrity as a diplomat – that they got on as well as they did. Albu summed up Steel as an 'old-fashioned Foreign Office type [who] had no more welcomed the Labour Government and my appointment than most of his colleagues', and when he met me he noted that I 'was one of the few British officials to welcome my appointment'.[23] Yet he and Steel were as one in thinking that there was a political hiatus in Hynd's headquarters in London (the Control Office for Germany and Austria, inevitably known as the hindquarters) that was to blame for the lack of political direction. Steel reported to the Foreign Office, and the Foreign Office had little contact with the Control Office. It did not escape Albu's eye that Montgomery issued policy statements 'of boy scout naïveté' without consulting or even intending to send a copy to Hynd.[24] I liked Albu, a reasonable, sensible, friendly man of warmth, and learnt a lot about the Labour movement from him. Bevin had made an imaginative appointment. I rejoiced that the Germans who met Albu would recognise that a Jew had been sent to help in the resurrection of their country.

So in the New Year I left for Lübbecke to set up the new unit's headquarters there. My task now became to do explicitly what until then I had had time to do only intermittently: namely to contact the emerging political leaders of the new Germany, to put heart into them, and to explain to Military Government how important these men would become.

Almost at once events in Berlin brought me back there. We were changing enemies.

❖

CHAPTER TEN

Fighting on Two Fronts

The events that drew me back to Berlin were the first manoeuvres in Germany by the Soviet Union in the Cold War which were to lead to the creation of West Germany as a state and an ally of those who had formerly been her enemies. The Soviet authorities were determined to amalgamate the German Communist Party with the social democrats. The idea of a united working class party had long been in the air, and had inspired the movement in Europe for a Popular Front before the war. Surveying the ruins of their country, the social democrats and old-guard communists recalled the days when they had torn each other apart in the streets as well as voting against each other in the Reichstag. Both acknowledged that their failure to unite in 1933 had brought Hitler to power. Throughout Germany social democrats discussed with communists the best methods of ensuring working class unity and of completing the destruction of their former enemies. In Hamburg and Frankfurt-am-Main there was much talk in social democrat circles of an *Arbeiterpartei* (Workers' Party) to replace the two parties. In Berlin, too, the social democrats took the lead in attempting to form a united workers' party. No doubt they hoped to gain for themselves the special favours which they judged the Russians would give the communists; but they were also encouraged by a declaration of the central committee of the KPD on 12 June, two days after Marshal Zhukov had permitted the formation of political parties in the Russian Zone. This stated that the KPD believed that it was wrong to impose the Soviet system forcibly upon Germany. The SPD took this as a sign that the KPD had abandoned the theory of the dictatorship of the proletariat and had undergone a lasting change of heart; and many socialists were to cling for long to this belief. On 15 June the SPD stated that it wanted to organise the German

workers into a single body, regarding this as a form of moral reparation for the political faults of the past, and four days later a meeting
took place between the leaders of the two parties. But the communist leaders, Pieck, Ulbricht and Wilhelm Ackermann, turned down
the social democrat proposals as firmly as they had ignored previous
approaches. They stated that amalgamation of the two parties was
premature. Before this could happen, a considerable period of collaboration must take place, 'involving joint discussions to elicit ideo-
logical questions'; otherwise, they declared, new rifts would open
and drive the parties further apart.

The SPD and the KPD in the Soviet Zone now began to build
up their party organisations on parallel lines. From the first the
KPD enjoyed enormous advantages; its press by the end of the year
had a circulation of some four million, while the SPD was only
granted sufficient newsprint by the Russians for a circulation of
one million. Paper for posters, party literature, etc. was allotted in
the same proportion. Moreover, the Russians appointed members
of the KPD to the majority of the leading administrative posts
throughout the Russian Zone, particularly in medium-sized and
small communities. Since many of these new officials proved to
be either incompetent or corrupt, the Russians found themselves
compelled to make continual changes, which hampered the efficient
working of the administration, and when provincial administrations
were set up they had no option but to call upon SPD members to
fill the leading positions. Indeed the Presidents of Brandenburg,
Mecklenburg-Vorpommern and Saxony were all social democrats.

Despite the disparity of treatment, the two parties continued
to co-operate, but it was soon acknowledged, even by the KPD
themselves, that the SPD was by far the stronger party. As its
membership increased and its relationship with the Russians
remained harmonious, the SPD regained its self-confidence. While
co-operation with the communists was still genuinely desired, little
further talk of amalgamation of the two parties was heard, and,
indeed, speeches by Pieck demanding equal representation of SPD
and KPD on workers' councils were greeted with robust laughter.
In the minds of all observers in Berlin in the autumn of 1945 there
was little doubt that the social democrats had the mass support of
the population, and that the KPD were regarded with suspicion as

the puppet of the much-feared occupying power, and as a party which harboured corrupt civil servants.

Then the first cloud appeared on the horizon. In September a communist leader delivered a speech that the sophisticated SPD intellectuals regarded as vulgar Marxism, and Grotewohl replied with a constructive speech about future policy. The Russians refused to allow Grotewohl's speech to be printed, and the Soviet liaison officer with the SPD – a graduate of the theological academy of the Orthodox Church in Moscow – said, smiling, 'Herr Grotewohl knows how to paint lovely pictures, but knows nothing of politics.'[1]

Throughout the autumn of 1945 the Soviets were content to use methods of peaceful penetration to achieve their ends in Berlin and the Russian Zone. The decisive anti-communist vote in the Hungarian and Austrian elections startled them. They realised for the first time the extent to which the USSR was feared, indeed hated, and saw that the Communist Party would be decisively defeated in free and fair elections even in countries which they had occupied. They accordingly decided to forestall any such eventuality in Germany. First they chastened the bourgeois parties: they called upon the leaders of the Christian Democrat Union to resign since their newspaper had criticised the method of enforcing land reform; got rid of the ineffective leader of the Liberal Democrat Party; and instructed the KPD leaders to press for a conference to discuss 'the strengthening of joint activities' between the SPD and KPD. On the day that the Christian Democrat leaders, Hermes and Schreiber, who had refused to resign, were peremptorily expelled by Marshal Zhukov, the Social Democrat central committee sat down to face the communist demands at a conference which was attended by two representatives of Russian Military Government in civilian clothes with their stenographer.

At first cautiously, and then relentlessly, the communists turned the screw in the Soviet Zone upon the SPD. All SPD meetings had to be held jointly with the KPD. Works Committees were convened to pass resolutions in favour of immediate amalgamation. Russian military commanders nominated pro-fusion members to run the local SPD party organisation. In Thuringia the local chairman, Dr Brill, was forced to resign and his place was taken by a Russian nominee, Hoffmann. In Mecklenburg a crowded SPD meeting passed a resolution in favour of an all-German referendum to decide the question; the party newspaper was forced to publish an article written by a communist which referred to all members of the SPD who supported the resolution as 'reactionaries' and 'saboteurs of unity'. The editor of *Das Volk*, who through an oversight of the Russian censorship had been able to publish a report of the meeting, was hauled over the coals by the Russian military authorities.

Before the SPD leadership sat down with the KPD they held a preliminary meeting on 19 December at which they decided to oppose fusion of the two parties in any one zone, and agreed that only a vote of the party in all zones could ratify the proposal. Meanwhile the KPD pressed for a joint list of candidates in elections and for amalgamation of local parties. In the conference on 20 and 21 December the SPD were harassed when they accused the KPD of oppression. Gustav Klingelhöfer quoted the case of an SPD member who had been kidnapped, shot in the neck and left for dead; Pieck heckled him. A joint declaration was passed: the two parties would prepare a programme for a united workers' party, but no mention was made of joint electoral lists or the amalgamation of local party organisations.

The SPD imagined that they had won a victory. Inheriting that fatal legalistic attitude towards political problems with which the party was cursed during the period of the Weimar Republic, the SPD leaders believed that their resolutions and speeches had solved their difficulties. But their defences had been breached. They had acknowledged before the occupying power their desire for the union of the two parties. *Das Volk* headlined the conference as 'the second step to the creation of a single Workers' Party'. From then on it remained only a question of time; and both the Russian military authorities and the communists immediately posed the question: 'Eventually – why not now?' The pressure mounted. SPD newspapers were censored. The Soviet military authorities refused to allow the decisions of the December conference to be circulated. Party secretaries who opposed immediate fusion were removed, or arrested, or found themselves in the Sachsenhausen and Oranienburg concentration camps where anti-Nazis had been imprisoned. All former local agreements with the KPD were cancelled. Every speech was taken down in shorthand and forwarded to General Kotikov of the KGB. SPD bookshops were ransacked for fascist literature.

When elections of trade union officials were held, SPD majorities were often overwhelming: in Saxony 174 SPD to 17 KPD; in Magdeburg 996 SPD to 112 KPD (the local Soviet commandant ordered the committee to consist of 113 KPD and 112 SPD); in Dresden ballot papers were forged. But in Berlin the communists scored a real victory, and the SPD, resting on their oars, were outwitted. Meetings were convened by communists at short notice, social democrat members were excluded and votes taken in their absence. Kaiser of the CDU thought the SPD were mainly to blame for the debacle. British civil servants in the Manpower Division (responsible for trade unions) ignored the elections; and some Foreign Office officials concluded that the SPD were too feeble to fight. Steel was asked by his Soviet colleague whether he thought the election had been fairly conducted, and had to admit he had no evidence to the contrary. 'M. Sobolev wore his most benign and casual smile.'[2]

The SPD leaders in the Soviet Zone and in Berlin realised they were up against it. Each solved the struggle of conscience in his own way. Max Fechner, the only surviving member of the 1933 SPD central committee, took to the bottle; as a reward the Soviet authorities provided paper for him to publish a book which, I judged, 'in these days of book shortage should set him up financially for the remaining years of his life'.[3] On the other hand Gustav Dahrendorf, one of the earliest supporters of the fusion of the two parties, was outraged. Until December he still hoped that the Russians might favour the SPD when they saw how few voters would support the communists. Now he declared that the methods the KPD employed made amalgamation impossible. He regretted that no radical measures such as land reform and the nationalisation of heavy industry had taken place in the West, but a visit there made him believe that 'the relatively open-minded attitude of the British' was more likely to get the economy going again than the reforms in the Soviet Zone.[4] But Dahrendorf had not always been so appreciative of British policy, and Steel fumed that he shot 'stinging darts' at him and was 'impertinent'.[5] But Austen Albu was impressed. So was I – and also by Dahrendorf's son Ralf, who had been apprehended by the Russians after saying at a youth conference that things were little better than under the Nazis.[6]*

Most unhappy of all was Otto Grotewohl, chairman of the party's central committee. A fine speaker, a charmer, adept at reconciling differences between members of a committee, perhaps almost too fluent and supple in argument, he was first and foremost a political boss. When Hermes was expelled, he feared he would be the next to go; and when Kaiser asked him what, after all, he was up to in the December conference, he remarked, '*Ich spiele ein grozes Spiel*' ('I'm gambling against heavy odds').[7] In December he told Steel he would dissolve the party rather than let it lose its independence; and on another occasion when he and Dahrendorf dined with Steel he told him of the pressure the Soviets exerted, and welcomed the idea of an independent SPD newspaper in Berlin. We learnt how Colonel Tulpyanov of the Russian Information Services Control had summoned Grotewohl to a series of conferences, at which he would be kept waiting for two hours and then alternately cajoled and flattered. Tulpyanov made no secret of the alternative that lay before Grotewohl; he had to choose between East and West. (These quite openly anti-Allied conversations took place at a time when German politicians like Schumacher were being rebuked by the British authorities for implied anti-Russian statements in their speeches.) Ambassador Simenov put forward a more diplomatic argument when he hinted that fusion might dispose Russia considerably to reduce her forces of occupation. At the beginning of February 1946 Marshal Zhukov himself saw Grotewohl. No Allied officer or German from a Western zone was allowed to enter the Soviet Zone, but Zhukov mendaciously told Grotewohl that since all Russian efforts to abolish zonal frontiers had failed, an all-German conference on amalgamation was impossible. There must be a speedy decision, and he hinted that if the decision were favourable, Russia would increase food supplies and aid the economic

* Ralf Dahrendorf subsequently went to Wilton Park, which enormously impressed him. After taking his doctorate in Germany, he entered the London School of Economics and became a formidable professor of sociology in America and Germany, returning to the LSE as its Director. As Lord Dahrendorf he later became Warden of St Antony's College, Oxford.

revival of Eastern Germany. Grotewohl set out on a tour of the Russian Zone. On his return he described to Steel and Albu what it was like to be tickled by Russian bayonets. The SPD provincial organisations were crumbling beneath the Russian and communist pressure; men who a fortnight before had been assuring him of their loyalty to an independent party were now begging him to get the business over so that they could be left in peace. He spoke, before Churchill's famous Fulton speech, of an 'iron curtain' descending in Europe.[8] Could we not remove the zonal frontiers? When we told him this did not lie in our power alone, he took the fatal plunge.

What, meanwhile, were the British doing? The picture that emerges from the two massive volumes, totalling 1370 pages, of Harold Hurwitz's *Demokratie und AntiKommunismus in Berlin nach 1945* is a study in chiaroscuro. There was no single policy. Different members of the Political Division and of the Foreign Office, and different members of the Parliamentary Labour Party, sought to impose their views. The *official* policy of His Majesty's Government was to abide by the Potsdam Agreements and work for four-power government of Germany – even if the French by their veto were making that impossible. This explains why for Strang the SPD posed 'a very awkward problem', which could become 'a serious bone of contention between the Allies'. The line I took, while not opposed to the official policy, assumed that we must not let the SPD in Berlin be overwhelmed or allow it to split. On 7 January I wrote to Steel that we should build up Schumacher in the British Zone, hint that he was our choice as leader of the party, but warn him that he could destroy it if he attacked the Berlin social democrats. By now I regarded Grotewohl as being on the run, but 'I do not think Grotewohl will resign the leadership of the party in order to keep in with us.' Could I, replied Steel, proceed 'tactfully, confidentially' to persuade Schumacher not to disown his comrades in Berlin – but not at the cost of accepting fusion?[9]

As Schumacher was determined to thwart Grotewohl's ambition to lead the national party, this was not all that easy. When

Grotewohl and Dahrendorf attended an SPD conference in Bruns-wick in early February, they had to admit that the KPD were doing their best by every action to show they were not sincere demo-crats.[10] I pleaded with Steel not to agree to any proposal to hold elections for all four zones simultaneously: the Russians would pro-crastinate and prevent us from holding elections in our zone for lack of quadripartite agreement.[11] On the day Albu arrived to take up his post, he dined at Steel's house with Grotewohl and Dahren-dorf. It was a dispiriting evening. Steel said he was 'at a loss to suggest how to help'. He suggested publicity in the British press, Albu offered a Labour Party statement. Grotewohl thought both would be unhelpful. Later when Kaiser, the CDU trade unionist, asked Steel whether he realised we were being squeezed out of Berlin, Steel replied that 'concrete measures were not easy to think of ... sympathy for Germans in England was not a very vigorous growth'. Ivor Pink, a career diplomat and by no means the most intellectually gifted in the Political Division, began to canvass sites for a new capital city – prophetically he picked on Bonn.[12]

The Foreign Office was equally despondent. It had been shaken by the news from the Soviet Zone, and reckoned the West had suffered a major defeat. Oliver Harvey, an influential figure there, wanted to conciliate the Soviet Union. Opposed to him was Con O'Neill, but at this juncture even he considered we should cut our losses in Berlin, build up the economy of our own zone and acknowledge Schumacher as leader of the SPD: 'The most depress-ing thing about these developments is that they already oblige us nine months after Germany's defeat to consider, in common pru-dence, Germany as a potential factor in power politics.' Bernard Burrows gave a typical 'balanced' diplomatic assessment. He hoped we had not yet got to the point of competing for German favours. He despaired of the American State Department: the number two on the German and Austrian Desk imagined that a fused party was no danger since the SPD would come out on top. Burrows added drily: 'I suggested that this was contrary to our experience in other places.'[13]

As I shuttled between the British Zone and Berlin, I became exasperated. If the SPD and the KPD fused and elections were held in Berlin, the Western Allies would function in a city run by a communist administration and a communist police force. Such a defeat for the West might increase the chance of a similar fused party forming in the Western zones; and even if the SPD remained independent under Schumacher, the party in the West might split. On 17 February I sent a memorandum to Steel. It was clear, I said, that it was war to the knife between East and West in Berlin. Tulpyanov lost no opportunity to point out that Berliners had a choice, and that they must choose the East. Why could we not come out in the open with a British-owned equivalent to the *Tagesspiegel*, the newspaper the French had licensed in Berlin, and start a press campaign? The Russian-controlled German press did not hesitate to vilify us. I admitted that the Foreign Office was following Steel's line that we must avoid 'a slanging match'; but had not the Foreign Secretary himself suggested on 16 January that we had been wrong to play it down when the CDU leaders were sacked? Schumacher asked us to sanction the formation of an independent branch of the SPD in our sector in Berlin. Why not? At all events we must license our own SPD newspaper, and see that it got into the right hands.[14]

I soon found that I had an ally – my new chief Austen Albu, who was head of the newly formed German Political Branch. He made contact with one of the editors of the *Tagesspiegel*, Karl Peter Schultz, and with Karl Germer, a member of the SPD central committee, both of whom were opponents of fusion. To help them were two sprightly young officers from the Berlin Intelligence section, David Royce and David Lancashire, whom Albu recruited. He and they proceeded to instruct the SPD in the, to them mysterious, technique (as Steel put it) of forming a breakaway party. These young officers, Steel added with genial cynicism, would soon be demobilised and could be disowned if things went wrong. The plan was to call for a referendum of all SPD members in Berlin, and put to them the simple question: are you for or against amalgamation of the party with the KPD? To avoid the charge of being reactionary, voters were also to be asked whether they favoured co-operation between the two parties.

The communist steamroller began to move. On 11 February Grotewohl proposed at the SPD central committee that a Zonal Congress including Berlin should 'enter into talks' aimed at fusing the two parties. Gustav Dahrendorf at once realised that if the motion was carried, fusion on communist terms was inevitable. He moved that it should be rejected, and won by nine votes to seven. At this point Grotewohl declared that the Russians would dissolve the central committee and appoint a new one unless the vote was declared invalid. When Dahrendorf returned to his flat in the American sector he found a summons to report to Soviet head-quarters. He at once asked the Americans for protection – which they were ready enough to provide, since they were smarting at the recent abduction in a Jeep of an Austrian politician from their sector in Vienna. Dahrendorf was not being alarmist. Between 1945 and 1960, 247 people were kidnapped – all of them for political reasons. I therefore arranged for him and his son Ralf to be flown next morning to Hanover and to be driven to see me in Lübbecke. We sat and chatted about events until the arrival of the car that I had ordered to take them to Hamburg, which Gustav Dahrendorf had represented in the Reichstag before 1933.

The day after the meeting of the SPD central committee the Russians rewarded Grotewohl by sending him six new cars and twenty food parcels from Marshal Zhukov, for distribution among 'the needy' of the party. But the rank and file of the SPD refused to be raped. They called for a referendum, and on 17 February numbers of local SPD meetings passed votes of no confidence in the central committee. Pieck declared that a referendum was undemocratic, since newly joined members could not decide an issue on which they were 'uninformed'. Realising that things were not going according to plan, the Russians sent 400 gallons of petrol and forty tons of newsprint: by mid-March Berlin was plastered with posters appealing for fusion – *'Ein Ziel, Ein Weg, Einheit'* ('One goal, one way, unity').

Austen Albu was roused. He asked me to persuade Schumacher to fly to Berlin and reinvigorate the local party. I had been trying to get Schumacher to do this for over a month, and he at last agreed on condition he might bring a bodyguard and sleep in a safe house. As so often in those days of permits and authorisations, the arrangements for the bodyguard went wrong, but a day late the two arrived and stayed for six days. His presence put new heart into the social democrats. Whereas Berliners had assumed the Western Allies would soon leave the city, they now took this as a sign that they would stay. Gustav Klingelhöfer of the SPD central committee formed an anti-fusion group with Kurt Schmidt and Arno Scholz and they howled down Grotewohl at a meeting on 1 March where 950 votes were cast against fusion and only fifty for it. They did not take to Schumacher. They found him too rigid, but in the unnumbered proposals and counter-proposals that were floated, Schumacher ensured that the SPD in the British sector must remain part of the zonal party and not go off on its own. He dined with Strang, and Albu, who thought him 'shrewd, sardonic, forceful . . . somewhat sobered by recent talks with Noel Annan', told him what was and was not possible under a Labour government.[15]

Albu next flew to London to obtain a public statement by the Government against fusion. Hynd would not agree: too many Labour MPs were still living in 1933, he judged, and favoured a united workers' party. The division of opinion in the Foreign Office now became even clearer. On the one side were the defeatists: Oliver Harvey wrote off the SPD as 'spineless – effect of last twelve years': a young diplomat, Andrew Franklin, minuted that their courage would probably ebb when it came to 'calling the card'; we should not risk making premature engagements 'likely to end in a dismal defeat'. On the other side was Con O'Neill: 'I don't agree we should give up Berlin without a battle.' Complete capitulation, he felt, would be a disaster. Somewhere in the middle stood Troutbeck and Strang, as usual proposing that we should wait and see.[16]

On 5 March Churchill spoke at Fulton. He electrified the young Turks, such as myself, as his speech justified what we had been saying. It also astounded Robert Murphy, General Clay's political adviser. As long ago as December I had been in touch with a dynamic and engaging American officer, Brewster Morris, who was such a hard-line anti-communist that Ivor Pink thought I, who was always willing to sit down with the zonal communist leader Max Reimann over coffee, might be shocked by him. But the Americans were even more divided than we were. Although in 1948 General Clay was to become the hero of the airlift when the Russians blockaded Berlin, he was in no mood in those days to play ball with the British. Steel told Albu that 'all agree Clay is a bastard', and that the Americans who had fought with us were all going home and their replacements none too pro-British. Strang thought the younger Americans were willing to help us, but were hampered by Clay's dislike of a gang-up against the Russians.[17] Strang was right. Robert Murphy, Clay's political adviser, at last gave Brewster Morris and Louis Wiesner their head, and they shot into action. In March Steel was to tell the Foreign Office how enthusiastic they were, and that 'they have set a good deal hotter pace than we have'. Morris got a press campaign going in the *Tagesspiegel* and sufficient newsprint for a million leaflets. When Ulbricht attacked the German administration in the British Zone, I found myself writing an article putting him in the pillory. I discovered that in 1940 *Die Welt*, a German communist newspaper edited in Stockholm, had published a piece of his praising the Nazi-Soviet pact. It gave the lie to his claim that he had always been opposed to Hitler. Louis Wiesner, the American trade union adviser, plastered the *Tagesspiegel* with stories of communist oppression in the Soviet Zone, even though General Clay had opposed such publicity. Wiesner went further. He charged the Soviet military administration with kidnapping and illegal arrest, and proposed protesting to Marshal Zhukov. Clay ignored him, but when Ulbricht denounced recent elections in the American Zone as undemocratic and rigged, even Clay was at last moved to act. On 25 March he stated that the SPD/KPD merger would be recognised 'only if demanded by party members rather than by a small group of party leaders'.[18]

The Foreign Office was still preaching caution. No point in protests to Zhukov – leave things to natural anti-Russian feelings – premature to take action now that Ulbricht has 'camouflaged' his attacks on the British – only if they became more outspoken would it be 'unwise to ignore them'. Andrew Franklin was gloomy, believing that Germany was lost to the West, and we would be lucky if we could extricate the Ruhr from the debacle. O'Neill said things were not as bad as that. Returning from leave on 16 March, Steel thought the situation had not improved: the SPD still expected us to perform a miracle. But when Patrick Gordon Walker, a minister in the Foreign Office, came to Berlin a week later he urged Steel and Albu to make even greater efforts to provide paper, telephones, cars – why not a hall for meetings? (This suggestion was abandoned when David Royce told him that the Russians would organise riots and the police would not intervene.[19]) Quite a number of the journalists in Berlin thought we were bound to lose and were satirical about my appearances with Schumacher. But as both sides poured food and drink into the mouths of the astonished SPD delegates, morale rose. The spectacle reminded me of a Hogarth print of election time in eighteenth-century England. On 26 March Steel thought the prospects of defeating fusion 'without any blatant intervention by ourselves were good'.[20]

Then came the most encouraging sign of all. General Sokolowski, the Russian chief of the Kommendatura, called on General Robertson. Speaking 'at great length and with much seriousness', he deplored the state of tension in Berlin, and acknowledged that the Soviets felt 'a natural affinity' between themselves and the Communist Party. The British Labour Government, he said, would feel the same affinity towards social democrats. Unfortunately the Germans were exploiting our differences: we should not let them stir up bad feeling between the Allies. Sokolowski gave his word that the Soviet administration would do nothing to promote the KPD/SPD merger. Robertson considered that the Russians had at last become disturbed, and had realised that their tactics might destroy four-power agreement. He believed Sokolowski 'genuinely wants to see co-operation between at least three of the four powers', although 'perhaps I allow myself to be taken in by my liking for General Sokolowski'.[21] Steel thought Sokolowski's *démarche* indicated how successful our support for the SPD anti-fusionists had been in shaking 'the Russian hegemony in Berlin to an inordinate extent. I sincerely trust we are not going to disinterest ourselves in Berlin politics. To do so would be a long step towards abdicating our vital politico-strategic position in Berlin.'[22]

I was delighted to see the line Steel was now taking. Then, and for some time afterwards, I felt that he had been too hesitant and at times pusillanimous; but he and Strang found themselves in an ambiguous position. Diplomats are trained to negotiate, not to direct affairs. They are also responsible for carrying out the policy of the Foreign Secretary; and though they could be certain that Bevin would not chide them for standing up to German communists, they remembered that he did not want to be blamed by his own party, or indeed by the Americans, for disrupting quadripartite government. But he never asked me to alter my line, and I now see him as a Daedalus anxious to lay a fatherly hand upon young Icarus and stop him flying too near the sun.

A few days before the referendum was due to take place the phone rang in my Berlin office. Austen Albu, who was at Lübbecke waiting to fly to London, had just heard on the BBC that a group of Labour MPs had sent a telegram to Grotewohl supporting the KPD/SPD fusion. These were the left-wing group – satirised as the Nenni-goats – who had previously sent a telegram of congratulation to the Italian socialist Pietro Nenni when he allied himself to the Communist Party. Albu told me to call a press conference at once and explain that these MPs were a tiny fraction of the Parliamentary Labour Party. This I did. When Albu arrived in London, he went at once to Westminster and a large number of Labour MPs signed a letter of support to the anti-fusionist SPD wing.[23]

At last on 31 March, a brilliant, warm spring day, the referendum took place. The electorate could read in the new British licensed newspaper, *Der Berliner*, an article by Albu simply urging them to vote. No polling stations were allowed to open in the Russian sector of Berlin. In the Western sectors 82.6 per cent voted against fusion, of a turnout of 71.8 per cent. Sixty-two per cent voted to continue co-operation between the two parties.[24]

The defeat of the communists' fusion campaign opened eyes in Whitehall. Arthur Street, Hynd's Permanent Secretary, saw at once that it was the prelude to the division of Germany. Bevin was apprehensive that if Germany were divided, the Americans might suddenly decide to pull out, and we would be left facing a communist central government. But Brewster Morris noted that until now the Russians had regarded the Berlin parties as merely part of the Russian zonal parties, and he and Wiesner understood that the British were changing their policy. Albu told him in effect that we had written off the Soviet Zone and 'will now build a high wall against the penetration of Soviet influence into West Germany'.[25] (It was, of course, not us but the communists who years later were to build just such a high wall.) Both Schumacher and Kaiser were appalled that this might be so. Where was the SPD majority to rule Germany to come from if the Eastern Zone were lost? Where was Kaiser to find the counterweight to black reactionary Bavaria? I used to tell them that we were not in principle against a united Germany, and would not surrender our position in Berlin, but Austria had shown that quadripartite government was cumbersome.

On 16 April I wrote a despatch on these stirring events.[26] In the last three paragraphs I urged that the government ought to bear in mind that the Russians were ahead in the propaganda battle to convince the German manual workers who their true friends were. The ability of the SPD to continue to draw votes away from the KPD, I argued, depended in part on the political and economic policy that the British adopted. I suggested that some of the reforms the Government was implementing in Britain should be applied in the British Zone. Why not set up regional production committees of employers and trade unionists, and joint production committees in factories? Was not land reform a card we could play to reward small farmers?

I look back on these proposals today with some embarrassment. Did land reform in Hanover and Westphalia really make any sense? But to my surprise, when I consulted the archives I found that Strang thought these suggestions, as he put it, 'carried considerable weight'; though he was wise enough to add that the time to consider such ideas was when it had been settled whether Germany could be ruled from the centre or by zones. My naive suggestions were prompted by a matter that has troubled me all my life. Why have we in Britain been so unable to improve industrial relations between management and workers? Already in Germany Hans Böckler's name was appearing in telegrams I sent to Steel and the Foreign Office. Under British guidance he invented a trade union structure that was to underpin the economic recovery of Germany. In their different ways the defeated powers, Germany and Japan, established harmonious industrial relations in which the workforce was brought into consultation with management and agreed upon the division of the profits that harmony produced. Years later I tried to treat the trade unions in my university as partners – without much success. The militancy of trade unions and the consequent obduracy of management ruined British industry and brought upon the unions the retribution of Margaret Thatcher's legislation and the end of full employment. It is a chapter in our history that I regard with aching sadness.

I returned to the British Zone to find that another matter which had never been easy to handle had got worse. This was the problem of de-Nazification, and its roots lay deep in the past.

The British and Americans differed on one profound problem upon which many theologians and political philosophers have pronounced. What is to be done to the wicked? The difference persisted long after the war, and in the 1990s Germans were again to face the problem – only then the wicked were not the Nazis but the communist secret police, the Stasi and their accomplices, in what for forty-five years had been East Germany. All through 1944 the British had been at loggerheads with the Americans about punishing the Nazis. Churchill's instinct was to execute the leaders and war criminals out of hand as speedily as possible. The Americans wanted a trial; they wanted to see the rule of law upheld, whether or not the accused recognised it. But how many were to be judged guilty? The Secretaries of the Treasury and of War were at loggerheads. Henry Morgenthau thought that every German who had furthered the war policy should be dispossessed. Henry Stimson said the objective – war crimes apart – was to obtain peace in the future, not punishment for its own sake. When the British tried to discover what precisely the Americans wanted they encountered the usual fog in Roosevelt's Washington. Each agency and department went its own way, hoping the boss would in the end come down on its side. The British Ambassador, Lord Halifax, compared American administration to a disorderly day's rabbit shooting: nothing comes out where you expect – and then suddenly something emerges at the far end of the field.

When Roosevelt died in April 1945 Morgenthau lost his protector and resigned. Stimson won the day. The Washington pashas regarded this as a victory for justice. Now there would be no lynch law. Wily defendants like Papen or Schacht might wriggle free, but at least many innocent people would not be the victims of crude revenge. The Nuremberg Tribunal required that to be proved guilty an individual had to know that the organisation which he joined was engaged in criminal activities, and this meant that thousands of hard-core Nazis would escape. But the Americans argued that trials would forever pin the responsibility for the war upon Hitler and provide an unforgettable record of Nazi infamy; and that was the more important issue.

The Americans were also intent on de-Nazification. Early on they were rocked by General Patton's gaffe when he said that he could not see much difference between a Nazi and a Democrat south of the Mason-Dixon line. They therefore conducted a mammoth purge to placate opinion at home. They were the only power which did not have to count the cost of their occupation: they had a seemingly inexhaustible supply of lawyers, officers and civilians who were willing to serve in Germany and cope with the enormous amount of paperwork involved in investigating whether those who were selected to occupy key positions in the German administration and economy had Nazi antecedents.

For the Russians de-Nazification was a straight political operation. German scientists and technical experts of all kinds were whisked to Moscow to work in relative luxury on rocketry and other matters. Some Nazis were liquidated or condemned to forced labour. Others – usually the little tyrants in the locality – were reinstated after a token disgrace: brown became red overnight. The Soviets used de-Nazification as a propaganda weapon to discredit the Western Allies whose zones were open to diplomats and journalists, whereas theirs was sealed. They suspected that the Western powers were plotting to revive Germany as an anti-Soviet force under German militarists who would claim to be the inheritors of the heroes of the 20 July plot. They therefore declared that the only heroes of the resistance were the communist working class. Their contention that democracy was synonymous with de-Nazification cut little ice with the Allies. The Nazis had destroyed multi-party government, and the Soviet Union's version of democracy similarly tolerated only one party.

The British could never make up their minds what they wanted. As late as 1945 Eden held out against show trials, but in the end had to give way. But as each SHAEF directive widened the grounds for removal of Germans from office and whittled away the grounds for discretion, Whitehall grew ever more anxious.

Die-hard Nazis, of course, should be removed and, if guilty of crimes, put on trial. But what about token Nazis? Were they to be removed but rehabilitated as soon as possible? Potsdam spoke of removing militarists. Did that mean excluding all former members of the German General Staff, some at least of whom had been anti-Nazi? Or was our policy even grander: to remove anyone with authoritarian traits – one of the reasons, it will be remembered, given for removing Adenauer and later the able Oberpräsident of the Rhine province Dr Lehr?

On these matters a chasm yawned between the political parties and their adherents in the Control Commission. Conservatives suspected that the governing classes would be lumped together with the Nazis; and later Churchill, in company with much-decorated British officers, was to subscribe to the defence costs of Field Marshal von Manstein and other generals whom they considered unjustly accused of war crimes. Labour, on the other hand, were delighted to see militarists as well as Nazis proscribed. But the left overreached themselves. Maddened by fellow-travellers such as Konni Zilliacus sniping at British negligence in de-Nazifying, Bevin became convinced that root and branch de-Nazification was yet another weapon in the Soviet arsenal to destroy the German economy, alienate the Germans and, if possible, persuade them that a better deal awaited them on the other side of the Elbe.

Whitehall was sceptical from the start. Old-school civil servants like Frederick Bovenschen, Permanent Secretary at the War Office, were obstructive: to him trials without precedent in Common Law were untidy. Meanwhile the deliberations of the Allied Control Council ground on; and on 12 January 1946 they published a directive designating ninety-eight groups of people who were to be removed and excluded from office. A further twenty-two groups, such as regular army officers and 'persons who represent the Prussian Junker tradition', could be removed on discretion. At this that independent-minded Foreign Office official Con O'Neill exploded: 'As an example of systematic and meticulous imbecility [this directive] would be hard to beat.'[27] The Treasury realised that if middling officials, police officers, bank managers, magistrates and the like were expelled, they would have to be replaced by British officials, and the British taxpayer would foot the bill. If they were not replaced, life in the British Zone would become nasty, brutish and short. Jackson, the chief American prosecutor at Nuremberg, was among those American officials who recognised that public opinion in a democracy can change with astonishing speed. The very people who demanded that the pips should squeak would be among the first to protest if there was mass starvation in Germany. There was never the faintest chance that the British and American people would endorse a policy of repaying barbarity with barbarity and giving the Germans a dose of Nazi medicine. They would not have been willing to starve millions to death, or use them as slave labour, still less pay for Germans to live in limitless idleness. As rationing in Britain grew more severe with every year of peace, it was elementary self-interest to restore the German economy to a state where it would no longer be a burden on Britain.

The German Political Branch became a punching bag. It was battered by zealots in Britain who had discovered yet another Nazi skulking under the protection of Military Government, and by officers in the zone enraged when I told them that their German officials, who claimed to be only nominal Nazis, had to be ousted under the Control Commission directives. Unless the fellow could be proved guilty of a crime, was he to be fired just for having joined the Nazi Party? Had he not in fact been obliged to do so if he was to retain his post? These were the arguments put to me time and again, and I was not best liked when I said they were unacceptable. In industry the process was ludicrous. In the Volkswagen factory, where cars were being produced almost entirely for the British, 179 employees and key executives were dismissed in June 1946; by February 1947, 138 of them had been reinstated on appeal.[28] Numbers of ardent Nazis learnt that their best chance was to lie low, to be employed as a clerk, and wait for the heat to die down. Soon Germans began complaining that the little men were being punished and the big fish had escaped the net. On the other hand I used to argue that it was precisely the petty fanatics, the *Blockleiter*, for example, who had made life hideous for the residents of a block of flats, who should now suffer as much as the *Bonzen* (big shots) already in prison.[29]

My experience of the long struggle it took to get rid of such an undeniable Nazi as the first Oberpräsident of Schleswig-Holstein province convinced me that the emerging German politicians who knew their former tyrants should be given the job of identifying them.[30] This view was to prevail. General Robertson endorsed the findings of a working party and set up German de-Nazification panels. Then the bureaucrats got to work. Appeals against the decisions of the panels could be heard by a German appeal body. Next Robertson ruled that the British had different aims from the Germans: we were concerned with security, they with justice and retribution.[31] So the findings of these two bodies could be reviewed and countermanded on grounds of security by a British court. The procedures to be followed were Byzantine. Every German under investigation had to fill in a questionnaire containing 130 questions, the fabulous 'Fragebogen'. Five categories of Nazis were decreed: from major and dedicated members to mere followers. The controversies between Whitehall, the different divisions within the Control Commission and the Military Government created an impassable swamp of directives, amendments, amplifications and explanations. By June 1946, 66,000 Germans had been arrested: by July 24,000 of them had been cleared and 42,000 were still in prison. Some 500 were put on trial. Towards the end of 1947 over two million Fragebogen had been evaluated, and nearly 350,000 Germans excluded from office.

This policy, if policy it can be called, fell between every stool. The British were determined to be fair. But a political purge can never be fair, nor is it susceptible to courts and appeals against sentence. Ernst von Salomon, a renowned reactionary of post-1918 Freikorps days, wrote a deadly book on his experience, entitled Der Fragebogen, exposing the absurdities of the questionnaire. So far from praising our sense of justice, the Germans became increasingly bitter about the confusions and absurdities of the British procedures. In the last despatch I wrote to the Foreign Office in 1946, I concluded that from being the least unpopular of the occupying powers, the British were now beginning to be hated and despised.

Nothing better illustrates the division of opinion over de-Nazification than the case of Hermann Abs. Years later Tom Bower, a trenchant critic of British policy, considered the employment of Abs by the British as particularly outrageous.[32] Abs was never a Nazi: as a Catholic he refused to join the party. But he had been head of the Deutsche Bank, which took over the assets of Jewish banks and of the Austrian Creditanstalt. During the war that bank financed huge industrial concerns which operated with slave labour. Abs saw to it that the bank's assets and records ended up in the British and not the Russian Zone, and Paul Chambers, the head of the British Finance Division, was determined to employ him to get the economy working again. The Americans, however, were determined to oust him, and in the end they succeeded and put him on trial. Prosecuted by American lawyers on charges of breaching laws which the Americans themselves had framed, Abs was acquitted. To Bower the case was evidence of the complicity of the British in letting the big fish escape. To Sigmund Warburg, head of the London bank, the British were right to employ Abs. Ah, a fellow banker would say that, wouldn't he? But then, Warburg was a Jew.

Bower had a stronger case in his allegations about the failure to trace and bring war criminals to justice. In May 1945 eight million Germans were interned. As British civil servants had forecast, the staff available to screen them was inadequate. The British adversarial system of justice operated horrifyingly, as Bower shows, in the trials of the concentration camp commanders and guards. British officers, or lawyers briefed for the defence, cross-examined the wretched inmates of the camps and without too much difficulty threw doubt on their evidence, with the result that the butchers were often acquitted by inexperienced officers acting as judges. (A High Court judge would have brought these amateur barristers up short and stopped this travesty of justice.) But there were even more sinister developments. By 1946 General Gehlen, former head of German intelligence on the Russian front, was working for the Americans, and Heinz Felfe, his deputy and a former SS officer, was working for the British.[33] Worse was to follow. I once asked a friend of mine in Intelligence what the Americans were up to on one particular case. 'You mean the OSS? They're a lot of cowboys,' was all he would reply. Making allowances for the animus that exists between rival organisations, it is perhaps significant that President Truman sacked the chief of the OSS, General Donovan, and broke it up. It now appears that numbers of the most odious war criminals were hired by the 'cowboys' as informants, or stay-behind agents against the day when, in the diseased imagination of that formidable and later manic CIA counter-intelligence officer James Angleton, the Russians would have invaded and be ruling Western Europe. Klaus Barbie, the SS chief in Lyon who tortured and executed resistance leaders and rounded up Jews including fifty-four children from an orphanage in Izieu, was allowed to escape and until extradited lived in Bolivia. Barbie was not the only example: others were also allowed to be spirited away to South America. Some among the Catholic hierarchy thought their duty was to help former Nazis start a new life: if a man has confessed his sins and does penance, the Church has no duty to hand him over to the civil authorities. The confessional keeps its secrets to itself. That baleful priest in the Vatican, Aloys Houdin, organised an escape route. How far MI6 were involved in these policies I do not know: of this villainy I never heard a word in those days.

To those, like Tom Bower, who saw the war as a Crusade in Europe – the title of Eisenhower's war memoirs – the aftermath of the war was a disaster. Thousands of those who committed crimes or knew about such crimes had escaped trial. Others sentenced for vile offences were released and rehabilitated as if they had been guilty of nothing worse than dangerous driving. Others successfully resisted extradition, or with disgusting arrogance displayed contempt for witnesses whom in former days they had tortured. Others managed to delay their trial, and were in the end exempted by statutes of limitation. German lawyers denied that there was such a thing as a Final Solution, and murderers were acquitted because the eye-witnesses to their guilt had gone to their graves during the trial. When one reads Sue Ryder's account of the German director of a prison in charge of displaced persons, some under sentence of death, shrieking at her for an hour, denouncing the British for starting the war and the Nuremberg sentences as wicked injustice, indignation surges; and it knows no bounds when she reminds us that the bodies of the Belsen guards Josef Kramer and Irma Grese, who made lampshades out of the skins of dead prisoners, were exhumed and reburied in Germany with full military honours.[34]

No reparation can ever be exacted for the murder of the millions.

Eschatological torments beyond the powers of Tertullian's devising could not even the score for the horrors of the concentration camps and the extermination of the Jews. The reparations that Adenauer made to Israel and to individuals who had been plundered by the Nazis could never be more than a token. The kind of justice Tom Bower demands is not to be had in this world. Justice is not synonymous with right. Nor is it the same as fairness. Justice will not give each his due deserts. It is usually the best of a bad job, as Shakespeare knew when he pictured it somewhere in the jar of the door which separates right from wrong.*

And the other side of the case? The SHAEF and Control Commission directives ignored the realities of life in Hitler's Germany. Nearly everyone in official life was obliged to join the Nazi Party: promotion was denied to those who did not. Businessmen who stood aside found they could not get permits, builders licences, decorators paint and even bakers flour. Some artists against their will were loaded with laurels. Refuse? Everyone who did so feared reprisals against his family. Hardly anyone in the Control Commission realised what it was like to live in a totalitarian police state. The wife and family of an executed July plotter was put in prison and held in isolation. Her pastor disobeyed the order and visited her. He was himself visited by the Gestapo. After they left they said he had 'committed suicide'. Marion Dönhoff said that the Allied directives on de-Nazification assumed that active resistance was to be taken as the norm: 'martyrdom was the standard to be expected of everybody'. In fact, as Robert Birley observed, thousands who were ashamed of the regime felt that resistance was futile and would land their dear ones in prison, or worse. Birley said that each of the education ministers in the four provinces of the British Zone had been an active resister, and that every time he met them

---

* Take but degree away, untune that string,
  And hark! what discord follows; each thing meets
  In mere oppugnancy . . .
  Strength should be lord of imbecility,
  And the rude son should strike his father dead:
  Force should be right; or rather, right and wrong –
  Between whose endless jar justice resides –
  Should lose their names, and so should justice too.[35]

Troilus and Cressida, I, iii.

he wondered 'whether I could have shown the courage they had shown'.[36]

The British record was not despicable. By Bower's own reckoning they executed hundreds of war criminals and sentenced thousands to long terms of imprisonment. I remember being surprised that in a ten-page memorandum which Kurt Schumacher wrote in May 1946 setting out what his party wanted the British to do there was, except for one request to remove a particular police chief, no reference to de-Nazification.

De-Nazification could cost lives – British lives too. On 20 February 1946 an explosion devastated a coalmine in the Ruhr. The British I Corps was galvanised to aid the rescuers, and men from the Durham Light Infantry, many of whom were miners, went underground. Eleven trapped men were only rescued three days later. Many safety officials had been de-Nazified. There was only one German with sufficient knowledge of the mine workings to direct operations, and he collapsed: he had been denounced by the communist workers a week earlier, and though he had been released from arrest, he was unnerved. The greatest fire-fighting expert was a Nazi: he came straight from gaol to direct the rescue. 418 men were killed. Three British officers were among them.[37]

Other European nations were racked with guilt about collaboration with the Nazis – especially France. Between D-Day and the end of the war at least 2500, and more probably 9000, Frenchmen were murdered – accused, as some no doubt were, of being collaborators. Special courts of justice were then set up to carry out épuration. They dealt with 58,000 cases, and another 70,000 were dealt with in other courts. By 1953 the French had had enough. A law of amnesty was passed and it became a criminal offence to name and accuse anyone of a war crime. The solidarity of the nation came first.

The sequel is disagreeable. The state thereafter avoided punishing Frenchmen responsible for rounding up Jews and sending them to Auschwitz (about a quarter of the Jews in France were murdered, and 10,000 Frenchmen were involved in helping the minimal Nazi staff to arrange the deportations). Jean Leguay, a brilliant young civil servant, organised these deportations with what can only be described as exemplary zeal. He never stood trial. He became an executive in an American firm in New York. Maurice Papon organised the round-up of Jews in Bordeaux. A case was brought against him but never concluded. Not until the late eighties did President Mitterrand bring Klaus Barbie to trial: none of Barbie's collaborators was arraigned.[38]

The enormity of Hitler's crimes against the Jews produced an even more overwhelming silence among Germans. Yet when the right-wing historian Nolte argued in the eighties that Auschwitz and the concentration camps were a more efficient imitation of Stalin's Gulags, a storm burst. The British writer Ian Buruma characterised the *Historikerstreit*, the war among the historians, as a denial by German historians that any historical explanation of the massacre of the Jews was possible – any explanation was to condone, even worse to justify, the crime.[39] During the war more Germans than cared to admit it heard rumours about the Holocaust. But many did not, and the Nazis took some pains to hide from the population what was going on. Michael Howard, the best British historian of the Second World War, has called on German historians to make as it were an act of contrition by explaining and analysing why the Holocaust took place, instead of recoiling from it in horror.[40]

Yet what do those who demand atonement expect? It is idle to hope that a nation will engage in continual acts of self-humiliation, whether it is Japan, or France after Algeria, or America after Vietnam, or the British in Ireland, or any communist power anywhere at any time. People cannot live with the sense of their guilt, and will do anything they can to rid themselves of it. That was what Christianity was once concerned with. Burke's aphorism is still unassailable: 'I do not know the method of drawing up an indictment against an whole people.'

Democracy in Germany could not be born unless it was delivered with the forceps of de-Nazification: but it was also important not to crush the infant. In the revival of German political life I never had any doubt about what came first. It was more important to see, as far as one could, that the parties and trade unions got into the hands of honourable men and did not splinter into factions, as had been the case in Weimar days. The British people, in however confused a way, wanted to rebuild a Germany with genuine democratic institutions and to live with her in Europe. The Western powers had to trust the German people to display some political sense and not vote for notorious Nazis or for parties which thinly disguised their sympathy for the past. It was not so much of a gamble as might appear.

CHAPTER ELEVEN

The Cold War

When I moved to Lübbecke I lived in a house that belonged to Herr Blase, a local cigar merchant and fervent Nazi, given to entertaining Brownshirts and on one occasion Göring and Himmler.[1] He was languishing in prison, not atoning for his beliefs, but because he had illegally removed some furniture when the house was requisitioned.* It was a curious house: every corner was rounded or bevelled. Downstairs was one vast gloomy room but upstairs was light and spacious, with hideous furnishings. Another entrepreneur, similarly dispossessed, was more resourceful than Herr Blase: within a year he had obtained permits to build five more houses, all without bathrooms and therefore unsuitable according to the regulations for requisition by the British. My immediate staff consisted of a parachute officer, Major Harcourt, fair-haired and good-looking until you observed his pig's eyes: I cannot remember whether he was posted to me or I selected him, but if I did, I made a mistake, for he turned out to be so doctrinaire and rude in his dealings with Military Government that the German Political Branch offended more people than it had to. Once again I became overwhelmed by paperwork, since I had to drive through the zone introducing Albu to German politicians and our Intelligence units, remonstrating with recalcitrant Military Government commanders, addressing youth meetings, seeing Adenauer and Schumacher regularly, and trying to reassure the refugees who had been forced to flee from the Soviet Zone or Sector that we would not abandon Berlin: they still hoped that a united Germany would emerge at the end of the occupation. After weeks of cajoling I got an extra post for a junior

---

* Herr Blase spent two further years in gaol in 1950–52 for tax evasion. He died in 1964 and a vast concourse of citizens followed him to his grave.

officer. There was only one to interview. He gave me an earth-shaking salute and was startled by my first question, whether he could read and write. Lieutenant Tracy was hired at once and proved to be excellent.

Throughout the zone one met or made friends. There was Jack Rathbone of the Legal Division, whom I had met with Raymond Mortimer and Desmond Shawe-Taylor, the literary and music critics of the *New Statesman*. There were the hospitable messes of the Intelligence detachments with whom I often stayed on my trips round the zone. At Brunswick there was a friend from the days before Staff College when I was attached to a brigade headquarters, another lawyer, Bernard Alexander. Bernard was supervising the administration of justice in Lower Saxony. Rotund, astute, ruthless, he purged the judiciary and then fought for privileges for those he retained. No one more enjoyed rooting out skulduggery, whether in Military Government or among German officials. (His wife Tania was the daughter of the redoubtable Baroness Budberg, H.G. Wells's constant companion.) I was also on the friendliest possible terms with my old colleague from MI14, Leo Long, an invaluable ally in my battles with Military Government, who sent me warm congratulations when I was given the OBE in June 1946. Whether he was still passing information to the Russians I do not know, but my activities in Berlin against the KPD, of which he can hardly have approved, did not affect our relations.

My favourite colleague at the Blase House was Cecil King, a gentle, laid-back cynic of the Foreign Office. When I asked him how he had entered the diplomatic service in the days before the war, he corrected me: 'Not the diplomatic; the consular service. I filled the lowest post that exists in the service. I was Vice-Consul in Bogota.' He mocked the self-confident and ignorant senior staff officers and his stuffier Foreign Office colleagues, and treasured remarks that should not have been made: there was the brigadier who referred to the SPD anti-Nazi refugees who had fled to England before 1939 as traitors; there was the German lady who said that just because the boilerman and the cook's husband had spent a few years in a concentration camp they seemed to think they had a right to be spiteful. One of Cecil's friends was a Swiss business-man, Fritz Zwicky, for whom he cut red tape to enable him to rebuild his business; another a German, Ilse Martos-Imhorst, who had prudently taken a Hungarian husband, had legs that matched Dietrich's and a temperament that was '*von Kopf bis Fusz auf Liebe eingestellt*' ('set up for love from top to toe'). Every so often she would flit in: whose bed she would choose for the night was a toss-up.

For the most part Austen Albu concerned himself with governmental problems on which he could speak with authority and deal direct with Hynd. He found Military Government trying to impose upon the Germans the British system of representation and of voting in elections ('first past the post'). Albu proposed a compromise that avoided the kind of proportional representation that hamstrung the Weimar Republic and yet prevented a body of opinion excluded from the elected assemblies that could cause trouble during the years of privation ahead. He also could speak with Hynd's authority on another important issue: the future governmental structure of a new Germany. Napoleon had reduced 300-odd states to thirty-nine; the Nazis reduced Germany finally to one centralised dictatorship. All the Western Allies agreed there should be some sort of federated decentralised state: the French wanted the loosest kind of confederation; the American political scientists could not envisage anything very different from the United States Constitution; and the British officials hardly understood the notion of federalism, despite the fact that the Colonial Office often imposed that form of government upon colonies that were gaining their independence.

Albu undertook the negotiations with the German politicians about the creation of new *Länder* (provinces) in the British Zone. Schumacher wanted the whole of the British Zone to be one *Land*; the small ancient principalities all wanted to be independent. Luckily the SPD Oberpräsident of Hanover, Heinrich Kopf, was a jovial conciliator. Albu got him to agree to let Hamburg and Schleswig-Holstein be a separate *Land*, and Kopf got Hanover, Brunswick, Oldenburg and Schammburg-Lippe to amalgamate as Lower Saxony. Lippe-Detmold, however, eluded Kopf. He had thrown a splendid party for its notables and, stupefied by Hanoverian hospitality, they voted to join Lower Saxony, backed by Military Government's regional Commissioner General McCready. But Albu had learnt the value of intelligence; he discovered that the leading citizens and trade unionists had previously said that they wanted Lippe-Detmold to belong to *Land* North Rhine-Westphalia, and he stuck to the original proposal.[2] He was later in 1947 to negotiate with the Americans about the exact powers of the central government and the countervailing powers of the *Länder*.

Albu was, of course, preoccupied with the fortunes of the SPD. He never warmed to Schumacher, whom he thought too harsh, uncompromising and nationalist: he preferred the more sophisticated and able Berlin social democrats such as the courageous first Oberbürgermeister of West Berlin Ernst Reuter, and the left-wing idealists of the CDU such as the trade unionist Jakob Kaiser. So I had much to do with Schumacher, responding to his request to set up an office in Berlin and provide in the British sector a flat, a car and a telephone linked to the military circuit (otherwise useless for interzonal calls) for the party's secretary Anne Marie Regner. When he dined with me on 4 June he asked me to prevent the dismantling of the docks in the north German ports, as it was through these ports that food for the British as well as the Germans was imported. Twenty-eight fishing smacks had been blown up by the British because they had been converted into torpedo boats: why couldn't they have been reconverted?[3] The SPD needed licences for a newspaper and a publishing house, and visas for returning émigrés. To get rid of police chief Schulte in Hanover was good, but why replace him with Engelmann, a militarist whom no democrat in Hanover would trust? Schumacher wrote a letter to Albu, which he made public, blaming Military Government for failing to impose a socialist economy upon the zone.[4] Some Military Government officers were involved in the black market, others were too friendly with 'the representatives of heavy industry, big financiers and landed gentry whose style of living no longer corresponds to present-day realities in Germany. Such a situation is unbearable.'[5] I used to tell him that these accusations made my task harder. He was wrong to suppose there was a Labour Government policy which contradicted that of Military Government. Many of his requests could not be met because he wanted nothing less than a peaceful revolution in which many functionaries in every department, from the police to agriculture, would be dismissed in addition to those already de-Nazified. Schumacher did at times rein in the mettlesome black horse within him, and on 29 April he told an audience in Hamburg that they could hardly expect the British to de-Nazify, as they themselves had done nothing to bring down Hitler.[6] His health troubled me. 'The old boy,' I wrote to Steel, 'is slowly cracking up. He now suffers from terrible insomnia and his stomach trouble is steadily getting worse. He never lets up for a moment . . . and seems physically and mentally exhausted.'[7] I arranged for his secretary to get medicines for him and extracted a promise that he would go to a sanatorium in August.

Schumacher was the indisputable leader of his party. Erich Ollenhauer, the leading SPD refugee in London, was a loyal supporter. When Labour Party activists asked why the refugees had not been brought back to form a government it was difficult to convince them that, hard as life was in Britain after the war, it was a paradise compared to life in Germany, and that the vast majority of exiled Germans never wanted to set foot in the country again. Impossible to convince them that the policy of the Soviet Union in imposing the regime of Ulbricht and fellow Moscow refugees was the negation of democracy. How could the British simultaneously promise free elections and genuine democratic choice while imposing upon the Germans a puppet government? Schumacher realised that he must not appear to be a British poodle, and was more openly critical of Military Government than Adenauer. At the same time it was true that in the first year of the occupation of Germany the SPD were monstrously under-represented in the administrative bodies Military Government set up; and if one attempted to remedy this, one was accused of partiality towards the SPD. Kit Steel wrote me a generous letter when I retired in which he said that 'The difference between you and the professional socialists is that they regard the SPD as *ipso facto* the only thing that matters and you I must say always looked on it as it should be looked on namely the most suitable instrument for regenerating Germany.'[8]

Adenauer was no less the indisputable leader of the CDU. On the occasions when I met him I tried to convince him that the British genuinely wished him well. This was not altogether easy for him to believe. Albu wanted to encourage the left-wing leaders of the CDU. When Military Government created a new *Land* by fusing North Rhine with Westphalia, Albu saw to it that Karl

Arnold – and not Adenauer's man, Lehr – was appointed to be its first Oberpräsident. Who could blame Albu for being taken with Arnold, a young man of character and intelligence, a sincere adherent of the left wing of the party and a friend of Jakob Kaiser, but quite incapable of winning the leadership of the party against Adenauer? Who could blame Adenauer for suspecting that British interest in Arnold and Kaiser was a further indication of hostility to him? Adenauer had a keen nose for unorthodox socialist utterances within the party: he noted such a speech by Arnold on 24 November 1945. He was quick off the mark to look for allies in building the CDU: as early as September in that year he was corresponding with Rudolf Petersen in Hamburg.[9] Whenever we met he rarely failed to insert a jibe that a British Labour government would naturally look after their esteemed colleagues in the SPD. (He was quite right to suspect the solicitude which Albu and myself displayed towards Schumacher; yet the most we did to help the SPD in the zone was on occasion to give their leaders lifts in Control Commission cars to major meetings.) I came to realise there was never any chance of placating Adenauer. Since 1918 his life had been devoted to coming to an understanding with the French, and he regarded Protestant England with the same scepticism as did de Gaulle.

By April 1946 I was advising the Foreign Office that the CDU was the most powerful party in North Rhine-Westphalia, and by July I reported that it was gaining ground in Lower Saxony and even in Schleswig-Holstein. Adenauer was now beyond question the most formidable figure. He still kept an eye on affairs in Cologne, and was said to spend three evenings a week with the Oberbürgermeister and one with Cardinal Frings. In the early days he had spoken of land reform, an astute move to capture the votes of the Catholic working class: it now became clear that by land reform he meant town-planning. His main appeal was to the professional classes, businessmen and small tradesmen, and his determination to free the Rhineland from Prussian rule was popular. He was shocked that the British did not choose all their leading administrators from the old *Beamten* or civil service class. Given the choice between an efficient official and nominal Nazi, and a man of no proved abilities but of strong dissident background, he chose the former.[10] The Catholic Church was his ally. When the ballot for confessional schools was held, parents were told their children would not get extra rations at school unless they voted with the Church; and Monsignor Wolkers, the head of the Catholic Youth Movement, denounced the Western Allies for the economic plight of their zones and their refusal to drive the Russians out of Germany. Adenauer regarded Kaiser's Christian socialism as a vanity: the man, he said, had been breathing too much oriental air. For Adenauer history was *Kulturgeschichte*. Today Germany east of the Elbe had been lost to Western culture – but then, had Prussia, uncivilised by Rome, ever belonged to it? What mattered now was to preserve civilisation west of the Elbe.

Events vindicated Adenauer's vision of politics. On 3 April Bevin and his Foreign Office officials considered whether we should continue to work for a unified Germany or set up a zonal government and press for a 'federal structure based on regional units with autonomous powers'. The arguments were evenly balanced. Germany was costing Britain £80 million a year, and we needed all the American material help we could get. On 7 May Attlee seemed to settle the matter by ruling in Cabinet that we could not afford to split from our Allies, despite the Soviet Union's determination to impose a communist regime in their zone. Both Attlee and Bevin were still reluctant to create anything that looked like an anti-Soviet bloc – not least because the Americans by no means accepted our apprehensions in Germany. Bevin had always to consider the state of opinion in the Labour Party. When Dick Crossman moved an amendment to the King's speech to repudiate Churchill's Fulton oration, no one voted for it, but 130 Labour MPs abstained, nearly all of them from the university-educated middle class.

But by July 1946 the cost of the occupation had derailed this policy. Britain had given 112,000 tons of wheat and 50,000 tons of potatoes from reserve stocks to feed the Germans. Bread rationing – unknown during the war – had been imposed in Britain. The British wanted to keep German steel production well above 10 million tons so as to export steel for hard currency. The other three powers in the Kommendatura forced us to settle for a figure of 5.7 million, with a let-out clause to raise production to 7.5 million in a crisis. The Soviets were now using reparations to cripple the economy of the British Zone.[11] Hugh Dalton, the Chancellor of the Exchequer and Germanophobe to the core, warned that occupation costs were draining our gold reserves and dissipating the American and Canadian dollar loans. Why pour money into this sink when our first priority should be socialist reconstruction at home – the creation of the Welfare State? Yet Labour Party theorists had always argued that poverty and slumps in the economy bred communism, and it seemed to be Soviet policy to keep Europe weak. Montgomery had warned Attlee that unless the German economy improved, a hostile population would look east. The Foreign Office noted that the establishment of a puppet regime east of the Elbe meant that we had waved 'goodbye to democracy on the Western pattern for what is practically half of post-war Germany'.[12]

In the summer of 1946 American policy also began to change. In July Bevin stopped reparations to Russia, insisted on an upper limit of 11 million tons of German steel production and refused to recognise the Oder-Neisse border with Poland until free elections were held in the Soviet Zone. Britain was going to break loose from quadripartite control and set up provincial (*Länder*) governments in its zone. Bevin soon had to approach America for financial help to run the British Zone and to take over affairs in Greece, where the communist EAM/ELAS party was waging a civil war. The next step was to amalgamate with the American Zone to form a 'Bizone'. Dedicated socialists lamented that this meant the end of their hopes to convert Germany into a peaceful democratic country.[13] The Bizone meant the triumph of American capitalism, and Bevin's hope for a body modelled on Roosevelt's Tennessee Valley Authority to run the Ruhr evaporated.

It was not only socialists who were dismayed. The 'low-level zealots' were appalled. Once elections began to be held it was inevitable that power would be transferred to the Germans. The writing was on the wall for the governors of Britain's newest colony. On New Year's Day 1947 General Robertson issued a brisk, emphatic directive: Military Government must stop issuing instructions to industry and to German officials in the *Kreise*. Even if this meant affairs were conducted less efficiently, his orders must be obeyed. Robertson spelt out many of the practices that were at the heart of British rule and added, 'This must now stop.' Many of the 26,000 officers in the Control Commission would not have their contracts renewed.

In March 1947, at the Council of Ministers in Moscow, Bevin argued for the last time for a centralised German government. Molotov demanded the disbandment of the Bizone and for reparations to be paid to Russia. Then came the decision by America that was to change the face of Western Europe. President Truman offered Marshall Aid to put the war-stricken countries on the road to recovery. Aid was offered to Russia and countries in Eastern Europe – indeed, Poland and Czechoslovakia came to the first two meetings. It has been alleged that Stalin's first reaction was to accept the offer and rebuild the ruined cities in Byelorussia and the Ukraine, but that Donald Maclean, the British spy based at that time in the British Embassy in Washington, sent a message to the KGB that the Marshall Plan was a ploy 'to ensure American economic domination in Europe', and that the price of restoring European productivity would be to put it under American financial control.[14] Accordingly Stalin prohibited any country behind the iron curtain to accept the American offer. This is highly improbable. Stalin's own belief in primitive Marxism determined his decision: as it had done when he refused in 1941 to listen to Churchill's warning that Hitler would attack him.

It was not the promulgation of a federal constitution for West Germany that caused the next crisis, but the currency reform which the Western powers instituted to break the black market. They insisted that the new currency should circulate in the Western sectors of Berlin. On 30 March 1948 the Berlin blockade began. On 16 June the Russians walked out of the Kommendatura, on 23 June they cut railway lines, and on 10 July they closed canals. The Americans and British pondered what to do. General Clay was for mounting a military convoy prepared to blast its way along the autobahn to Berlin. But the Western Allies faced a legal difficulty. In the Potsdam agreements there was no mention of access by road to Berlin for the West: right of access had simply been assumed. But there was a written agreement about the right to free air passage. When Bevin asked whether the Americans could supply Berlin by air, the US Air Force general at the meeting doubted whether it was possible: the transport aircraft of the American air force were scattered over the Far East and the Mediterranean. Bevin turned to him and said genially, 'That is the first time I have ever heard an American question whether something is possible.' That settled it. It was a challenge that no American could resist; and the Americans with the help of the British mounted one of the most remarkable demonstrations of improvised air power in the post-war era. Two and a half million people were fed and supplied for eleven months: one quarter of the tonnage and one third of the flights were British. Bevin had no need to worry about the support of Labour Members of Parliament: the communist coup in Czechoslovakia in February 1948 shocked the left, and its idol Aneurin Bevan supported the decision to feed and supply Berlin by air. Had the Western Allies not stood out in 1946 against the forcible amalgamation of the SPD and KPD, the airlift could never have succeeded. Under a communist administration the distribution of the supplies would have been blocked even if the airfields had continued to operate.

The final act was played out next year. When the Russians armed the German militia in their zone in October 1948 the establishment of NATO and the emergence of a German army became inevitable. In September 1949 the Western zones became the Federal Republic of Germany, still nominally under the control of an Allied high commission in Berlin but in effect governed by federal and *Land* ministries answerable to elected assemblies.

German historians usually stress that the British always put their own self-interest first; but that their policy was so inconsistent that intelligent Germans became exasperated and said: 'All we ask is that you should govern; but if you can't, get out and let us do it.' When I read again the despatches and telegrams of those days, I see the hesitations and contradictions in British policy springing from the change of enemies. Those contradictions were never better displayed than in the first speech on Germany Austen Albu made in the House of Commons after he had resigned from the Control Commission and been elected a Member of Parliament. He began by saying that little change had taken place in the German mentality, and quoted a German newspaper discussing all sorts of reasons why the Germans were unpopular – except one: that Germans had killed between eleven and thirteen million of their fellow

Europeans.[15] Even so it was no longer possible, if it ever had been, to transport and impose our own style of democracy upon another country. Yes, German governance must be decentralised, *but* central government must have the power to finance the rebuilding of the economy. Yet that meant that Britain had to face uncontrolled competition from German industry financed by American capital. Albu concluded – with foresight – that Britain's best hope was to integrate the German into the European economy and plan our own economy to be complementary to theirs.[16] That piece of elementary self-interest was rejected by the Labour government, the Conservative opposition and in those days by the Foreign Office and the Treasury.

I left Germany in August 1946. One of my last acts was to accompany Adenauer and Schumacher to Berlin so that, as an act of common courtesy, we could inform them of the decision to create four self-governing *Länder* and detach the British Zone from the rule of the Kommendatura. So, on a windy afternoon, I found myself on an airfield near Lübbecke. Beside me was Adenauer, impassive, in formal dress, overcoat and homburg hat, as always dignified and calm. I never failed to be struck by the intelligence and the mischievous delight with which, in an elegant turn of phrase, he would allude to some example, as he saw it, of British stupidity, his eyes shining in that expressionless oriental face.* On the other side stood Schumacher, his thin hair blowing in the wind, hugging, as he often did, the stump of his right arm with his left hand, his body twisted by torture in the concentration camps, each gesture revealing his demonic energy and sardonic, impatient disposition. Schumacher was every bit as devoted as Adenauer to the creation of a Western democratic Germany, but narrower in his single-minded vision and less flexible in accommodating himself to the realities of life in Germany in 1946. You noticed how emaciated he looked, his sallow colour, his bad breath. I watched the two men to see how they would greet one another. In Britain the leaders of the two opposing parties would probably not have liked each other,

---

* Talking to Sir Ivone Kirkpatrick, later High Commissioner in Bonn, Adenauer said, '*Gott hat die Klugheit aber nicht die Dummheit der Menschen begrenzt*' ('God has limited man's intelligence, but not his stupidity').[17]

but they would have exchanged civilities. Throughout the journey, in the aircraft and then by car, neither Adenauer nor Schumacher spoke a word to the other.

Adenauer naturally accepted the proposals for *Land* governments, and made an admirable impression upon the senior British officials. Schumacher rejected them in a series of sarcastic interjections. None of the British could understand his bitterness. I do not remember how I then interpreted it, but I was aware of a paradox in the development of German politics. Adenauer, with his scarcely veiled contempt for British policy, was already coming to terms with the occupying powers, maintaining his distance and advertising his independence from them, but learning how to exploit them to the advantage of his country. What he had predicted would now come true. Berlin would not be the political capital of Germany because Germany would not be united. The Western Allies would be forced to develop a separate policy for West Germany, and there would now be West German political parties. The dreams of Hermes and Kaiser for the CDU and of Schumacher for the SPD would dissolve. In every speech Adenauer proclaimed his dedication to the ideal of a united Germany. By every action he did his best to make it politically impossible. Why should he want the traditionally socialist Germany east of the Elbe to thwart his scheme of a Catholic-dominated West Germany?

Schumacher, on the other hand, refused to join the Zonal Advisory Council, and now dedicated himself to implacable opposition to his best source of help because he believed that the creation of a West Germany, and in particular the amalgamation of North Rhine and Westphalia into a single *Land*, would return the CDU to power in perpetuity. When men talk of 'perpetuity' they mean, whether or not they know it, the next twenty years, or their own lifetime – whichever is the shorter: and therefore Schumacher was not all that inaccurate. Adenauer's policy for Germany cannot be faulted: and it became inexorably the policy of the Western world.

And yet I never felt more affection for Schumacher than I did at that meeting. I had got to know him well. I understood how he felt, and was touched to see how he responded to warmth and sympathy. Most of the time he did his best to reject friendly overtures, but if he felt that friendship came from the heart, he responded. He was the sort of man whom intellectuals understand: very fierce, very pure, unwilling to compromise with the truth as he saw it, hating his enemies and none too appreciative of his friends. Yet at the same time he had suffered tortures rather than renounce his faith. I felt affection for him because I saw that he was doomed to defeat at the hands of a man who possessed all the political skills which he lacked, and who would outwit him at every turn. In my mind's eye I see myself smiling and grasping Schumacher's hand and shaking my head reproachfully, while to Adenauer I bowed in respect and admiration. Adenauer was cunning, sometimes ruthless, always an authoritarian, most unlike his countrymen in his scepticism towards – indeed contempt for – ideas, very tenacious, yet at the same time never rigid, conscious of his goals and above all a man of limitless patience. Unlike Gladstone he was an old man *not* in a hurry. Like Roosevelt, he set his most able political supporters at each other's throats; he had no scruples about selecting scapegoats and scuppering rivals. His sense of ridicule was highly developed and not at all kind, and I have to admit that he made me laugh. When I left Germany to take up my Fellowship at King's he wrote me a letter in which, among other things, he said: *'Ich hatte immer da empfunden, dasz Sie bei aller Wahrung der britischen Interessen doch den ehrlichen Willen hatten, unserer Lage nach Möglichkeit gerecht zu werden. Das Zusammentreffen mit Ihnen war mir immer eine Freude'*[18] ('I always had the feeling that despite your devotion to British interests, you always had the desire to be as fair as you could to our situation. Meeting you was always a pleasure').

I never saw him again. In 1952, on an official visit to Britain, he was taken to Cambridge, and naturally as a young don I was not invited to the lunch party. But Adenauer had not forgotten me; and I received a letter saying that he was sad we had not met, and that if I came to Germany I should call on him.[19] I never did. I decided I could not keep up with German political affairs. My research, my life, my interests were all leading me in other directions; and who was I to waste his time? But I am glad to have known him in those years. For Adenauer and de Gaulle were the saviours of their countries – countries whose morale was broken: in the case of Germany, by the destruction of her cities, by the Allied occupation, and by the appalling shame of the concentration camps; and in the case of France by the aftermath of collaboration, by die-hard colonialism and by ineffective governments who let inflation soar. Each of them – Adenauer and de Gaulle – resurrected his country and gave it self-confidence and pride; and they also created a Europe which, until they reached their famous *entente*, had been at odds with itself.

As a minor combatant in what came to be called the Cold War, I have to ask myself: was it necessary, was it inevitable? When did it begin? Choose your date. In 1917 and at Versailles when the West built a *cordon sanitaire* against Bolshevik communism? Conservatives and liberals regarded the existence of the Soviet Union as a threat to their possessions, their social system, their class and their freedom. Isaiah Berlin remembered Sir John Simon when he was Foreign Secretary in the early 1930s being pressed by some of the younger Fellows at All Souls' to impose sanctions on Italy at the time of the Ethiopian war, saying, 'You young men want me to bring down Mussolini. And what will happen then? Communism in Italy.' Perhaps the Cold War began with the Nazi-Soviet pact in 1939? Certainly the partition of Poland, for whose independence Britain had declared war on Germany, contained the seeds of the conflict. When Stalin agreed to Poland's resurrection he was determined to put in office a puppet government under Marshal Rokossovsky's tanks and refuse to recognise the credentials of the London Poles. Or was the Cold War caused by a misinterpretation of Ultra that led General Marshall and Field Marshal Sir Alan Brooke to tell General Antonov at Yalta that the Sixth Panzer Army (withdrawn after its defeat in the Ardennes and transferred to the southern part of the Russian front) would attack at Torum in Poland, when in fact it attacked in Vienna and halted Marshal Tolbukhin? Or perhaps it was brought about by the machinations of the master spy Kim Philby, who used to boast that he had frustrated attempts by Allied negotiators, or neutrals or Germans such as Field Marshal Kesselring, to accept a surrender in the West but not on the Eastern Front?[20] Did Philby's reports inflame Stalin's mind by suggesting that the *pour-parlers* had been initiated by the Western

Allies? That could account for the furious and biting messages Stalin sent to Churchill and Roosevelt in March 1945, reproaching them for bad faith. Despite their assurances, Stalin never retracted – and indeed the OSS were in contact with German emissaries, though neither of the Western leaders had any intention of abandoning unconditional surrender.

Timothy Garton Ash, however, believed that unwittingly Churchill was a cause of the Cold War. Churchill liked to beguile people, and thought that by using the language of dictators he could beguile Stalin. When he flew to Moscow in October 1944 and concluded his 'percentage agreement' with Stalin (e.g. 90 per cent of Romania to the USSR, 10 per cent to Britain, and vice versa in Greece) he used language that sold the pass. He adopted a cynical, offhand tone of voice when he alluded to the defeat of the Polish resistance under General Bor in Warsaw – although he knew the Russian army had stood by and watched. Churchill next told Stalin he approved of President Beneš coming to terms with Russia: why couldn't the Poles do the same? Why not a loose confederation of Poland, Czechoslovakia and Hungary? That showed how little he understood Eastern Europe. He gave Stalin a false idea of his beliefs and principles: 'There can be few sights more depressing,' wrote Garton Ash, 'than that of a democratic statesman using the language of brutal and cynical "realism" to justify a policy which is not even realistic.'[21] No wonder Stalin ignored Churchill's reservations about Soviet policy in Poland, and underestimated the force of British public opinion in Parliament. No wonder he told the Polish delegates who referred to Churchill's speech in the House of Commons asserting the right of the London Poles to join a new government in Poland that 'serious politicians should ignore parliamentary gobbledygook'. Even after the war Churchill continued to nurse the illusion that Stalin and Molotov broke their word after Yalta only because they were overruled in the Central Committee of the Party. Yet in the end Garton Ash has to admit that the real reason that Eastern Europe was Sovietised was simple: the Red Army got there first.

Somewhat naturally, Britain's most distinguished Marxist historian, Eric Hobsbawm, saw things differently. People imagined that they lived in the shadow of nuclear war; but it was not so.

Both America and the Soviet Union accepted the division of the world after 1945 and did their utmost to avoid war, whether over Iran, Berlin, Korea or Cuba. They growled at each other, however, because both were alarmed by their own weakness. The Russians surveyed the wreckage of their war-stricken and impoverished country; the Americans expected a post-war slump that would make Europe a breeding-ground for communism. That was why neither country would compromise. But Hobsbawm argued that of the two, America was the more dangerous. Whereas seasoned diplomats like George Kennan and Frank Roberts did not consider the Soviet Union to be an active aggressor as Hitler had been, in a democracy politicians had to whip up hysterical anti-communism to get re-elected. Egging them on was the conglomerate of interest groups that President Eisenhower referred to as the 'military-industrial complex'. In both countries the livelihood of large numbers of officials and workers depended on arms production, for their armed forces at home and for sale abroad to client states. Most historians put the Cold War confrontation down to fear, and the more sensible agree that both sides were to blame. But that is not the whole story. It was only in America that presidents were elected on an anti-communist ticket. It was only America that demanded supremacy in numbers of nuclear weapons; and the NATO governments, though not inspired as America was by the ideal of 'destroying communism', followed their master.[22]

What are we to make of this? Practically everyone agrees that the Cold War was inevitable. States are bound to confront each other when they measure their power against each other – as they did in the eighteenth century and before 1914. But they are even more likely to collide when they are inspired by opposing ideologies – as Catholic and Protestant states were in the late sixteenth and early seventeenth centuries, or in Napoleon's time, when his armies spread the ideas of the French Revolution. But Hobsbawm's analysis loses sight of a tiny interstice in history. From late 1944 until the autumn of 1946 Stalin could have made a deal with the United States. It was then that America ostentatiously detached herself from Britain.

For a brief moment Truman looked as if he might follow Churchill's tougher line against Russia; but he then fell under the influence of Joseph Davies, the former US Ambassador in Moscow. Well known though Truman later became for giving quick and clear decisions, he was now indecisive.[23] America compromised over Poland and on a number of other issues at Potsdam. Davies was not the only weathercock pointing to a significant change in American policy. When SHAEF broke up Bedell-Smith warned Strong that the Anglo-American alliance would dissolve: America would now look to Russia to be her new partner. Even after American policy hardened towards Stalin, America offered him and the East European countries Marshall Aid on the same terms as others. For Hobsbawm, Marshall Aid was yet another ploy in the American plan to exert an economic hegemony over other states, and Stalin could not be expected to accept it, or allow his satellites to be swung out of their Soviet orbit. But the terms on which Marshall Aid was offered were totally different from those imposed on Britain in 1946 as a condition of being offered a loan. Then indeed Britain was treated as a client state and forced to accept convertibility – which meant that dollars drained out of Britain as soon as they flowed in. Marshall Aid was different. It was not a loan but a grant. Marshall Aid bore no resemblance to the trade agreements between the USSR and her satellites, which imposed a pattern of industry upon the client states that was not in their own interests.

Hobsbawm declares that Stalin did all he could to convince the West that he wanted the anti-fascist alliance to continue: he dissolved the Comintern in 1945, advised Tito to keep King Peter on the throne of Yugoslavia and refused to help the communist guerrillas in Greece.[24] But Stalin was too convinced a Marxist to believe that there could be an 'alliance' with capitalist powers after the war. Frank Roberts in Moscow (where later he returned as Ambassador) remembered the *Daily Worker* correspondent telling him that agit-prop teams had been sent out to Russian factories directly the war was over to tell the workers that America and Britain were no longer allies, but agents of capitalism and imperialism.[25] Stalin saw events in terms of the inevitable conflict between capitalism, which was doomed, and communism, which would triumph. Nor was it in character for him to trust the West. His life was governed by suspicion. He trusted no one. Conspiracies sprang up like weeds in his mind. If events did not go to his liking, someone in authority in Russia must be punished, and someone abroad must be thwarted. Hugh Thomas was correct when he declared that the Cold War was essential to Stalin. He needed an enemy.[26]

Stalin was in fact the first to make a public declaration of Cold War. On 9 February 1946, before Churchill spoke at Fulton, Stalin delivered in the Bolshoi Theatre at once a demand for the reimposition of Party unity and an uncompromising statement that the enemy today was capitalism.[27] Hobsbawm is right to refer to American hysteria. In McCarthy's time or in the early days of Ronald Reagan's presidency grotesque and monstrous things were said and done. Of all the countries in the world, America was the least likely to suffer a communist coup. But Hobsbawm does not allude to the events that triggered the hysteria. When Igor Guzenko, a Soviet officer in military intelligence (the GRU), defected in September 1945, he revealed the depth of the Soviet penetration in Canada and America, and Britain as well. As spy after spy fell like skeletons out of the cupboard, indignation rose that the Soviet Union should have organised such networks of agents and sympathisers to steal secrets from their Allies during the war. At first the spies seemed to be connected solely with the atom bomb, but the cases of Alger Hiss in America, and in Britain of Burgess and Maclean, revealed that officials in the highest reaches of government were spies. In America a witch-hunt began, and hundreds of innocent people lost their jobs. In Britain there was no witch-hunt: the Establishment imposed a pall of silence. But the journalists were to have their revenge, and the subsequent exposure in the sixties of Vassall, Philby and later Blunt disintegrated the trust that was once placed in the old governing class of men who had been to a public school and to Oxford or Cambridge. The Beaverbrook press and the left-wing periodicals rejoiced that they had been rumbled, and succeeded in discrediting them. To this the West could make no riposte. It was almost impossible to plant agents in Russia or its satellite states when security was so intense that diplomats were not free to travel where they wished. Yet although the *nomenklatura* were reluctant to learn that the working class were not starving in the West, the steady stream of defectors, some from the KGB itself, showed that truth did penetrate the Soviet defences.

Stalin waged war on two fronts: the Cold War and the Class

War. Some Western trade unions were led by communists, others were subverted internally by them. The militants did not need to incur odium by supporting the Soviet Union. They might call themselves Trotskyites, or belong to splinter groups of the left, such as the International Socialists, the International Marxist Group, the Red Front, the Workers' Revolutionary Party and so on. They were soldiers in the class struggle. In Britain, and for some years in France, they hamstrung industry, fuelled inflation and disrupted public confidence as successive governments tried vainly to appease the unions. Militant unionism was, arguably, the most immediate cause of Britain's post-war economic decline.[28] By their nature democratic states with representative institutions were at the mercy of the communist tactics of capturing branch after branch, meeting after meeting. Not only in trade unions. Youth organisations, cultural bodies, international committees and the like were on the list to be captured. No such fifth column could operate in the Soviet Union. On this Hobsbawm is silent.

The Soviet diplomats were quick to accuse the Western Allies of breaking the Yalta and Potsdam agreements, but they themselves broke the agreements in letter and spirit. While the fighting continued in 1945, they liquidated or imprisoned thousands of middle-class people in Romania and Bulgaria. They might justify that by citing Churchill's percentage agreement, but in Greece, though Stalin kept his word in not aiding the communist attempt to take over the country, he found Yugoslavia and Albania ready to do his work for him. Hobsbawm does not mention the revulsion that ordinary citizens in the West felt when they learnt of the execution of a *class* of people; of the Polish officers murdered at Katyn in 1939, of the trial and imprisonment of the sixteen Polish leaders of the Home Army who were tricked into discussions with the Russians and then put on trial. During the little skirmish in Berlin I have described, the most sinister occurrence was the disappearance of prominent social democrats who sometimes, if they were lucky, reappeared in the concentration camps they had occupied as anti-Nazis. Yet, perhaps, nothing in the countries behind the Iron Curtain was as repulsive as the system of compelling ordinary people to inform and spy upon their own neighbours and colleagues. Perhaps not until the collapse of Eastern Europe in 1990 did people in the West realise how all-embracing were the tentacles of the Stasi in East Germany and the secret police forces in the other communist states, reaching out over citizens' lives, feeling them, fondling them, sucking statements from them at the same time as others were informing on them. When Western leaders protested that they favoured 'freedom' or 'free elections' they were not being hysterical.

How far then did each of the four powers achieve their aims in Germany? At first sight the French failed in all of theirs. They opposed a centralised German government, and failed to break Germany up into a confederation of sovereign states. They failed to internationalise the Ruhr and set up a separate state west of the Rhine. And yet in the end, by the Schuman Plan for integrating the coal and steel industries of France, Germany and Benelux, and the *entente* with Adenauer, they got what they wanted: a Western European union with Germany as a willing and subservient partner ready to accept French leadership, while watching their former ally Britain, who during the war had wounded their pride, exclude herself from the new Europe because she failed to understand how much the world had changed.

The Soviet Union failed in its main objective. In politics all nations put self-interest first, and must do so: but they may misjudge where their self-interest lies. The Soviet aims were comprehensible. They wanted a Germany with the Ruhr under four-power control and a communist-controlled government in Berlin. Yet on whatever issue, whether it was Turkey, Greece, Poland, Eastern Europe or Germany, Molotov refused to compromise. Or if he did, he would go back on the deal. Or if he gave in on one point, he expected capitulation on all others. Or if Stalin used his charm and seemed to be willing to break the log-jam, Molotov would insist on the same points as if his master had not spoken. So in the end the Soviets lost Western Germany and, owing to the indomitable Bevin and the resolution of General Clay, they were humiliated and forced to lift the Berlin blockade. They seemed unable to understand that the tactics that had served them well during the war could never be acceptable to their former allies once peace had come.

The Americans came out best, because they adapted quicker to the realities of the situation, and held most of the cards in the game of poker. They had fine diplomats in Kennan, Acheson and Douglas, who were susceptible to the difficulties the British and French faced. The diplomats defeated the War Department and that independent warlord in Berlin, General Clay, on the issue of who should control policy in Germany. The Americans were from the start indifferent to the unification of Germany. What they wanted was an independent *laissez-faire* state which was not a threat to peace. In achieving this they gave little away to their allies, either to Bevin, who wanted to nationalise German coal and steel, or to the French Foreign Minister Bidault, who wanted guarantees against a German nationalist resurgence. They admired the German capacity for hard work, and were the most popular of the occupying powers. Conversely, the new Germany was influenced in its style by American methods – and language: the advertisements one reads in Germany are often written in Americanised German. The very fact that the counter-culture that built up in the 1960s was anti-American, hostile to the doctrine of the market and consumer culture, was only confirmation of American influence.

And the British? They too could congratulate themselves. After all, West Germany became a peace-loving country, locked into the Western alliance of NATO: indeed, in the sixties the German people elected a social democratic government. The British, over-whelmed by their own financial disasters, were unable to impose their 'first past the post' electoral system. Nor could they impose their system of local government – a system that in the eighties Margaret Thatcher tried to cut down to size. The dreams of the Control Commission idealists dissolved.

But perhaps not quite. The post-war Germans were different from those of 1914 or 1939. Something of the spirit of Robert Birley remained behind. The 'bridges' that he built multiplied. With no other country in Europe was there a more conscious attempt to create friendship and understanding between those who might well be the leaders in the future.

The British were misled by the miserable performance of the succession of French governments that flickered across the screen of history in the forties and fifties. But Adenauer was not misled.

Since Britain had thrown into the gutter the leadership of a European Community that was hers for the asking, those two enemies of Britain, Adenauer and de Gaulle, saw to it that the journey for the British to obtain entry to the European Community would be humiliating and, when they did get in, extremely expensive. In the sixties and seventies it was the turn of Britain to have a succession of governments whose weakness in foreign negotiations was an echo of her financial and industrial debility. By the end of the century it looked as if the three great powers in Western Europe had become two: Britain had become irrelevant to France and Germany.

The achievement of the Germans in the aftermath of their defeat is beyond praise. The squalor of life in the cities was degrading; children shared books and were lucky to find chairs and desks in unheated schools; their parents worked long hours building hovels from the ruins after their day's work. As if to accentuate their misery, they saw their conquerors beside them living and feeding well, and soon claiming yet more of the few habitable houses to accommodate their wives and families. They saw their factories dismantled for reparations, yet they got production going again. They soon realised how hated and feared they were across Europe, and learnt, as they became prosperous and were once again able to travel abroad, a quality for which before the war they were not renowned: tact. No doubt the British helped to establish freedom of speech. They allowed *Die Zeit* to criticise the policies of the occupying powers (to the irritation of the Americans), and licensed Augstein's *Der Spiegel*. They permitted Hugh Greene to encourage Nordwest Deutscher Rundfunk occasionally to twit Military Government. No doubt Germany's economic recovery could not have begun without the currency reform imposed by British initiative. When I reflected fifty years later on the change in Germany's fortunes and the reunification of the country that in my time there became divided, my mind went back to the days with which this book began in my Officer Cadet Training Unit, where we were taught (to our satirical comments) that the three essential requirements for an officer were Personality, Initiative and Drive. These were the virtues the Germans displayed, coupled with a self-discipline that astonished the world.

Ernest Bevin was a redoubtable Foreign Secretary – redoubtable because he negotiated from a position of terrible weakness as financial crisis succeeded financial crisis. He was loved by his officials because he followed their advice. That advice was fatal in Palestine, but successful in the Cold War. But his very success blinded the British to reality. Decade after decade, despite Suez and de Gaulle's veto, the British went on behaving as a great power when much of their power had long ago evaporated.

'All the world is in trouble,' said Bevin in 1945, 'and I have to deal with all the troubles at once.' In 1945 he had no choice. How much wiser the Germans were during the years when they built up their strength not to take the troubles of the world on their back.

Epilogue

Of the many visits I have made to Germany since I left the Control Commission, three stand out in my mind.

The first was in the summer of 1948, when the Russians began the blockade of Berlin and the Western Allies organised the airlift to preserve their right to govern their sectors as they wished. Each of the four powers decided to make a cultural demonstration in the city. The Russians sent a 400-strong Cossack choir to sing in the Alexanderplatz. The British Council pondered. Every professional orchestra and theatrical company was engaged for months ahead. Their response was in the end delectably in character. They mounted an *Elisabethanisches Festspiel* for a fortnight. The Cambridge University Madrigal Society were to sing, and the Marlowe Society to act *Measure for Measure* and Webster's *The White Devil*. At the performances programmes were distributed by the matrons of the Control Commission and officers' wives attired in Elizabethan costume. My great friend and mentor at King's College, the Shakespearean scholar George Rylands, who directed the plays and knew I spoke some German, implored me to come and bring with me my future wife, Gabriele Ullstein, who was born and bred in Berlin. In my student days I had acted in the annual Marlowe Society Jacobean production. Would I not now play, he suggested, the part of Cardinal Monticelso in Webster's tragedy? The Cardinal has a fine speech directed at the White Devil, which begins 'Shall I expound the word, whore, to you: sure I shall'; and as he is made Pope in Act IV, I thought my acting career could go no higher.

We flew in to Tempelhof, the old airport in the south of the city, down a narrow corridor. For the last two miles the aircraft seemed to be level with the top storey of the houses on either side. The hostel where the cast stayed was in the Grunewald, and the only flower in the garden was that depressing specimen Love Lies Bleeding. It was August, and each day was sweltering. We had the luck to be near the Blauweisz club, where before the war the Wimbledon stars Gottfried von Cramm and Henner Henckel had played: and there we swam in the pool until the time came to go to the little gem of a theatre where we were to perform.

The house managers and stage hands of the Renaissance Theater welcomed us as if we had been professionals, and made our get-in much easier than we had thought possible. Occasionally one of them would keel over from heat and hunger, for the Berliners were on minimal rations as stocks of coal and food were being built up, and no one knew at that time whether the city could hold out. An old master of his craft made me up each night, taking pleasure in seeing how closely he could make me resemble Philippe de Champaigne's portrait of Cardinal Richelieu.

There were, of course, parties and festivities. One of them was given by Robert Birley in the house in the Grunewald that had been occupied by Sir William Strang when I was in the Political Division. It had in fact been built by Gabriele's father Louis Ullstein, the businessman and most prestigious of the five brothers who owned the publishing house Ullstein Verlag. She had lived there only a short time: her father died a few months after Hitler became Chancellor. Mother and daughter later came as refugees to London. During the Occupation the house became the residence of our ambassadors, and years later two of them, with characteristic solicitude, invited us to stay there and sleep in the room that was Gabriele's as a child. Now it looked strange, filled with economy furniture, the bookshelves boarded up to stop theft.

The division of Berlin was symbolic as well as real. Germany has always looked east as well as west, and the rivalry between the two sectors produced marvellous productions in both of Berlin's opera houses and witty, imaginative theatre in the Schauspielhaus in the Western sector. Berliners are famous for their wit. Even in the darkest days of the war irreverent verses circulated:

> *Mein Auge strahlt, mein Herz es klopft,*
> *Ich singe ein Te Deum*
> *Ich sehe Adolf ausgestopft*
> *Im Britischen Museum.*

(My eyes shine, my heart beats,
I am singing a Te Deum
I can see Adolf dead and stuffed
In the British Museum.)

Berliners are mischievous as elves – but heavy-lidded, cynical, impertinent elves. Some evenings when we were not performing, we would go to a nightclub, Die Stachelschweine (The Porcupines), where a minute cast put on satirical political sketches. Eight of them would sit opposite each other as in a third-class railway carriage and imitate the sound of the train as it rumbled through the countryside where they were going to barter illegally goods for potatoes. '*Kartoffeln, Kartoffeln, Kartoffeln, Kartoffeln,*' they would murmur and then, miming the train as it went through a tunnel, they would shout '*Politzei, Politzei, Politzei!*'

The cast of a professional theatre company paid us the compliment of coming to see our productions, and in return we were invited to their dress rehearsal of Goethe's *Egmont*, directed by the famous Jurgen Fehling. When one of us coughed, Fehling shouted, 'If you want to cough, get out. Any more coughing and I'll clear the auditorium.' We also met some of the cast, including the noble Walter Suessenguth, later director of the Hebbeltheater in Berlin. The discipline, the attention to detail, the dedication to drama as an art, the contempt for exhibitionism and reverence for the text that inspired the German company were exemplary. George Rylands was already well known as the director of John Gielgud in *Hamlet* during the war and for his determination to make his cast speak Shakespeare's verse as verse, and I was fascinated to hear Suessenguth on Laurence Olivier. Of course he expressed his admiration for Olivier as an actor, but his comment on Olivier's movie of *Hamlet* was unerring: '*Kolossal: spricht aber Oscar Wilde*' ('Marvellous: but speaks it as if it was Oscar Wilde'). Not everything was earnest. One of our number managed within forty-eight hours to have a fling with the German *jeune premier*. But the intelligence and boundless capacity for hard work that the German actors displayed should have given me warning of the *Wirtschaftswunder* (economic miracle) to come.

The second of the three visits I recall was to a different Berlin.

In September 1974 the city was no longer blockaded, but divided by the Wall that the East German Communist regime had built in 1961 to stop the drain of skilled workers and the professional classes to the West. The occasion was not political but domestic, the centenary of Ullstein Verlag, to which members of the family had been invited.

The house of Ullstein was the most famous publishing house in Central Europe before the war. Under the imprint of an owl the Ullsteins published books, magazines and newspapers. The *Vossische Zeitung*, the leading liberal paper, almost the equivalent of *The Times*, was the flagship of the firm, but the *Berliner Morgenpost* and the *B.Z. Mittag* sold more copies. There was a raft of magazines: the avant-garde *Querschnitt*, the fashion magazine *Die Dame*, a precursor of *Picture Post* called *Die Illustrierte*, and weeklies – one for farmers had come in handy for First World War widows to advertise for new husbands who could manage a farm. The books were of every variety, including great illustrated editions of history and art history. The Ullsteins were originally orthodox Jews, but had long ago converted to Lutheranism. Not that that saved them from Hitler. The Nazis seized the plant and expropriated the family.

The celebration of the Ullstein centenary began by being somewhat tense. A day or so earlier Hanns-Martin Schleyer, the head of the Confederation of Industries, had been murdered by the terrorist group the Red Front. The Chancellor of the Federal Republic who was to have spoken at the meeting cancelled his visit, and the audience assembled with armed police surrounding the building. Nevertheless, the descendants of the five Ullstein brothers foregathered, each *Stamm* represented, some coming from America, others from England, some already having returned to Germany and Austria from the exile to which Hitler had condemned them. There were to be speeches, and between them the famous strings of the Berlin Philharmonic were to play. Frederick Ullstein spoke. The Bürgermeister of Berlin spoke. So did Bach and Vivaldi. My programme told me we were about to hear the last piece, the second movement of Haydn's 'Kaiser' Quartet. How often had I heard that air, transposed and vulgarised, blared out by a brass band. But now the tender strings wrapped themselves around the melody and softly and slowly played the air we know as '*Deutschland, Deutschland über*

Alles'. I happened to glance at some of the elderly members of the Ullstein family. Tears were running down their cheeks. What were they thinking? Of friends in their youth who had perished in the concentration camps? Of their good fortune in escaping? Or of the memories that air, so delicately phrased, evoked? – of the city in which they grew up, of their country that had once meant so much to them and still was precious, of their country that, despite the horrors inflicted upon their race, was still dear to them?

Once again in September, but this time in 1994, came the final dénouement. The end of the Allied occupation of Berlin was being celebrated, and I was invited to attend the opening of an exhibition (it was hoped that it would become a permanent museum) which recorded the history of the Occupation and marked its end. Tactfully the Russian army had marched out the previous week. This week it was the turn of the three Western Allies. A German military band played. The limousine bearing Chancellor Kohl appeared and, like a noble tanker edging towards its moorings, the Chancellor arrived on the dais flanked by his tugs, the three ambassadors. He spoke, unusually for him, with emotion – and with gratitude too – to the three powers for preserving the independence of Berlin. He remembered those who had given their lives to maintain the city so that it could become once again the capital of a united Germany. Murmurs of '*Grossartig*' (splendid) on all sides. Each ambassador made an admirable speech.

The following evening a former American and a French officer, together with the veteran diplomat and ambassador in Bonn, Sir Frank Roberts, and myself, appeared on the same dais to answer questions about our time during the Occupation. When it was over I wandered through the exhibition looking once more at the photographs of the days long ago that I remembered, the ruined city and the inhabitants already clearing sites and rebuilding it. The next day I drove out of the city and saw road signs to the Schumacherdamm and Jakob Kaiser Platz. The Occupation was over.

I realised I had become a speck in history.

Notes

CHAPTER 1

1 Patrick Howarth, *Intelligence Chief Extraordinary* (1986), 116.
2 F.H.N. Davidson, Memoir, G. Liddell Hart Archive, Davidson MS.
3 Kenneth Strong, *Intelligence at the Top*, 16, 34. See Ralph Bennett, *Behind the Battle* (1994), 4–24 for an account of our military unpreparedness, especially in intelligence.
4 Sapper, *Jim Maitland*, 'The Rottenness of Lady Hounslow'.
5 Hugh Trevor-Roper, *The Philby Affair* (1968).
6 Christopher Andrew, *Secret Service* (1985), 307–11.
7 F.H. Hinsley et al, *British Intelligence in the Second World War* (BISWW) (1979), Vol I, 61–3.
8 Ibid., 71.
9 Howarth, 112.
10 BISWW, Vol I, 292.
11 Ibid., 93.
12 Peter Calvocoressi, *Top Secret Ultra* (1985), 45.
13 Andrew Hodges, *Alan Turing: The Enigma of Intelligence* (1983), 295.
14 Ralph Bennett, *Ultra in the West* (1979), 15–16.
15 F.H. Hinsley and Alan Stripp (eds), *Codebreakers: The Inside Story of Bletchley Park* (1993).
16 Bennett, *Ultra in the West*, 12; *Behind the Battle*, 72–3.
17 Calvocoressi, 8–9.
18 Hodges, 221.
19 Howarth, 128.
20 BISWW, Vol III Pt 2, 384–6.

CHAPTER 2

1 P.B. Earle, Diaries, 4 April 1945, Imperial War Museum.
2 Gerald L. Weinberg, *A World at Arms* (1994), 180.
3 Ibid., 985 fn.14.
4 BISWW, Vol I, 263–4.
5 F.H.N. Davidson, Memoir.
6 BISWW, Vol I, 303–4.
7 BISWW, Vol III Pt 2, 20, 767.
8 Ibid., 75.
9 Earle, Diaries.
10 BISWW, Vol I, 432.
11 Ibid., 353. John Colville, *Fringes of Power* (1985), 305.
12 BISWW, Vol I, 419–20.
13 Bennett, *Behind the Battle*, Appendix 11, 281–4.
14 Weinberg, 233.
15 BISWW, Vol II, 422.
16 E.T. Williams, Unpublished paper in Imperial War Museum, 1.
17 Hinsley and Stripp, *Codebreakers*, 38.

CHAPTER 3

1 Earle, Diaries.
2 Alanbrooke, Diaries, 10–12 July 1942.
3 David Fraser, *Alanbrooke* (1982), 571–2.
4 Alanbrooke, Diaries, 20 May 1942.
5 Weinberg, 358.

6 Earle, Diaries.
7 Alanbrooke, Diaries, 19 August 1943.
8 Fraser, 295.
9 Alanbrooke, Diaries, 12 April 1942.
10 Weinberg, 354, 1023; Alanbrooke, Diaries, 28 March 1942.
11 Michael Howard, *Grand Strategy*, IV, 561.
12 Alastair Horne with David Montgomery, *The Lonely Leader: Monty 1944–45* (1994), 183–94; Earle, Diaries, 19 April 1944.
13 Alanbrooke, Diaries, 31 March 1942.
14 Elizabeth Longford, *Wellington: The Years of the Sword* (1969), 218.
15 Alanbrooke, Diaries, 3 December 1942, 13 January 1943, 21 January 1943, 10 July 1943.
16 Ibid., 24 August 1943.

CHAPTER 4

1 Howarth, 134 (Hinsley does not record this note of dissent: BISWW, Vol I, 185).
2 Ibid., 134.
3 Ibid., 163; Anthony Cave Brown, *Treason in the Blood* (1994), 215–18.
4 See Patrick Beesley, *Very Special Admiral: The Life of Vice-Admiral J.H. Godfrey, CB* (1980), 223–37.
5 Howarth, 165.
6 Andrew, 195.
7 Weinberg, 434.
8 Letter to the author from Francis Ogilvy, 16 January 1944.
9 BISWW, Vol III Pt 1, 7.
10 Ibid., 114.
11 Ibid., 117.
12 Ibid., 175.
13 Ibid., 176.
14 Howarth, 177.
15 BISWW, Vol III Pt 1, 154–6.
16 Martin Gilbert, *Winston Churchill*, Volume VII (1986), 513.

17 Fraser, 366–7.
18 Earle, Diaries. Yet only a week before Churchill was importuning Brooke to withdraw troops from the Mediterranean to enable Mountbatten to land forces on the tip of Sumatra (Alanbrooke, Diaries, 1 October 1943).
19 BISWW, Vol III Pt 2, 130.
20 Alanbrooke, Diaries, 28 October 1943.
21 Ibid., 28 March 1942.
22 Ibid., 14 August 1942, 28 November 1943.

CHAPTER 5

1 R.V. Jones, *Most Secret War* (1978), 388.
2 BISWW, Vol III Pt 1, 301.
3 Ibid., 297.
4 Ibid., 293.
5 Ibid., 172.
6 These telegrams were not decrypted until May 1944, and therefore did not affect the assessment by the JIS. BISWW III Pt 1, 306–8.
7 Albert Speer, *Inside the Third Reich* (1971), 392.
8 BISWW, Vol III Pt 1, 549–50.
9 Bennett, *Behind the Battle*, 156.
10 BISWW, Vol III Pt 1, 318, 321.
11 Jones, 425.
12 Ibid., 435–40.
13 BISWW, Vol III Pt 1, 363–455.
14 S. Zuckerman, *From Apes to Warlords 1904–46* (1978), 143, 405.
15 Ibid., 211.
16 Earle, Diaries.
17 Zuckerman, 248.
18 President Roosevelt to Prime Minister, No 587, 11 May 1944.
19 W.W. Rostow, *Pre-Invasion Bombing Strategy* (1981), 70.
20 Zuckerman, 256.
21 Spaatz refused to sabotage the Transportation plan by advocating

an alternative. When General
Cabell of the Eighth Air Force,
using Churchill's argument about
French casualties, warned him that
the Americans would be blamed if
they bombed marshalling yards, he
was sent away with a flea in his ear
(Rostow, 45).

22 Zuckerman, 271, 349–50.
23 Ibid., 289–90.
24 Ibid., 302.
25 Howarth, 189; BISWW, Vol III Pt
2, 497–514, 913–23.
26 Rostow, 30; Zuckerman, 343.
27 BISWW, Vol III Pt 2, 532.
28 Ibid., 531.
29 Ibid., 522.
30 John Grigg, *The Victory that Never
was* (1980), 44.
31 John Colville, *The Fringes of Power*,
(1985) 520.
32 David Irving, *The Destruction of
Dresden* (1963), 93.
33 Ibid., 99–100.
34 Charles Kingsley Webster and
Noble Frankland, *The Strategic Air
Offensive in Germany* (1978), III,
108.
35 Gilbert, 1173.
36 *Foreign Relations of the United States:
Conference of Malta and Yalta 1945*
(1955), 641–5, 800–1.
37 Ibid.
38 For his book *The Destruction of
Dresden*, Irving had no access to
Ultra.
39 Gilbert, 1219, 1257–8.
40 BISWW Vol III Pt 2, 61.
41 Earle, Diaries, 6 February 1944.
42 Grigg.

CHAPTER 6

1 BISWW Vol III Pt 2, 894. See
David Astor, 'Adam von Trott: A
Personal View', in Hedley Bull
(ed.), *The Challenge of the Third Reich*
(1986), 17–34; Astor, 'The Man
Who Plotted Against Hitler', *New
York Review of Books*, 28 April 1983,
16–21.
2 Alexander Stahlberg, *Bound in Duty*
(1990), 239–46.
3 Weinberg, 754.
4 Klemens von Klemperer, *German
Resistance Against Hitler* (1992), 386,
390.
5 Ibid., 428; 484 fn.
6 Patricia Meehan, *The Unnecessary
War* (1992), 384–403.
7 BISWW Vol III Pt 2, 369; Fraser,
443.
8 Ehrman, *Grand Strategy* Vol V,
401–2.
9 L.F. Ellis, *Victory in the West* Vol
II (1968), 95; Nigel Hamilton,
*Monty: The Field Marshal 1944–
1976* Vol III, 103.
10 Hamilton Vol III, 35.
11 Bennett, *Behind the Battle*, 264.
12 BISWW Vol III Pt 2, 384.
13 Letter to the author from Sir
Andrew Noble, 5 July 1945.
14 Arthur Marshall, *Life's Rich Pageant*
(1984), 162.
15 Strong, 164.
16 Weinberg, 755–6.
17 The evidence is set out excellently
in Bennett, *Ultra in the West*, 180–
90.
18 BISWW Vol III Pt 2, 430. A
detailed account of Ultra traffic will
be found 402–438.
19 BISWW Vol III Pt 2, 407.
20 Ibid., 409, 414–15.
21 Ibid., 428.
22 Bennett, *Ultra in the West*, 189.
23 Strong, 177.
24 But Bedell-Smith remembered him
also mentioning Alsace as a
possibility. Charles B. Macdonald,
The Battle of the Bulge (1984), 73.
25 BISWW Vol III Pt 2, 438.
26 Macdonald, 76. The only other
officer to claim he had foreseen
the attack was Colonel Bussey of
G2 (Intelligence) in US Seventh
Army in the Strasbourg sector. He

was told, understandably enough, that SHAEF, US First and Third Armies 'had lots more information than we do, and they are not arriving at that judgement' (BISWW Vol III Pt 2, 436 fn.).

27 BISWW Vol III Pt 2, 430.

28 Bennett, *Ultra in the West*, 15, 190.

29 Bennett, *Behind the Battle*, 270–2; Zuckerman, 357.

30 E.T. Williams, Memorandum, Imperial War Museum.

31 Weinberg, 762.

32 Meehan, 207–11. Schwerin had no luck: after the war, when the USSR formed a paramilitary police force in their zone, General Robertson and his Foreign Office chief Christopher Steel approached him and put his name to Adenauer, who asked him to form a centre for national service. This was the beginning of the most sensational reversal of Western policy, the rearming of Germany. Schwerin was dismissed for giving advice contrary to Adenauer's liking. Michael Thomas, *Deutschland, England über Alles* (1985), 261–4.

33 George Bailey, *Germans* (1991), 55–6.

34 Weinberg, 816.

CHAPTER 7

1 Walter Laqueur, *World of Secrets* (1985), 291.

2 Bennett, *Behind the Battle*, xviii–xix.

3 See R.J. Overy, *War and Economy in the Third Reich* (1994).

4 Gilbert, 1095; Weinberg, 727.

5 J.P. Stern, *Hitler: The Führer and the People* (1975). See also Ritchie Robertson, 'Difficult Truths: An Essay review of J.P. Stern', in *Comparative Criticism, The Heart of Europe*, Vol 16 (1994), 247–61.

6 Isaiah Berlin, *Personal Impressions* (1980), 11–32.

CHAPTER 8

1 *Foreign Relations of the US*, 614; D.C. Watt, *Britain Looks to Germany* (1965), 37–45. For a detailed account of the negotiations about the division of Germany into zones see Tony Sharp, *The Wartime Alliance and the Zonal Division of Germany* (1975).

2 WM(44) War Cabinet, 123 PRO FO/371/35453.

3 JCS 1067 (1944).

4 F.S.C.V. Donnison, *Civil Affairs and Military Government in North-Western Europe 1944–46* (1961), 205.

5 Ibid., 264–89.

6 Alan Bullock, *Ernest Bevin, Foreign Secretary* (1983), 15.

7 Ibid., 25.

8 Ibid., 90.

9 Pelly, Yasamee and Bennett (eds), *Documents on British Policy Overseas* I, V, 43–6.

10 John Cloake, *Templer, Tiger of Malaysia* (1985), 149.

11 Ibid., 139–40.

12 Donnison, 334, 342.

13 *Documents on British Policy Overseas* Series I, v. no. 89, 409–13; Historical Branch Occasional Paper, November 1989, Margaret Pelly and Gillian Bennett, 'Occupation and Control: The Administration of the British Zone of Germany in the Second Half of 1945', 17–24.

14 Barbara Marshall, *The Origins of Post-War German Politics*. See Ulrich Reusch, 'The British Control Machinery for Germany in London and the British Zone'.

15 See Goronwy Rees, *A Bundle of Sensations* (1960) and *A Chapter of*

Accidents (1971); Jenny Rees, *Looking for Mr Nobody* (1994).

16 *Documents on British Policy Overseas* V, 129.

17 William Strang, *Home and Abroad* (1956), 234-5. Goronwy Rees accompanied him on this tour and gave me this independent account of that meeting.

18 Roy Jenkins, *A Life at the Centre* (1991), 182-4.

19 FO 1030/317 XC157229; 4-5.

20 FO 1030/317; 9.

21 FO 1030/317; 14-15.

22 Pelly et al, 198; Barbara Marshall, 97.

23 cf. Barbara Marshall, 90-104.

24 Ibid., 110.

25 Watt, 77.

26 Ulrich Reusch, 'Versuche zur Neuordnung des Berufs Beamtentum', in *Deutsches Beamtentum und Britische Beratzung* (1985). See also Watt, 78.

27 Annan to Steel, 10 April 1946, 22/233/KC.

28 Lothar Kettenacker, 'Grossbrittanien und die Zukunftige Kontrolle Deutschlands', in J. Foschepoth and R. Steininger, *Britische Deutschland – und Bezatzungspolitik 1945-1949* (1988), 27.

29 David Welch, 'The Political Re-Education of Germany After World War II: A Need for a Reappraisal?', *Journal of German History*, Winter 1987. See also Lothar Kettenacker, the doyen of German historians on the British Occupation, for an authoritative chapter in Nicholas Pronay and Keith Wilson (eds), *The Political Re-Education of Germany and her Allies* (1985), 59-81.

30 FO 371/46894, Steel to Troutbeck, 3 May 1945.

31 FO 953/1285 of May and September 1952, quoted by Kurt Jurgensen in Pronay and Wilson, 93.

32 *British Zone Review*, 12 October 1946, quoted by Welch.

33 Welch, fn.24.

34 Arthur Hearnden (ed.), *The British in Germany: Reconstruction After 1945* (1978), 53. See Rolf Lutzebäck, *Die Bildungspolitik der Britischen Militäregierung in Spannungsfeld zwischen education und re-education in ihrer Bezatzungszone in Schleswig-Holstein und Hamburg in den Jahren 1945-47*, Teil 1 (1991).

35 Ibid., 147.

36 Ibid., 169-71. See also David Welch, 'Priming the Pump of German Democracy', in Ian Turner (ed.), *Reconstruction in Post-War Germany: British Occupation Policy and the Western Zones 1945-55* (1989), 223; Cecil King to author, 12 July 1947.

37 Welch in Turner, 233; Kurt Jurgensen in Pronay and Wilson, 90-2.

38 Barbara Marshall, 136.

39 Ibid., 52ff.

40 Donnison, 234.

41 Cloake, 166; *Documents on British Policy Overseas* V, 6.

CHAPTER 9

1 Adenauer's recollection of our meeting differs from mine, and I believe that he conflated two meetings he had with British officers at that time. But we agree that after we met the ban on his political activities was lifted. Konrad Adenauer, *Erinnerungen (1945-1953)*, 33-8.

2 Cloake, 159.

3 Donnison, 234.

4 Michael Thomas, 130.

5 Ibid., 137.

6 Ibid., 142–4.
7 *Documents on British Policy Overseas*, 197.
8 Harold Hurwitz, *Demokratie und Antikommunismus in Berlin nach 1945* I, 232–6.
9 Ibid., 486.
10 *Documents on British Policy Overseas*, 198.
11 FO 1050/130, 29 November 1945.
12 FO 3571/46910. 84914, 29 December 1945; printed in *Documents on British Policy Overseas*, 473–6.
13 Hugh Thomas, *Armed Truce* (1986), 348.
14 FO 371/46910.
15 Raymond Ebsworth, *Restoring Democracy in Germany: The British Contribution* (1960), 26ff.
16 FO 371/46910, 9.
17 See Barbara Marshall, 38, 163.
18 FO 371/46910, 11.
19 See Barbara Marshall, 'German Reactions to Military Defeat 1945–47', in V. Berghan and M. Kitchen (eds), *Germany in the Age of Total War* (1981), 218.
20 FO 371/46910, 12.
21 E.H. Carr, *Conditions of Peace* (1942). For years Carr was always invited to review books on the Soviet Union for the *Times Literary Supplement*, and it took some time before the new generation of Kremlinologists such as Leonard Shapiro at the London School of Economics and Robert Conquest could make their voices heard.
22 For instance, on 25 August 1945 he suggested to Montgomery that the time had perhaps come when individual Commanders in Chief might cease to send personal directives to the Germans: why not let such communications be signed by the four powers? *Documents on British Policy Overseas*, 73.
23 Unpublished memoir by Austen Albu, Chapter III, 3.
24 Ibid., 2.

CHAPTER 10

1 Hurwitz I, 509. For another account of the events of 1946 see Henry Kirsch, *German Politics under Soviet Occupation* (1974).
2 Hurwitz II, 766, 777.
3 FO 1049/326, 75139.4.
4 Hurwitz I, 523.
5 Ibid., 545; II, 797.
6 Ibid. II, 873.
7 Ibid., 687.
8 Ibid., 796; FO 1049/326.4, FO 370/55360. Churchill had used the phrase in the House of Commons on 16 August 1945 (Hansard Col 1291).
9 FO 1049/322; Hurwitz II, 693.
10 Hurwitz II, 831.
11 Ibid., 695.
12 Ibid., 812–13.
13 Ibid., 802–3.
14 FO 1049/324.
15 Hurwitz II, 975.
16 Ibid., 992.
17 Ibid., 807, 930.
18 Ibid., 1259.
19 Ibid., 1118.
20 Ibid., 1181.
21 FO 371/55364/C3762. Letter to Sir Arthur Street.
22 Albu, III, 17.
23 FO 1049/325; Hurwitz II, 1182–5.
24 The actual figures as given by Albu were: entitled to vote, 33,247; voted 23,755. The percentages are given by Hurwitz II, 1220.
25 Hurwitz II, 1263–5; FO 321/55586/C3992.
26 FO 1049/326.
27 FO 371/55534/C740 (28 January 1946).
28 Turner, 258, 261.
29 FO 1005/1387, Appendix A (16 March 1946).

30 FO 1005/1387, SCDP (46/21) (12 April 1946).
31 FO 371/64352/C3969 (7 March 1946).
32 Tom Bower, *Blind Eye to Murder* (1981).
33 Hugh Thomas, 336.
34 Sue Ryder, *Child of My Life* (1986), 199, 185.
35 *Troilus and Cressida*, I, iii, 109–18.
36 Donnison, 369-70; Marion Dönhoff, *Observer*, 17 July 1955.
37 Donnison, 416–17.
38 David Pryce-Jones, 'The Holocaust and its Consequences in France', *British Journal of Holocaust Education*, I, Winter 1992.
39 Ian Buruma, *The Wages of Guilt* (1994).
40 *London Review of Books*, 8 September 1994, 9.

CHAPTER 11

1 Albu, III, 3.
2 Ibid., 21–5.
3 FO 1049/328/75238.
4 In November 1946 Military Government did in fact arrest eighty leaders of heavy industry in the Ruhr, interning them on the grounds that they were, in the words of the Potsdam Declaration, 'a danger to the Allied occupation and its interests' (*Documents on British Foreign Policy Overseas*, 443).
5 Letter from Schumacher to Austen Albu, Hanover, 20 May 1946.
6 Barbara Marshall, 86–7.
7 FO 1049/328/75238.
8 Letter from Steel to the author, 18 August 1946.
9 Horst Walter Heitzer, *Die CDU in der Britischen Zone* (1988), 57, 67, 122fn.
10 Ebsworth, 18.
11 See Dietmar Petzine and Walter Eucher, *Wirtschaftspolitik in*

britischen Besatzatungsgebiet 1945– 49 (1984), 69-72.
12 D.C. Watt, *FCO Occasional Papers*, November 1989, 39; FO 371/55586 PREM 8/216.
13 See W. Friedmann, *The Allied Military Government of Germany* (1947), 240.
14 Cave Brown, 351. This story emanates from the suspect source General Sudoplatov of the KGB. Sudoplatov said Maclean declared that this information came from Ernest Bevin (with whom Maclean was not in touch), and that Maclean's code-name was Orphan (in fact it was Homer). Robert Cecil, Maclean's biographer, makes no mention of such intervention.
15 Hansard, 29 March 1949.
16 Albu, III, 42.
17 Lord Bridges, in *FCO Historical Branch Occasional Papers*, 3 November 1989.
18 Letter from Adenauer to the author, 19 August 1946.
19 Letter from Adenauer to the author, 29 May 1952.
20 Cave Brown, 338–44.
21 Timothy Garton Ash, 'From World War to Cold War', *New York Review of Books*, 11 June 1987, 49. Alan Brooke considered that the 'levity' with which Churchill spoke to Stalin at Tehran about the fate of Germany and Poland was 'alarming' (Earle, Diaries).
22 Eric Hobsbawm, *Age of Extremes* (1994), 226–56.
23 Hugh Thomas, 121–36.
24 Hobsbawm, 168.
25 Frank Roberts, *Dealing with Dictators* (1991), 90–1.
26 Hugh Thomas, 543–50.
27 Ibid., 7–17, 481–91.
28 See Frank Chapple, *Sparks Fly* (1984); Andrew Roberts, *Eminent Churchillians* (1994), 243–84.

Index

Ranks and titles are generally the highest mentioned